DOLLARS FOR RESEARCH

Science and Its Patrons in Nineteenth-Century America

Dollars for Research

Science and Its Patrons
in Nineteenth-Century America

HOWARD S. MILLER

University of Washington Press

Seattle and London

For Marlo, Eric, Kurt, and Andrew,
who would rather go camping

Preface

F E W Americans today would seriously question the value of basic scientific research. Science has become the foundation of industrial development, an instrument of national survival, the peril and hope of the world. Scientific knowledge has become a vital national resource. In 1968 alone, Americans devoted $3.6 billion to basic—as contrasted to applied—research. Of that total, the private sector supplied nearly 40 per cent.

The massive, systematic support of scientific research, so characteristic of twentieth-century American life, was unknown a century ago. In that earlier time there was no well-defined, recognized niche in the occupational structure for a man who devoted his life to research. The descriptive noun, "scientist," though coined by an English philosopher in 1840, was uncommon in the American vocabulary until the closing years of the nineteenth century. In contrast to present-day Big Science with its rich array of foundation grants and government subsidies, nineteenth-century science had few established sources of financial support. The resulting logistical problems, the men who helped solve them, and the institutions they created are the subjects of this study.

By the second quarter of the nineteenth century the pursuit of science was fast becoming an esoteric quest. During the colonial period and well into the formative years of the new nation science had been, along with Latin, Greek, and moral philosophy, an integral part of a gentleman's cultural heritage. Men of Thomas Jefferson's circle worked at science as they worked at politics, polite letters, and farming. Within a few decades, however, the advancement of knowledge overwhelmed gentlemanly, amateurish science, just as it overwhelmed the crude, Baconian empiricism that had served as scientific method in America since the seventeenth century. The time of transition varied from discipline to discipline, but by mid-century science as a whole had become the property of specialists. The generation of the 1840's, represented by Joseph Henry, Asa Gray, Alexander Dallas Bache, and Benjamin Peirce, was the first in America for whom professional competence was at once possible and necessary. Such men were pioneers of basic science, investigators whose personal and patriotic ambitions prompted them to revise the aims, the structure, and even the meaning of science in the United States. For their predecessors a well-stocked "Cabinet of Curiosities" had been the visible sign of a scientific calling. For the younger generation original research and publication were the highest goal.

The new men of science were supremely confident, frankly elitist, and aimed to reform American science from the top down. Circumstances might occasionally call for what Joseph Henry termed "a few oblations to Buncombe," but otherwise they strove "to pour fresh material on the apex of the pyramid of science, and thus to enlarge the base." As a plaything of eighteenth-century savants science had at times been elevated above common understanding. As the discipline of nineteenth-century specialists it grew foreign even to the liberally educated. Already in the 1840's men of science and men of letters perceived a divergence into two cultures, and this alienation would continue to perturb American intellectuals into the twentieth century.

The growing complexity of the sciences posed special problems for their social relations in general and their financial support in particular. Removed from everyday experience, scientific enterprise could not expect the same gratuitous interest and public sentiment that other more obvious social activities received as a matter of course. Few philanthropists had enough first-hand knowledge to subsidize the pursuit of science effectively. In some cases their interest in the cause had to be stimulated; in almost all cases it had to be cultivated, nurtured, and directed into some special branch of investigation.

Men of science consequently had to act as their own entrepreneurs, availing themselves of every opportunity to secure patronage and general recognition for basic scientific research. Their success lay principally in their ability to capitalize upon the contingent and the unforeseen. Save for their unremitting efforts, there were no general principles governing private philanthropy for scientific purposes. Special circumstances and idiosyncratic individuals gave a unique flavor to each case. Fortuitous family connections between men of science and men of wealth, a comet passing in the latitude of Boston to spark enthusiasm for astronomy, an industrialist's realization that economic development created new career opportunities in science and technology, a patrician's concern for the cultural status of his community, a robber baron's bid for respectability, the winning personality of a Louis Agassiz, the whims of an eccentric old lady who became the first patron of the American Association for the Advancement of Science: these were characteristic elements in the story of how science won its support, and its lasting position in American life.

Coming at a moment when institutional forms were yet plastic, the early gifts for science were particularly significant. They established precedents and projected lines of development. By a process of institutional aggrandizement the first scientific schools, observatories, and laboratories created their own need and perpetuated their own kind. They began the process by which the informal mechanisms of private support evolved into lasting social institutions. The great research endowments and private foundations of the early twentieth century owed their structure to general trends in American economic development, but their programs and policies derived from traditions reaching back into the 1840's.

Institutional organization, a principal goal after the 1880's, introduced a greater degree of security and regularity into the life of science. The new research-oriented universities gave the scientific community a base of operation. A philanthropic foundation managed by a professional administrator freed the creative scientist from the responsibility of acting as his own business manager and public relations expert. A foundation could also command the resources necessary to drive onward in the increasingly complicated and expensive search for knowledge. But organization brought problems as well. The question of individual versus collective research accompanied the trend toward bigness; the question of whether science was best promoted by centralized team research or by widely dispersed individual effort was as much an issue for the founders of early foundations as it would be for the administrators of those foundations a half century later.

In sheer quantitative terms, during the nineteenth century as during the twentieth, public appropriations outweighed private donations for scientific research. But qualitatively, in the nineteenth century financing from the private sector did much to give tone and tempo to American scientific work. Federal and state agencies encouraged investigations that promised useful results, and under utilitarian guise government scientists often conducted important original work. But politicians were unimaginative, and frequently timid. Inertia, ignorance, partisan politics, and a gnawing fear that government support of science was somehow unconstitutional weakened public efforts at the advancement of knowledge.

Private support helped make possible the first steps in the social organization of modern science in America. Individual philanthropists underwrote new and abstract researches, investing hard-earned dollars in what Thorstein Veblen called "idle curiosity." Their commitment was a commentary on the status of pure science in a pragmatic society, and a suggestion that blanket condemnations of "anti-intellectualism" in American life need to be revised.

For the support of science, as for most other American enterprises in the nineteenth century, the distinction between the public and private sectors was more apparent than real, more rhetoric than substance. Scientific research demanded and received assistance from both. But if private philanthropy was often as uncertain as public patronage, the common source of science funds abroad, it had the redeeming grace of flexibility. If intermittent in their support, private benefactors were free to innovate, to experiment, to venture capital on the unknown.

Often historians, no less than scientists, owe their subsistence to private philanthropy. In my case a Richard D. Irwin Doctoral Fellowship saw me through the initial phase of research. Research grants from the University of Wisconsin and the University of Southern California assisted materially in mid-passage, and a Summer Research Fellowship from the latter institution saw the manuscript to completion.

During the course of my research a number of individuals unselfishly shared with me their understanding of American science, and clarified my thinking on a number of points. Merle Curti, Richard H. Shryock, Richard J. Storr, Robert V. Bruce, George H. Daniels, Whitfield J. Bell, Jr., Nathan Reingold, and Helen Wright were particularly helpful. I would also like to thank the following institutions for permission to consult and quote from manuscripts in their possession: the Massachusetts Historical Society, Harvard University, the Library of Congress, the Smithsonian Institution, the American Philosophical Society, the University of Chicago, the Franklin Institute, the California Institute of Technology, the State Historical Society of Wisconsin, Yale University, and the Henry E. Huntington Library and Art Gallery. Finally, I am grateful, as always, to Chancellor Irvin G. Wyllie of the University of Wisconsin, Parkside, for his encouragement, his good sense, and his ruthless blue pencil.

H.S.M.

Los Angeles, California
June 1969

Contents

Illustrations

DOLLARS FOR RESEARCH

Science and Its Patrons in Nineteenth-Century America

1
A Bounty for Research

In this Democratic Country we must always do
what we can, when we cannot do what we would.
. . . We must recollect that great changes are seldom or never produced *percaltum* and that we
frequently waste our strength in endeavouring to
suddenly overcome an obstacle which will gradually give way under a gentle constant pressure.

Joseph Henry, 1864

ON the first of April, 1844, a scientific congress convened
in the First Presbyterian Church of Washington, D.C.
It was hardly surprising that the meeting attracted hordes of
curious townspeople as well as the delegates, for it was the first
such assembly of national scope in American history. The
delegates and spectators took their seats, the Marine Band
rendered an appropriate air, President John Tyler offered an
official greeting, and the delegates settled back for a week of
scientific papers and conviviality.[1] Several days later Alexander
Dallas Bache, Superintendent of the United States Coast Survey, addressed the congress on "the condition of science in
Europe and the United States." Much of what he said merely
rehearsed the familiar themes of cultural nationalism. But those
in the audience who knew his intent, or who grasped the
implications of his message, realized that Dallas Bache was
calling for a dramatic shift in the character and direction of
scientific enterprise in America.[2]

"What are the wants of science in the United States," he
began; what conditions have produced the present situation?
Molded by foreign ideas and domestic circumstance, American

3

science had passed through several phases. Before the Revolution, science had shared a colonial status with other institutions. With few exceptions it had been derivative and utilitarian, subservient to the European scientific Establishment. The American Revolution had ushered in the second period, punctuated by demands for cultural as well as political independence. Impelled by the promise of the American experiment, new colleges sprang into life, "and if they were neither rich in endowments in students or in learning, they might become so: Our youth were preparing in them for better things." Meanwhile, settlers had penetrated far inland, unveiling a richness of new plants and animals, unknown minerals, and strange geological formations, all of which demanded classification. Such a bewildering array of raw material "drew the attention of men of science especially to descriptive Natural History." Natural history societies flourished as American savants scoured the country in search of specimens, and a well-stocked cabinet of curiosities became the visible sign of a scientific calling. Yet, Bache reminded the delegates, Americans had advanced few original scientific ideas in spite of their frantic activity. "Experiments made abroad were repeated here, & men acquired a reputation for mere repetition."[3]

Bache attributed the meager output of original scientific work to a want of solid institutional support, and to a widespread misconception of what the pursuit of science actually entailed. Because Americans tended to confuse research with teaching, discovery with its dissemination, few colleges or universities made provision for faculty research. Because legislators lacked scientific understanding, they often bungled public appropriations which might otherwise have been turned to good account. Private agencies modeled on the Royal Institution of London (founded in 1800 by the American expatriate Count Rumford) presented a hopeful alternative, Bache admitted, but here too instruction might supplant discovery. The Lowell Institute of Boston was a case in point. John Amory Lowell's subsidized lectures might keep Bostonians in touch with the scientific community, but the institute did not directly advance human knowledge. "It offers a bounty for good lectures; we want a bounty for research."[4]

To secure financial support for research, either within or outside the existing framework of higher education; to provide more and better scientific journals; to improve the general reputation of science and its practitioners: these were the needs of science in the United States. If they hoped to meet such needs, Bache declared, Americans must cease their fawning dependence on Europe and strike out on their own. It was an old appeal; such patriotic sentiments had stimulated American savants for nearly a century. But what followed was new, for Bache suggested that the future of science in America rested with the professional specialists, not with the gentlemanly scholars who made up the bulk of his audience. The amateur, the learned hobbyist, was losing his place, outdistanced by the sheer pace of discovery. Already there was evidence of change in the character of scientific endeavor; the time had come to seize the initiative and sustain the impetus. "Is it the diffusion of science, or the encouragement of research that American science requires? Is it sympathy and kindly communication of which we have the most need? Acquaintance with each other and our several doings? Or opportunities, means, and appliances for research? Do we need talkers or workers?"[5]

Historical discourses often told less about their subject than about the speaker's own times. Dallas Bache saw in the colonial and early national periods what he wanted, and wanted others to see; he minimized the contributions of earlier generations in order to point up the importance of his own. American savants had in fact shown considerable vitality during the early years of the republic, and many an old-time college, though formally committed to the twin ideals of mental discipline and moral philosophy, had been the scene of creditable original research. What Bache did describe accurately was the episodic, eclectic quality of early American science. Provincial society had failed to produce a solid institutional foundation for scientific enterprise. In the new nation there was no ready-made occupational niche for a man of science. Many Americans who called themselves men of science were physicians, clergymen, public servants, and country squires for whom the pursuit of science was part of their heritage as gentlemen. Typical for his breadth of interest, if remarkable for his energy, was Samuel Latham Mitchell of New York. Respected as a physician, editor, paleontologist, essayist, chemist, geologist, and ichthyologist, he also found time for politics and, in Henry Adams' words, "supported the Republican party because Jefferson was its leader and supported Jefferson because he was a philosopher."[6] Though extreme in Mitchell's case, eclecticism was the norm in Jefferson's day. In 1828 Noah Webster noted, "*Pure* science, as in Mathematics, is built on self-evident truths; but the term science is also applied to other subjects founded on generally acknowledged truths, as *metaphysics;* or on experiment and observation, as *chimistry* [*sic*] and natural philosophy; or even to an assemblage of the general principles of an art, as the science of *agriculture*, the science of *navigation*." In common parlance science still implied what it had in Samuel Johnson's day: the general "comprehension or understanding of truth or facts by the mind."[7]

The modest accomplishment of early American science was due only partly to unfocused energy and institutional deficiencies. Involved too were the inherent limitations of the "Baconian" empiricism then in vogue. American savants had taken Francis Bacon as a patron saint, convinced, as he had been, that his inductive method would invariably lead to Truth. A sufficient number of facts, so they argued, would arrange themselves into a scientific law. If error crept in, it was the result of careless induction, and might be corrected by the accumulation of still more data. Thus assured of ultimate certainty and equipped with an almost mechanical method that all diligent men might employ, Americans had pursued science since the seventeenth century. "At the present day, as is well known," wrote Edward Everett in 1823, "the *Baconian* philosophy has become synonymous with the true philosophy."[8]

The Baconian method had been eagerly embraced by natural

historians confronted with the taxonomic nightmare of a new world. It had afforded scientific status to Puritan divines, plantation owners, and inquisitive laymen alike, for in a wilderness of unknown creatures, exotic plants, and bewildering geological forms every observation might indeed yield an important discovery. But the very strength of the Baconian philosophy was also its fatal weakness. By the fourth decade of the nineteenth century industrious Baconians had discovered so much that the accumulated data threatened to smother them. Unguided by conceptual imagination, which doctrinaire practitioners stigmatized as mere speculation, the diligent pursuit of facts led nowhere. Brute empiricism revealed no clear path through what seemed increasingly "the vast labyrinth" of Nature.[9] The cabinet of curiosities, long regarded as an essential tool of science, seemed destined to become a burdensome museum of useless artifacts. Just a few decades after Edward Everett had celebrated Baconism as the true method of science, the inductive philosophy had lost its appeal. The rising generation of scientific men, when it looked to tradition at all, aligned itself not with Lord Bacon but with Sir Isaac Newton, Galileo, and other symbols of theoretical insight. Few complained in the 1850's when the editor of Bacon's scientific works termed his method "practically useless," nor was Dallas Bache criticized when he told the American Association for the Advancement of Science, with evident relief, that research was no longer "stifled by empiricism."[10]

Their dramatic repudiation of Baconism and their strident, professional stance set Dallas Bache and his generation apart from their older colleagues. Self-conscious reformers bent upon improving both the quality and the quantity of scientific research in America, they frequently ridiculed their Baconian predecessors as "charlatans," and "Old Fogeys." Joseph Henry, the nation's leading physicist, voiced their common complaint: "We are overrun in this country with charlatanism. Our newspapers are filled with puffs of Quackery and every man who can burn phosphorous in oxygen and exhibit a few experiments to a class of young ladies is called a man of science."[11]

Small as it was, the rising scientific generation was by no means monolithic. Personal feuds, professional disagreements, shifting alliances, and petty in-fighting over academic appointments and government jobs lent a decidedly political cast to scientific enterprise. During the crucial two decades following Dallas Bache's address, he and his friends dominated the scene. Calling themselves at various times the Florentine Academy or the Order of the Scientific Lazzaroni (the latter, appropriately enough, after the poorest class of Neapolitan beggars), they fancied themselves the nation's sole custodians of scientific culture. Constantly intriguing to marshal support for research, and for each other, they corresponded constantly and met to plan grand strategy at "one good great happy annual winter feed."[12] The core of the group included Bache, the "Chief"; Joseph Henry; the Harvard mathematician Benjamin Peirce and his protégé, the astronomer Benjamin A. Gould; Oliver Wolcott Gibbs, a chemist; John F. Frazer of Philadelphia, another chemist and one of Bache's former students at the University of Pennsylvania; and the Swiss-American zoologist, Louis Agassiz. At the outer fringes of the Lazzaroni circle were a number of quasi-members, fellow travelers, and sometime allies, including the Yale geologist, James Dwight Dana; Benjamin Silliman, Jr., a Yale chemist and co-editor of the *American Journal of Science;* Cornelius C. Felton, a Harvard professor of classics and Agassiz's brother-in-law; James Hall, another Albany geologist and paleontologist; and the encyclopedist Francis Lieber.

For a variety of reasons the Lazzaroni pointedly excluded a number of equally qualified men from membership, notably Henry Draper, William and Henry Rogers, and Asa Gray. Whether they were inside or outside the Lazzaroni circle, however, the young men of science all agreed that the only route to scientific respectability at home or abroad lay in the direction of original research. And since all men were not equally endowed with scientific talent, the reform of science would necessarily diverge from the democratic reform movements of the day. As a matter of strategy, admitted Joseph

Henry, it might occasionally be necessary to court popular favor and "make a few oblations to Buncome." But this was strategy only; the proper course in the long run was "to pour fresh material on the apex of the pyramid of science, and thus to enlarge the base."[13]

All devoted cultural nationalists, the young men of science viewed the advancement of knowledge in part as a patriotic duty. Sidney Smith's jeering question of 1820, "Who reads an American book?" still taunted them, and invidious comparisons with European science were hard to avoid.[14] Yet Europe could serve as a source of inspiration as well as a goad. Long before the allure of a Continental Ph.D. drew large numbers of American students abroad, scientific men had made lasting personal and institutional contacts in European (especially English) scientific centers. Even the usually reserved Joseph Henry was dazzled by the world of Sir David Brewster and Michael Faraday. "England," he confided to Asa Gray, "is to us a fairy land."[15] On his return in 1838 Henry told Dallas Bache that reform at home was imperative. "I am now more than ever of your opinion that the real working men in the way of science in this country should make common cause and endeavour by every proper means unitedly to raise our scientific character, to make science more respected at home, to increase the facilities of scientific investigators and the inducements to scientific labours."[16] What Henry envisioned was a kind of research agency patterned on the Royal Institution of London and the Parisian *Institut*. The model was clearly European, and the first hope for its realization came from the old world as well, for in 1826 James Smithson, an eccentric English gentleman-chemist, had died leaving the residue of his estate in trust to the United States "to found at Washington, under the name of the Smithsonian Institution, an Establishment for the increase & diffusion of knowledge among men."[17]

No one knew precisely what Smithson had had in mind. Some sought guidance in the vague phrasing of the will; others, like old John Quincy Adams, were content to see "the finger of Providence, compassing great results by incomprehensible means."[18] If not providential, the bequest had come at a propitious moment for the post-Baconian generation. The pursuit of science was still an uncertain vocation in America. At once a private trust and a public agency, the Smithsonian might combine the independence and flexibility of the one with the resources of the other.[19]

Late in August 1838 the packet *Mediator*, forty-three days out of London, had sailed into New York harbor with Smithson's bounty safe in her hold. Converted into American currency the eleven iron-bound boxes of gold amounted to $508,318.46. The following December Martin Van Buren directed the Congress to seek the advice of "persons versed in science, and familiar with the subject of popular education," and carry out the object of the bequest.[20] Nearly eight years, four Congresses, and three presidents later, on August 10, 1846, James K. Polk signed the bill establishing the Smithsonian Institution.

The lawmakers had been delayed for a variety of reasons. Debate was bound to be sporadic during those depression-ridden years, when the press of economic and political considerations left little time for pondering the increase and diffusion of knowledge. Moreover, the gift was unprecedented; it required considerable argument to overcome long-standing constitutional scruples against appropriations for scientific and philanthropic purposes. John C. Calhoun and other southerners raised the states-rights bogy against the proposed national establishment, and also objected on the ground that it was "beneath the dignity of the United States to receive presents of this kind from anyone."[21] The Treasury Department complicated the disposition of the bequest still further by investing the fund in speculative western state bonds. Except for John Quincy Adams, whose persistent fretting over the trust finally prodded Congress into action, Smithson's half million might have been lost forever when the states repudiated their indebtedness in the early 1840's. But the greatest obstacle was simply that the lawmakers were at odds over the institution's proper design. Educators and persons versed in science, the two groups singled out as consultants in the enterprise, disagreed with each other and among themselves, and they were but two groups of many who regarded the Smithsonian bequest as their exclusive treasure. With little experience in applying a fund for the increase and diffusion of knowledge, congressmen found many paths but few guideposts in the tangle of petitions, reports, and memorials that cluttered the legislative docket.

A many-sided contest over the institution's character developed as soon as debate wandered from the propriety of accepting the trust to the possible methods of carrying it out. In what was to be their final bid for national recognition, Baconians lobbied for a museum, a great cabinet of curiosities and scientific lore. Their younger colleagues replied with demands for a research institute. Educational reformers urged a national university, normal school, or a super-lyceum. Scholarly statesmen like Senator Rufus Choate of Massachusetts insisted that "a grand and noble public library" would best embody the donor's intent. Practical-minded congressmen like Isaac Morse and Benjamin Tappan countered with the proposition that the American people, "whilst they entertained a proper respect for . . . the sciences taught in the Universities of Europe," would better appreciate agricultural experiment stations or prize essays on useful topics.[22]

In March 1840 John Quincy Adams offered one of the first constructive proposals for the disposition of the bequest. Although his personal scientific tastes were relics of an earlier age, Adams understood better than most of his contemporaries the scientific ideals and professional aspirations of the rising scientific generation. Overlooking the stinging ridicule that had defeated a similar plea fifteen years before, Adams urged the establishment of a great astronomical observatory. "There is no richer field of science opened to the exploration of man . . . than astronomical observation," he declared. "The physical relations between the firmament of heaven and the globe allotted by the Creator of all to be the abode of man are discoverable only by the organ of the eye."[23] In spite of his eloquent argument, buttressed by an informed global survey of existing astronomical apparatus, few legislators shared the vision. Although he revived the scheme periodically as late as 1844, Congressman Adams found as little support for "lighthouses in the sky" in the 1840's as had President Adams in 1825.

Although the proposed observatory was lost in debate and amended into oblivion, John Quincy Adams made two important contributions to the final character of the Smithsonian. Justifiably fearful that the institution might be stillborn, exhausted by initial building and organizational expenses, Adams insisted that the capital fund remain intact, invested at 6 per cent to yield a perpetual income for annual operations. Once introduced, his fiscal scheme became a permanent feature of the plan, and assured the Smithsonian financial security and institutional permanence whatever its particular design might be.

Adams' second contribution helped to define the institution's sphere of operation. Admitting that "the first impression upon the public mind, whether learned or illiterate" had been that Smithson meant to invest his fortune in the cause of education, Adams came out strongly against such a plan even before the gold arrived from England. In 1840 he explained to the House that there were already nearly one hundred colleges and universities in the United States, not to mention innumerable academies and common schools. Adams argued that education was a civic duty in America, not the responsibility of philanthropic foreigners. Furthermore, the ultimate object of all educational institutions was instruction, "the communication of knowledge already possessed—and not the discovery of new truths or the invention of new instruments for the enlargement of human power." Original investigation, not the rehearsal of old information to new listeners, should be the goal of the Smithsonian. To dissipate the fund on any form of educational establishment, Adams concluded, would be a perversion of the trust.[24]

Such a suggestion required both imagination and courage in an age when domestic rhetoric celebrated the glories of free manhood suffrage and the common school. The ex-president, however, was no stranger to unpopular causes, and at seventy-three he still held to the whiggish ideals he had tried to implement on the eve of the age of Jackson. Opposed equally to pedagogical and narrowly utilitarian schemes, Adams strove to make the Smithsonian an intellectual agency of the first rank, an establishment for the increase and diffusion of knowledge among scholars. Though frustrated in his own pet observatory project, Adams successfully introduced the idea of a research institution before congressional discussion had polarized around other alternatives.

Between 1841 and 1844 a national museum seemed the most likely contender for the fund. In 1840 the National Institute for the Promotion of Science had risen from the ruins of its predecessor, the Columbian Institute, as the hopeful nucleus of scientific life in the nation's capitol. Conceived by such politician-savants as Joel Poinsett, Levy Woodbury, and Francis Markoe, Jr., and endorsed by Peter S. Duponceau, the venerable president of the American Philosophical Society, the institute was a monument to Baconian empiricism. Its promoters assumed care of the treasures brought back by the United States (Wilkes) Exploring Expedition in 1838, and supplemented this horde with an additional stock of natural curiosities. A typical list of donations, received in December 1841, included one pitcher of pickled fish, five birds, four squirrels, one leaf from a Siamese book, one whale tooth, five copper coins, one hornet's nest, one rock, and an arctic wolf, presumably stuffed.[25] Already custodians of the nation's cabinet of curiosities, Poinsett and the others banked on gaining control of the Smithsonian bequest, and in an effort to impress Congress they staged the April 1844 gathering of scientific men in Washington.

Their efforts were an exercise in futility. The National Institute, or, more properly, the style of science it represented, was already an anachronism. The laboratory, not the attic, was now the scene of discovery. The younger men of science had long since concluded that a "promiscuous assembly" of old-style scientists "would only end in our disgrace," and they

attended primarily "to direct . . . the host of pseudo-savants
. . . into a proper course."[26] It was in this context that Dallas
Bache lectured the delegates on the shifting direction of scientific endeavor. His call for professional specialization, together
with the strong implication that the days of groping empiricism were numbered, laid out the new course as plotted by the
younger generation. Outmaneuvered in the politics of scientific organization, unable to cope with the exponential growth
of technical knowledge, weakened by internal stresses, the
National Institute had little remaining influence by the time
the Senate resumed debate on the Smithsonian in the summer
of 1844.

On June 6 Benjamin Tappan of Ohio offered a new Smithsonian bill. In place of a great national museum, Tappan called
for an agricultural experiment station, the creation of "professorships" of natural history, chemistry, geology, and astronomy, and a complement of miscellaneous laboratories. The
museum function was reduced to the custody of whatever
government-owned "objects of natural history" happened to
be located in Washington. Tappan was not overly critical of
the museum as such; his real objection to the National Institute
was that it was a private, self-perpetuating clique, responsible
neither to Congress nor to the public at large. Tappan's bill
offered a more democratic alternative by vesting control of the
Smithsonian in a board of managers selected by Congress, and
left the management of the institution to a secretary elected by
the board. The National Institute saw its expectations of exclusive control slashed to the sole privilege of naming two managers to the Smithsonian board.[27]

With minor amendments, the Tappan bill dictated the institution's final administrative form. The senator's utilitarian emphasis upon "agriculture, horticulture, and rural economy,"
however, touched off a series of new debates in both houses.
The Senate began serious discussion of the Tappan bill in
January 1845. Rufus Choate of Massachusetts immediately rose
in opposition. "On the basis of a somewhat narrow utilitarian-
ism," he complained, Tappan proposed to confine the increase

and diffusion of knowledge to instruction in the practical applications of science. "This is knowledge, to be sure," Choate remarked condescendingly, "but it is not all knowledge, nor half of it, nor the best of it." A far better plan, thought Choate, speaking for men of letters everywhere, was the creation of a "grand and noble public library." Surely no one could doubt that such an institution was best adapted "to the actual literary and scientific wants" of the country.[28]

Choate assumed a harmony of interest between men of letters and men of science. The ensuing debate over the library proposal suggested instead a growing rift in the American intellectual community. Although they might still join forces to defend the life of the mind from outside attack, men of letters and men of science were separating into two cultures.[29] For many congressmen, however, such nice distinctions were meaningless in 1845. A year before Senator William Rives had sensed the drift of debate, and had rejected any categorical distinction "between the moral and the physical sciences." Men of letters and their spokesmen in both houses were particularly suspicious of attempts to restrict "all knowledge, all science, to the numerical and quantitative values of material things."[30] Laboratory experiments were merely "the dry bones of science," insisted George P. Marsh, an ardent bibliophile and leader of the library faction in the House. True science depended upon meditation, on the search for "that higher knowledge which served to humanize, to refine, to elevate, to make men more deeply wise."[31]

In a new and fluid situation American men of letters had clung to the traditional understanding that science embraced all departments of human knowledge. While champions of popular culture indicted Benjamin Silliman for making his *Journal* too abstruse, literary intellectuals had criticized him for restricting its pages to "what is, rather arbitrarily, called science." The same spirit motivated their efforts to make the Smithsonian an establishment for the liberal arts, a bastion against the encroachments of specialized, technical knowledge. For their part, men of science considered the speeches of

Marsh and other library boosters "a whole sale, gratuitous, and absurd attack on physical science."[32] In such an atmosphere conflict was almost inevitable. Communication was breaking down between the two cultures, and the outcome was a divergence of sympathy and understanding that would complicate the social relations of science well into the twentieth century.

For the present the contest between books and laboratories could be resolved by compromise. No single faction, whether museum, library, or scientific institute, could muster enough strength to drive its own bill through both houses. Yet it was obvious that Congress had to act. Two decades had passed since the death of James Smithson; the failure to implement his trust had already become a national disgrace. "Let us take one step—let us do something," pleaded George Rathbun of New York in April 1846, "and if any blunder should be committed, experience would enable us to correct it."[33]

When it emerged four months later the final version of the Smithsonian bill was a patchwork measure. The act provided for a durable building "without unnecessary ornament" to house a chemical laboratory, a museum to receive the government's "objects of art and of foreign and curious research," a library, and lecture rooms. It authorized the thirteen-member Board of Regents and the secretary (a full-time director) to make an appropriation "not exceeding an average of twenty-five thousand dollars annually, for the gradual formation of a library composed of valuable works pertaining to all departments of human knowledge." Surplus income might be distributed in any manner deemed "best suited for the promotion of the purpose of the testator."[34]

Poorly drawn, purposely vague at critical points, passed by a narrow margin in both houses, more than anything else the Smithsonian Act of 1846 reflected congressional willingness to leave the precise formulation of policy up to the regents and the secretary. At first it seemed unlikely that the regents could succeed where Congress had failed. On the board sat Rufus Choate, guarding the library interest. Robert Dale Owen now worked diligently on plans for the building, incorporating his conviction that medieval Norman architecture best captured the American spirit. Representative William J. Hough, who had drafted the final bill, could be expected to work for compromise, as could senators George Evans and Isaac Pennypacker, who evidently took little interest in Smithsonian affairs. An observer might have anticipated the course of future events, however, when the National Institute named its regents. They were Colonel Joseph G. Totten, chief of the United States Engineers, and Alexander Dallas Bache.

Although at forty the youngest trustee, Dallas Bache soon emerged as the most influential member of the board. As befitted the great-grandson of Benjamin Franklin, he moved easily in both governmental and scientific circles. His vigorous superintendence of the United States Coast Survey already had made Bache the chief liaison between Washington and the scientific community. Chief of the Lazzaroni, a confidant of congressmen, and now a regent of the Smithsonian Institution, in the winter of 1846 Bache was in a unique position to implement the plans he and his scientific colleagues had been discussing for a decade. Their success illustrated what a small group with a dynamic program could accomplish in the political and administrative underworld of scientific enterprise.[35]

Early in December, with the help of Robert Dale Owen, Bache engineered the passage of a resolution stipulating that the yet-unnamed secretary was to be a man who had already earned an international reputation as an investigator "capable of advancing science and promoting letters by original researches and effort."[36] Such qualifications narrowed the field to the new generation of scientific men. In particular, Bache had in mind his friend, Joseph Henry of the College of New Jersey. Henry's electromagnetic researches had brought the fifty-year-old professor favorable notice from Europe, and had made him by all counts the nation's leading physical scientist. For several months Bache had been grooming his friend for the post. Henry had not sought the position. He left his Princeton laboratory only at the insistence of his professional peers, who prevailed upon his sense of duty and barraged him with reminders that "the Scientific men of the Country and others of good practical judgment" would have little confidence in the Smithsonian unless he assumed control.[37] On December 3, 1846, Henry won the secretaryship over his nearest rival, Francis Markoe of the National Institute. "Hurrah!" wrote Bache the next morning, "Science triumphs in you my dear friend and come you *must*. Your position here would be most favorable for carrying out your great designs in regard to American Science."[38]

Henry had formulated the design even before his election. The preceding September he had composed a long memorandum containing the kernel of what subsequently grew into basic Smithsonian policy. He noted that no institution in the United States supplied the fundamental requirements for original research—time for thought and money for experiments. It was up to the Smithsonian to supply these deficiencies. "Select from the scientific men of the country a few in the different branches who have already distinguished themselves by original discovery," Henry wrote, "and furnish them with all the means of prosecuting their researches." A general library was undesirable, as well as a costly and unnecessary duplication of the congressional library a few blocks away. A museum would be equally burdensome unless it directly aided new research. Above all, the limited income should not be wasted on an impressive building. The institution's contributions to knowledge, not a "monument of brick and mortar," should perpetuate the donor's name. The secretary's famed Programme of Organization, adopted late in 1847 as the guiding statement of institutional policy, was only an elaboration of his earlier private reflections.[39]

Given the heterogeneous complexion of the Board of Regents, Henry and Bache could not immediately concentrate upon what they were pleased to call the "active operations" of research and publication. Unable to reconcile the conflicting viewpoints that had carried over from congressional debate, in January 1847 the regents adopted a series of compromise resolutions. Under this plan, to go into effect after the building was completed, the library fund was to receive fifteen thousand dollars per year, while other operations would receive "the remainder of the annually accruing interest."[40] Publicly the secretary acquiesced in the compromise. A brilliant experimentalist, Joseph Henry was also an adept administrator. He understood, as he later put it, that "in this Democratic Country we must do what we can, when we cannot do what we would."[41] Privately, he felt that the arrangement compromised science and cramped his administration. "I do not think that we shall adhere rigidly to this arrangement," he vowed, "since we shall require more money to develop the plans of the Institution."[42]

The secretary and his allies on the Board of Regents engaged in two basic maneuvers. The organic act of 1846 had stipulated that an average of twenty-five thousand dollars was to be allocated annually for the library. By a deft turn of legal logic Henry interpreted the sum as a limiting clause, a figure he was not to exceed. To the dismay of Regent Choate, nothing like twenty-five thousand per year was ever spent for books. After four years of operation the total library expenditure (and that only for basic works of reference), was a fraction over eight thousand dollars. And each year the unofficial but operative retrenchment policy freed more "surplus" revenue for Henry's scientific projects.

The other tactical scheme involved the building. The compromise would not become effective until the building was completed. Resentful of Robert Dale Owen's grandiose, turreted, red sandstone castle rising on the Capitol Mall ("that abortion of a building," snorted Benjamin Peirce from Harvard), Henry and his friends spread construction costs over seven years instead of the expected two or three. Each year the delaying maneuver channeled more income into the fund for research and publication, and incidently postponed the judgment day when the library and museum could demand their share.[43]

By 1850 the active operations had born fruit. The *Smithsonian Contributions to Knowledge*, an elaborate series of technical memoirs, had set new standards for scientific publication in America. Henry could boast with considerable justice that the institution's system of international exchanges had made the Smithsonian a major avenue of scientific communication between the old world and the new. Moreover, the program of active operations had the backing of the scientific community. His policy apparently vindicated, and with the building looming to completion, Joseph Henry began in 1850 to urge repeal of the compromise, to demand official sanction for a program devoted almost exclusively to research and publication.

He opened the offensive in his *Annual Report* for 1850. The plan of active operations was admittedly unusual, he wrote, so novel that only scientific men could fully appreciate its worth. It was unfortunate that Congress had not given complete discretion to those "entitled with the management of the bequest." Two years later Henry grew more outspoken, declaring that it was the duty of Congress to rectify earlier errors and impel the Smithsonian "in the right direction." According to the *Annual Report* for 1853, the institution's "prominent design" was "the promotion of abstract science."[44]

As he redoubled his efforts "to get rid of the Museum and library," the secretary was consolidating support on the Board of Regents. Since 1846 many of the original members had been replaced either by close friends like Jefferson Davis and Representative James A. Pearce of Maryland, or by congressional nonentities who seldom attended meetings. Bache, Totten, Pearce, and Davis almost constituted a quorum themselves, and they could usually count on support from several other regents as well.[45]

At the secretary's instigation, in March 1853 the regents appointed a special committee to review the compromise. Considering that James Pearce served as chairman and that six of the seven members were Henry's allies, their findings were hardly surprising. The sole representative of the library faction was George Marsh's protégé, Representative James Meacham of Vermont. He could only register an ineffectual dissent when Pearce presented his report, a trenchant defense of active operations and scientific men. The very idea that the Smithsonian should be a library, Pearce wrote tersely, was "palpably absurd." Congress had not intended to purchase a hoard of books with Smithson's bounty; the lawmakers had realized that such action would be "the *hiving* of knowledge, not its increase and diffusion." The secretary and the regents had merely acted in accordance with their discretionary powers in emphasizing active operations. After rehearsing what had become the stock arguments for Henry's program, Pearce called for the repeal of the compromise of 1847. In the future, he suggested, each of the institution's functions should receive "such sums as its intrinsic importance and a compliance in good faith with the law may seem to demand." The formal phrasing scarcely concealed the intent.⁴⁶

"The coming session of Congress is going to be a stirring one," wrote Spencer F. Baird to George Marsh six months later. Baird was Henry's assistant in the museum, and while his own relations with the secretary were satisfactory, he had seen the effects of active operations at first hand. "I would not be much surprised to hear of attacks being made on the Smithsonian by persons dissatisfied with the administration of its funds."⁴⁷ Among the most displeased were Marsh himself, James Meacham, and above all, Rufus Choate, who, though he had left Congress in 1845, had continued to serve the Smithsonian as a regent-at-large. On the whole, the champions of the library had relaxed after 1847, settling back comfortably to watch the institution evolve. Content with a legislative victory, they overlooked the possibility of an administrative defeat. Not until active operations were thoroughly entrenched did they discover that they had been outflanked. In January 1855, Henry's supporters acted on James Pearce's recommendation, overruled the opposition, and repealed the compromise.⁴⁸

Spencer Baird was right. In an attempt to save the library from annihilation, the library faction staged a last-ditch battle in the Thirty-third Congress. The day after repeal Rufus Choate quit in protest. He charged that the secretary and the regents had subverted the will of Congress, employing questionable discretionary power to create an institution "substantially unlike that which it intended."[49] Choate's charges of misfeasance were serious, and in large part, justified. Though the advocates of active operations had remained scrupulously within the letter of the law (as they read it), they had violated its spirit by relegating the library to an inferior position. Horace Greeley's contention that Joseph Henry was empire-building, converting the Smithsonian into "a lying-in hospital for a little knot of scientific valetudinarians," was not entirely unwarranted. The Senate Judiciary Committee, however, ruled that Choate's charges were groundless. The chairman, Andrew Butler of South Carolina, took special pains to commend scientific research and publication as the best possible application of Smithson's bounty.[50]

In the House, Rufus Choate deputized his friend, Charles W. Upham, a Unitarian clergyman turned Whig politician, to speak in his behalf. "I entreat you to do two things," he instructed Upham in February 1855. "1. Vindicate the sense of the law. 2. Vindicate art, taste, learning, genius, mind, history, ethnology, morals—against sciologists, chemists, & catchers of extinct skunks."[51] Upham carried out his mentor's instructions, attacked Henry's active operations, and in so doing, intensified the controversy between men of letters and men of science. James Smithson, he argued, would have been astounded by the turn of events. "The word science is getting to be quite generally used to denote what are called the physical sciences, excluding political, moral, and intellectual science—excluding history, the arts, and all general literature."[52] Upham was correct, but apparently few other congressmen shared his concern. As in the Senate, the House Committee sustained the regents' action in abolishing the compromise, thus legitimatizing the policy of active research and publication. For Joseph Henry's conception of the sciences as specialized disciplines, and for the secretary personally, it was a decisive vote of confidence.[53]

Charles Upham had, unwittingly, offered a capsule summary

of American scientific development during the first half of the nineteenth century. What he bewailed as the shrinking sphere of legitimate "scientific" inquiry was the inevitable consequence of an exponential increase in technical knowledge. The future belonged to the specialist, not the universal savant, however disruptive such a division of labor might be to the ideal of a community of scholars. "No one can be learned in all branches of thought," declared Joseph Henry, a few months after his policies were vindicated, "and the reputation of an individual therefore ought to rest on the appreciation of his character by the few, comparatively, who have cultivated the same field with himself."[54] The difficulty was that in the United States the scientific few had to depend for their support upon the unscientific many. As discovery advanced direct lay participation necessarily declined. Men of science could not expect spontaneous interest and support for investigations that had little apparent relation to everyday life. Interest therefore had to be stimulated, and support guided into productive channels. For Joseph Henry's generation, the Smithsonian Institution provided such a channel and, perhaps more importantly, provided an institutional focus for a new style of scientific enterprise. Well-entrenched, self-confident, determined to "keep pace with Europe in Science . . . by going ahead of her," Henry's generation had worked a revolution in the social relations of science.[55] Amateur scientists, men of letters, and the public at large might still cling to the scientific style of the eighteenth-century savant, but they would never again set the tone or the tempo of science in the United States.

2

The Works of Creation

The laws of motion and gravitation are known absolutely. Physical astronomy has reached an exalted state of simplicity and perfection. The analytic machinery for the resolution of the mighty problems of nature, is comparatively perfect; and what is now required is to give to the analyst exact data from the heavens, precise positions, exact quantities of mass and distance, in short, a true report of nature as she exists.

Ormsby MacKnight Mitchel, 1856

ONE of the prominent subjects of discussion among our savans," reported the Boston correspondent of the *Athenaeum* in the summer of 1840, "is the establishment of *Observatories* of a character suitable to our standing as a civilized nation, and still more to our exigencies as a practical, and especially as a commercial community." It spoke well for a young, bustling republic, for astronomy was the queen of the sciences, and its cultivation a sure sign of cultural accomplishment.[1]

During the colonial period the vogue of natural theology alone would have guaranteed a continuing interest in astronomy. Inspired, like Isaac Newton, by a fertile union of piety and natural curiosity, colonial savants from John Winthrop to David Rittenhouse had peered at the heavens and wondered at the works of creation. Colonial astronomy reached its zenith in the activities of Rittenhouse, a self-taught mathematical instrument maker of Philadelphia. In 1769 he led American participation in the great international scientific venture of the eighteenth century, observing the Transits of Venus.[2] Two decades later his orrery, a working scale-model of the solar system, made him something of a cultural hero for the revolutionary generation. "He has not indeed made a world," wrote an admiring Thomas Jefferson, "but he has by imitation approached nearer its maker than any man who has lived from the Creation to this day."[3]

Jefferson's extravagant praise helped obscure the fact that the orrery *was* imitative; as a piece of demonstration apparatus it embodied and perhaps diffused astronomical knowledge, but it did not increase it. Similarly, while the efforts of Rittenhouse and others to observe the Transits of Venus demonstrated their scientific zeal, their over-all failure to produce sufficiently accurate data demonstrated their personal and instrumental limitations. Self-taught science and makeshift apparatus might satisfy a gentleman's curiosity, provide material for sermons, or illustrate collegiate lectures, but it was an uncertain foundation for serious scientific research.

During the early decades of the nineteenth century astronomy temporarily lost ground. Public apathy on the one hand, derision on the other defeated several public and private attempts to establish observatories suitable for research. As late as the 1830's even the well-stocked cabinet of Harvard College did not contain "a single instrument which was adapted to making an astronomical observation which would have any scientific value."[4] Part of the difficulty stemmed from the increasing sophistication of the science itself. The grand work of Newton's age, reducing all the phenomena of the solar system to the law of gravity, had largely been completed in 1799 with the publication of Laplace's monumental *Mécanique céleste.*[5] Astronomers now faced the even more exciting and exacting task of extending gravitational theory beyond the solar system to include the sidereal universe. But to do so required incredibly precise measurements. When projected millions of miles into space, a hairsbreadth error in a telescope could easily render months of work worthless. Discriminating seconds of arc and seconds of time required a degree of instrumental sophistication and individual talent rare in the new nation. Few Americans who had the skill also had the funds for a transit instrument and a clock, the barest essentials for serious research. Fewer still could outfit a complete observatory. Moreover, as Benjamin Peirce would point out in the 1840's, the astronomer had to be a professional man of science. "He cannot live two lives; if he works while others sleep, he must sleep while others work. While he sustains science, we must sustain him."[6] Astronomy, then, was critically dependent upon outside support. European astronomers could rely upon a long tradition of government subsidy. Their American counterparts, however, sought aid primarily from private patrons.

In the 1830's there was a dramatic renewal of public interest in astronomy. A succession of brilliant comets and meteoric displays turned attention skyward. Piety, scientific and patriotic ambition, and a variety of practical needs combined to make astronomy the most richly supported of the physical sciences in the United States. Though many were modest institutions, by mid-century Americans could boast of more than a dozen "light houses of the sky."

In 1838 Albert Hopkins, professor of mathematics and natural philosophy at Williams College, established the first permanent astronomical observatory in the United States. Three years before the college trustees and his brother Mark, the college president, had sent Hopkins to Europe with four thousand dollars to procure philosophical apparatus. He returned in the spring of 1835 with a small transit instrument, a sidereal clock, and a reflecting telescope, all of the best London manufacture, and began work at once on an observatory. The reappearance of Halley's Comet six months later may have generated interest in the enterprise, for after Hopkins had invested nearly five hundred dollars himself, the trustees contributed twelve hundred, and four merchants came forward with four hundred more.[7]

The Hopkins Observatory was a transitional institution. It was equipped for original investigation, but it lacked the trained personnel and a firm commitment to research. Years later John Bascom, class of '49, recalled that the Williams faculty was more concerned with affirming the known than exploring the unknown. "The instructors of my college life were little more than the driven stakes to which we were tethered. They defined the circuit of our range, but did nothing to expand or to enrich it."[8] But if weak in creative research, Williams was strong in piety. There, as in most American colleges of the period, it was difficult to distinguish natural philosophy from natural theology. Called upon to dedicate the observatory in June 1838, Hopkins declared that its prime task was to "impress upon the mind the idea of a superintending power," and thus "subserve the interest, not merely of sound science, but of spiritual religion." Over the north entrance, on a tablet quarried in the neighboring hills, Williams and his colleagues invoked the Prophet Isaiah: "Lift up your eyes on high and behold who hath created these."[9]

Other motives combined with the religious impulse as a succession of new observatories followed Albert Hopkins' pioneering efforts at Williams College. Some Americans, haunted by a nagging sense of cultural inferiority and smarting from invidious comparisons with Europe, fostered astronomical research as a matter of national pride. Others mingled patriotism with practical necessity. Navigational charts and nautical almanacs, not to mention accurate surveys of the public domain, all depended upon astronomical observations to establish standards of time and geographical position. For want of a transit instrument to rate their chronometers, navigators in the 1830's sailed from ports like Philadelphia unable to reckon their longitudes at sea within fifteen miles—an uncomfortable margin of error in unfamiliar waters.[10] Moreover, in the years after the War of 1812 the American merchant marine had to rely upon foreign, especially English, navigational aids. Merchants joined intellectual leaders in demanding a national nautical almanac which would at once advertise cultural independence and lower marine insurance premiums. An American ephemeris, said the whiggish *American Review*, would enable the nation's seamen to ply the oceans "in patriotic reliance upon the calculations of their countrymen."[11]

Both patriotic and personal ambition urged American men of science to make the most of the situation. Revolutionary discoveries at the great European observatories of Königsberg, Dorpat, and Pulkowa were constantly opening new areas of research and speculation, and served to remind domestic observers of their own instrumental deficiencies. When the brilliant German astronomer, Friedrich Bessel, detected stellar parallax in 1837, thus revealing the immensity of stellar space, the way seemed open for investigations "of which astronomy has before only dreamed."[12] Determined to advance American science and their own careers, American astronomers began an active search for patronage.

Private, rather than public support took the lead in the organization of astronomical research. Some public institutions, such as the observatory of the Philadelphia High School (a by-product of Alexander Dallas Bache's European tour) made important contributions by introducing the latest European techniques and the best Munich instruments. But on the national level ingrained prejudice stymied even applied astronomical work. The national observatory so long championed by John Quincy Adams became a reality in 1842, but only as the surreptitious creation of Lieutenant James M. Gillis and other naval officers. In time the Naval Observatory became a leading research center, but it began without Congressional blessing, "an illegitimate concern, smuggled into existence under the name of a 'Depot of Charts and Instruments.' "[13]

Immune to legislative hostility and unburdened by governmental inertia, private munificence raised two major observatories between 1840 and 1843. At Cincinnati and Harvard, American astronomers first achieved instrumental equality with their European counterparts. The two institutions, each founded on a fruitful union of individual zeal and public enthusiasm, illustrated both the advantages and limitations of informal, private patronage. Their establishment also revealed that the almost hypnotic attraction of the heavens affected Americans of all ranks, from Cincinnati tradesmen to New England merchant princes.

When Ormsby MacKnight Mitchel arrived in Cincinnati on a bleak November day in 1832, an astronomical observatory was the furthest object from his mind. A West Point graduate, class of 1829, he had taught mathematics at the Academy for two years, served a brief and unhappy garrison duty in Florida, and recently had resigned his commission. Now he returned to his native state of Ohio to read law. Admitted to the bar in 1834, Mitchel soon found legal practice as unrewarding as military service. As his clients and his interest dwindled, he put his Academy training to good use tutoring private students in mathematics and serving as chief engineer of the Little Miami Railroad. Within a year Mitchel had given up his practice altogether for the professorship of mathematics, civil engineering, mechanics, and machinery at the recently resuscitated Cincinnati College. In spite of his lack of scientific training beyond the usual West Point fare, in spite of the fact that he had never made a formal astronomical observation, the former attorney found himself moving toward a career in science.[14]

Several years of teaching improved Mitchel's astronomical knowledge and considerably sharpened his scientific ambition. Like other Americans of his generation, he resented the common charge that "whatever advances might distinguish our country and countrymen in the arts of getting money, in the sublimer researches of science they must, from the very nature of our institutions, forever remain grossly ignorant." Somehow he would prove otherwise by settling "the great question, as to what a free people will do for pure science."[15] Mitchel's opportunity came in the winter of 1841–42, when a local Society for the Diffusion of Useful Knowledge invited him to lecture on the solar system. After weeks of preparation, the young professor faced his audience with a battery of lantern slides and a half-formed plan by which Cincinnati might acquire a telescope "in all respects comparable with the finest in Europe."

Mitchel was a seasoned and effective speaker. His oratory, highlighted by illustrations of nebulae, comets, and galaxies, turned the trick. "On the first evening my audience was respectable, on the second evening my house was filled, and on the third it was overflowing."[16] A winter's program on the solar system expanded into an elaborate series of astronomical lectures lasting well into the spring. Throughout the series Mitchel reiterated the majesty of the heavens "as seen through the great telescopes abroad." Meanwhile he had investigated the cost and construction of the Dorpat Equatorial, the source of many of his illustrations. The great telescope, purchased by the Russian Crown in 1824 for five thousand dollars, was universally recognized as one of the finest astronomical instruments in the world. Setting his own goal at seventy-five hundred dollars, at the conclusion of his last lecture Mitchel made an appeal to a capacity crowd of three thousand.[17]

Mitchel elaborated on a patriotic and republican theme. "While Russia with its hordes of barbarians boasted the finest observatory in the world," he declared, "our own country with all its freedom and intelligence . . . had literally done nothing." Foreign governments vied with one another in subsidizing astronomical research, but in America "no representative would risk in its defence his reputation for sanity." Little wonder then that Europeans decried American culture, and ridiculed "profound republican ignorance." National honor was at stake. If government patronage was out of the question, if scientific men were "too few and too poor" to support their own researches, if the wealthy were "too indolent and too indifferent," ordinary people would have to sustain science in America. Mitchel proposed a novel plan. He would divide the seventy-five hundred dollars into three hundred equal shares, payable when the entire amount was subscribed. With each twenty-five-dollar share came membership in the Cincinnati Astronomical Society and the privilege of viewing the heavens through the best telescope obtainable. "I am determined to show the autocrat of all the Russias," he concluded in a patriotic flourish, "that an obscure individual in this wilderness city in a republican country can raise here more money by voluntary gift in behalf of science than his majesty can raise in the same way throughout his whole dominions."[18]

The response was immediate. One in four contributed as Mitchel "perambulated the streets with his subscription book." He approached all classes, all occupational groups. The learned professions were naturally well represented on the rolls, but Mitchel had even more remarkable success among the public at large. He enrolled more grocers than physicians, more landlords than lawyers, more carpenters than clergymen. Within a month he had collected three hundred subscriptions. In June 1842, fully a year before his projected departure date, he sailed on a "scientific pilgrimage" to the Old World.[19]

Armed with letters of introduction from American statesmen and men of science, Mitchel gained easy access to European scientific circles. English and Continental savants willingly demonstrated their apparatus and offered advice, though many were quietly amused by the idea of democratic science on the banks of the Ohio. His quest took Mitchel from London to Paris and finally to Munich, where Joseph Fraunhofer and his successors had long led the world in optics and instrument design. At the Fraunhofer Optical Institute Mitchel found a twelve-inch objective already polished, tested, and pronounced perfect. It was even more powerful than the Dorpat Equatorial. "My journey was at an end," he later recalled. "True, its magnitude and power were beyond anything I had dared to hope or anticipate; and what was a matter of far greater importance, the price was nine thousand dollars." Dazzled by the image of the great refractor, Mitchel hurried back to Cincinnati and another round with the subscription book.[20]

In Mitchel's absence economic depression had all but halted the collection of subscriptions. The Astronomical Society possessed neither money for the refractor, a site for the observatory building, nor the $6,500 required for its construction. Within a month, however, Mitchel had collected $3,000, the first installment on the telescope. In February 1843 he began in earnest to collect old subscriptions while continuing to enroll new ones. A few wealthy patrons paid in cash on demand, but increasingly Mitchel found himself a broker for due bills payable in dry goods, carpenter work, and groceries. "I frequently made four or five trades to turn my due bills . . . into cash." Even so, by July he had forwarded $9,437 to Munich; Nicholas Longworth, a local philanthropist and land speculator, had offered a hilltop site; and old John Quincy Adams had agreed to dedicate the observatory.[21]

In spite of heavy rain, November 9, 1843, was a festive day in Cincinnati. Stores and schools closed, thousands turned out to see the cornerstone laid atop Mount Adams, named in honor of the old statesman. The summit was "covered by an auditory of umbrellas, instead of faces" as the ex-president delivered the dedication address. At first Adams had been reluctant to attend. Nearly eighty and racked with "old man's cough," he was in no condition to hazard a western journey. Moreover, at their first meeting in 1842 Mitchel's "braggart vanity . . . which he passes off for scientific enthusiasm" had annoyed him. Whether charlatan or man of science, however, it was now undeniable that Mitchel had kindled popular passion for astronomy. Under the circumstances, Adams could not refuse. "This invitation," he wrote, "had a gloss of showy representation about it that wrought more on the public mind than many volumes of dissertation or argument. I hoped to draw a lively and active attention to . . . the importance of patronizing and promoting science." It was one of his last public efforts in behalf of science in America. Returning home from Cincinnati "in a state of debility and exhaustion beyond description," Adams never fully regained his health.[22]

There was still a great deal to be done in Cincinnati. The instruments were due to arrive in a year, and work on the building could not begin until spring. Consolidating his few remaining resources, Mitchel began work in May 1844. Hiring workmen by the week, exchanging shares in the Astronomical Society for lumber, quarrying his own stone to reduce construction costs, contributing from his own salary and savings, he was "sometimes rendered almost desperate" by the effort.[23] Finally in the spring of 1845 the observatory opened; it seemed that the young promoter had reached the point "when I might be permitted to enter the career of observation and research, in the possession of as perfect instruments as art and money can afford."[24]

Mitchel's own lack of skill and training, economic realities, and the problems inherent in piecemeal patronage frustrated his dreams. Without permanent endowment, the observatory lacked the continuing revenues necessary for sustained research. Mitchel himself lost his source of livelihood when the Cincinnati College burned in 1845; he took to the winter lecture circuit in order to support his family and the observatory.[25] Industry also came to Cincinnati, and with it came smoke. Soon Mount Adams, hardly more than a hillock, was shrouded in haze, the great telescope usable only a few evenings each month. Above all, the observatory had been founded on a genuine, but transient enthusiasm. When Mitchel limited visiting hours in the interests of research, he came under fire "for not throwing open the doors of the Observatory to all those who might choose to present their dime and demand admittance." The tedium of exacting astronomical observation appealed little to "the intelligent mechanics of Cincinnati" who had underwritten the enterprise. They had wanted to view heavenly bodies, not pinpoint their positions.[26]

Yet if it did not fulfill its promise, the Cincinnati Observatory was an important symbol of the place of science in American life. In one sense, Ormsby MacKnight Mitchel had realized his goal. He had demonstrated what a free people would do—and would not do—for pure science. Well equipped, if not well endowed, the observatory also introduced new standards of construction and instrumentation that would influence subsequent efforts. Upstart Cincinnati, not the older, richer cities of the Atlantic coast, built the first major American astronomical observatory. It was a creditable accomplishment for a backcountry river town in the 1840's. Moreover, it was a fact which New England men of science would use to good advantage in their own campaigns for financial aid. Even before his observatory was completed, Mitchel began to hear reports from the East of "munificent donations" for astronomy. "I am almost tempted," he sighed, "to wish Boston instead of Cincinnati was my theatre of action."[27]

Mitchel had relied upon lantern slides and oratory. Harvard men of science were more fortunate; in New England the heavens themselves furnished the necessary spark to fire public enthusiasm. At high noon on the last day of February 1843 a brilliant comet blazed out in the southeast sky. Bright enough to show clearly beside the sun, with a tail nearly two million miles long, the comet had just swept past perihelion at 366 miles per second on its periodic orbit around the sun. The news traveled rapidly; within a week crowds gathered nightly on Boston Common to view the phenomenon. "It comes nearer to the idea of the splendid comets described in the books," reported the *Boston Advertiser*, "than any thing which has appeared for several years past." The Great Comet of 1843, in fact, would remain one of the nineteenth century's most brilliant celestial displays.[28]

The comet captured public attention and imagination. As Bostonians peered through spyglasses and disputed who had first sighted the visitor, newspapermen ground out editorials and science fiction stories relating a cometary collision with the earth. Amid public wonder and apprehension, meanwhile, watchers for the Second Coming rejoiced and distributed their worldly goods. The timing was uncanny; years before, the Millerites had predicted that the first of March 1843 would herald the millennium. Perhaps the comet was indeed "the judgment car."[29]

As the faithful prepared to meet the Lord in the air, other citizens deluged the Cambridge Scientific Corps with requests for reliable information. William Cranch Bond, the Harvard College Observer, had done his best to follow the comet from its first appearance, but instrumental limitations had frustrated him at every turn. Struggling along on a two-thousand-dollar subscription raised in 1839, equipped in part with borrowed

Coast Survey instruments, the Dana House Observatory was unequal to the task of plotting a comet's orbit and computing its period. By the second week in March it was obvious that Harvard's observations could never "rival those which can easily be made with a proper equatorial telescope."[30] Anxious to improve their facilities, hard pressed to satisfy local curiosity, the Cambridge men of science made the comet's appearance the occasion to carry their appeal to the public.

Benjamin Peirce had been reiterating the need for a suitable telescope ever since his election as Perkins Professor of Mathematics and Astronomy in 1842. It was the responsibility of the college and the community, he insisted, "to provide such instruments as are necessary to enable us to enter the lists with foreign astronomers." During the summer of 1842 he had memorialized the Harvard Corporation, intimating that several wealthy gentlemen were willing to assist in the project. At his urging the corporation had dispatched agents to Munich to study telescopes "constructed in a manner most approved by the astronomers of Europe." Now, thanks to the comet, the college could act on their agents' report.[31]

On March 22 a thousand people filled the Odeon to hear Peirce lecture on the comet. Reassuring his audience that comets were not, as Cotton Mather had said, "scythes to cut down the wicked," Peirce ranged over accepted fact and current speculation regarding their nature and behavior. He then moved to the heart of his message. The Great Comet, he declared, underlined the need for precise observations and demonstrated Harvard's inability to supply them. Holding one of Bond's telescopes aloft to dramatize its diminutive size, Peirce pointed out that the Philadelphia High School possessed better astronomical instruments than Harvard University. Even more embarrassing to Boston's cultural reputation was the fact that the citizens of an upstart Ohio river town had recently subscribed ten thousand dollars for the most powerful telescope in the nation. "Massachusetts is not wont to lag behind," Peirce asserted. "I trust it is only necessary that the public should know the want to relieve it."[32]

Massachusetts responded within the week. At the suggestion of J. Ingersoll Bowditch, whose famed father, Nathaniel, had translated *Mécanique céleste*, the American Academy of Arts and Sciences called a public meeting "to consider the felt want in this community of a Telescope."[33] Alive to the cultural and commercial advantages of a front-ranking observatory, merchants, manufacturers, and marine insurance underwriters met with representatives of the college and the scientific community. Abbott Lawrence presided. William Appleton, John Pickering, Josiah Quincy, Samuel Eliot, and Benjamin Peirce spoke for the enterprise. Success seemed assured when David Sears, a wealthy Boston manufacturer, offered five thousand dollars for a mounting pier provided others came forward with twenty thousand dollars for the telescope. Announcing that "the reputation of a great commercial city, and the interests of commerce and science" demanded an observatory, the group set about at once to fill a subscription list.[34]

A week later the comet had disappeared. "After electrifying the nervous—puzzling and ever quizzing the scientific—frightening the timid, and confirming the fanatics" it was "off again to illimitable space, tail and all."[35] But in its wake the Great Comet of 1843 left David Sears's contribution, an active subscription committee, and a reservoir of public concern for the state of astronomical science. By May twenty thousand dollars had been subscribed, the corporation had purchased a tract of land for a new observatory, and a fifteen-inch refractor had been selected from the cabinet of the Fraunhofer Optical Institute in Munich.

The ninety-five names on the subscription list represented a fair sampling of the region's public men and business leaders. Although Peter Brooks, reputedly the richest man in New England, offered one thousand dollars, most individuals gave half that sum or less.[36] Their motives were varied and numerous. Anticipating improved navigational aids, Boston insurance underwriters together contributed nearly four thousand dollars. Many subscribers were imaginative merchants and manufacturers who had built vast fortunes, then retired from active business to lives of travel, public service, and benevolence. Habitual philanthropists, a significant number had assumed the support of science and learning as their special charge. John Amory Lowell, Abbott and Amos Lawrence, and Samuel C. Gray all had close ties with the American scientific community. Samuel and Nathan Appleton took a lively interest in their city's cultural life, and the latter had himself contributed an original geological paper to *Silliman's Journal*. Nathaniel Thayer, who in a few years would also give thousands to Asa Gray's Herbarium and Louis Agassiz's zoological researches, was one of Harvard's regular patrons. David Sears, sharing Thayer's interest in Harvard, supported the observatory because it strengthened the university. For others, like William Lawrence, scientific research was one of many outlets for the philanthropic impulse. "My income is very large: I must give a good deal of it somewhere. The only question with me is, where can I bestow it best."[37]

Instruments, however, were only half the story. "Without practical astronomers," wrote Benjamin Peirce, "America can have no astronomy." The observer who spent his nights at the telescope could not spend his days earning a living. Because of the nature of his research, the astronomer had to be a full-time man of science. The matter of salaries was critical at Harvard, for William Cranch Bond had already served seven years without pay. Fortunately he had been a watchmaker by trade, and while acting as College Observer supported his family by regulating marine chronometers and doing contract work for the Coast Survey.

The promise of a new observatory heightened the need for permanent endowment, both for salaries and for ongoing institutional expenses. Already strained by fiscal problems of its own, the college treasury could do very little to help. Once committed, however, Harvard's patrons of science kept on giving. In 1846 thirty-three individuals subscribed five thousand dollars to meet current expenses. The next year, when the instruments were installed and the observatory commenced operations, David Sears added another five thousand dollars to his previous contribution. He earmarked the income from his second gift for salaries and the purchase of apparatus.[38]

In 1848 Edward Bromfield Phillips unexpectedly bequeathed Harvard one hundred thousand dollars as a fund for observers' salaries. It was an astounding gift, "one of the largest in this part of the world to the cause of pure science." The donor had lived a brief and unhappy life. Born in 1824, the son of the Deacon of Old South Church, he belonged to one of New England's oldest and wealthiest families. Phillips inherited more than seven hundred thousand dollars upon his graduation from Harvard in 1845. His classmates recalled him as shy, "of a curiously awkward appearance," and often the object of ridicule. He apparently had had few friends, the closest being his neighbor and classmate, George P. Bond, son of the Harvard College Observer. Although newspapers speculated on an unhappy love affair, no one knew why the young man retired to a water cure at Brattleboro, Vermont, and there in June 1848 shot himself to death. It seemed clear to Harvard officials, though, that his friendship with the younger Bond accounted in large measure for the observatory's first major endowment.[39]

By 1855 the Cambridge astronomers could point to a well-equipped observatory and three permanent funds for its support. In that year Josiah Quincy, Jr., gave ten thousand dollars in his father's memory for one of the institution's "present wants and permanent interests," the publication of researches. The Sears, Phillips, and Quincy funds helped guarantee that Harvard Observatory would become a center for continuing astronomical research. Though working astronomers would always plead poverty in the hope of securing additional support, at Harvard the study of the stars had achieved firm institutional backing and could expect future patronage from the community at large.[40]

The founding years of the Cincinnati and Harvard observatories illustrated a special application of Joseph Henry's dictum that the increase and diffusion of knowledge were distinct, and occasionally antagonistic functions. Exacting astronomical research was one thing, star gazing was quite another. Cincinnati and Harvard differed in many particulars, but none was so important as the contrasting expectations of their respective patrons. The former was a republican observatory, founded on the desire of ordinary people to look at the stars. It was prompted in part by the same thirst for self-improvement that sustained the lyceum and the mechanics institute. Harvard's support, on the other hand, came from wealthy and, on the whole, sophisticated businessmen who were proud of Harvard University and appreciative of the value of science. These patrician philanthropists, while eager to peer through a telescope, were also willing to support men of science in their tedious, abstruse, often unspectacular investigations.

The friction between lay participation and scientific efficiency grew more pronounced as American astronomers became better informed and more fully committed to original research as a professional ideal. In the late 1850's the clash between laymen and scientific men broke into open warfare at the Dudley Observatory in Albany, New York. Fed by personal animosities, competing expectations produced a controversy that scandalized scientific circles, split Albany into factions, and for a time threatened to jeopardize the support of scientific research throughout the country.

The observatory at Albany originated in a grand scheme to establish a national university. The city was a logical location for such an enterprise; the Mohawk-Hudson valley region had produced many of America's scientific men, Albany was equally convenient to Boston and New York, and the Erie Canal had made the city an economic and cultural center. During the winter of 1850–51 scientific circles buzzed with excitement as men in every field made plans to join in the venture. Louis Agassiz, Benjamin Peirce, and Joseph Lovering agreed to leave Harvard, John P. Norton and James D. Dana would desert the scientific school at Yale, Ormsby Mitchel would come from Cincinnati. As New York State Geologist, James Hall was already on the scene laying foundations for local and state support. The university at Albany promised to become the intellectual capital of the United States, "glowing with American fire, pulsating with American aspirations, and, strange as the words may sound to us to-day, radiating with what will then be American scholarship, American depth of research, American loftiness of generalization."[41] In April the organizers secured a state charter. In August the American Association for the Advancement of Science lent prestige by holding its annual meeting in Albany. "While New York has become the London of the western hemisphere," noted the *New York Times*, "Albany will soon be its Gottingen and Leipsic."[42]

From the beginning an observatory had figured prominently in the plan. Dr. James Armsby, Albany's leading physician, and Thomas Olcott, the principal banker, were prime movers in the university project. They called in O. M. Mitchel as an experienced observatory promoter. During the AAAS meetings, Mitchel selected a site on land donated by Stephen Van Rensselaer. Meanwhile, Armsby and Olcott solicited financial support. Primarily through the latter's efforts, in September 1851 Mrs. Blandina Dudley, the elderly widow of a former Albany mayor and United States Senator, agreed to contribute ten thousand dollars as a memorial to her husband. Astronomy had found a wealthy and willing patron.[43]

Plans matured rapidly, impelled by Mrs. Dudley's gift. The larger university scheme foundered for want of funds, but by the spring of 1852 Armsby and Olcott had obtained twenty-five thousand dollars in observatory subscriptions and a charter from the New York legislature. O. M. Mitchel, one of the incorporating trustees, was also to design the building, select the instruments, and act as astronomer in charge.[44]

As the building neared completion in 1855, Mitchel found that his Ohio obligations (especially his work as director of the Cincinnati Observatory), prevented him from assuming control at Albany. In August the trustees, suddenly responsible for a headless observatory, sent Dr. Armsby to the AAAS meetings in Providence to consult with the assembled scientific men. Benjamin Peirce, as always, was ready with advice. Peirce had just proposed a method for the accurate determination of longitude which involved the use of a heliometer. No American observatory possessed such a delicate instrument, the same device employed by Bessel to detect stellar parallax. "It is much to be desired, therefore, that this important instrument may be obtained for one of our observatories."[45] Dr. Armsby rose to the bait, declaring that Albany would supply the deficiency. He also agreed with Peirce that Benjamin A. Gould, currently the head of the Coast Survey's longitude department, was the logical successor to O. M. Mitchel. Soon after Armsby's return to Albany, the trustees announced that Mrs. Dudley had come forward with fourteen thousand dollars for the new instrument.

The trustees could scarcely appreciate the consequences of their action. By substituting Gould for Mitchel and a heliometer for a general purpose telescope, they had radically shifted the character and purpose of their institution. As originally conceived, the Dudley Observatory would have been another Cincinnati, albeit better financed. A heliometer, however, symbolized the most exacting astronomical researches and was fitted for no other use. Benjamin Gould, moreover, was the most dedicated and uncompromising of scientific men. But in the autumn of 1855 such distinctions were not readily apparent. The trustees, awed and flattered by their interest in the venture, appointed Benjamin Peirce, Joseph Henry, Gould, and Dallas Bache an advisory Scientific Council to manage the observatory's affairs.[46]

Considering the differences in training and outlook, some misunderstanding between the trustees and the Scientific Council was almost inevitable. These might not have led to open conflict, however, except for Gould's personality. He had graduated from Harvard in 1844, Benjamin Peirce's star mathematics student, and had proceeded to Germany to study with Karl Friedrich Gauss and Friedrich W. A. Argelander. Young, vigorous, and inordinately proud of his Gottingen doctorate, Gould had returned to the United States in 1848 full of "serial plans for Science in America." One of his first projects was a research journal modeled closely on the German

Astronomische Nachrichten. "The columns of the Astronomical Journal," he declared in a revealing passage, "are designed for scientists rather than philanthropists. Its province being exclusively the advancement of science, its design has been rather to aid and serve astronomers, than to interest lovers of astronomy."[47]

Driven by a single-minded devotion to original research, Benjamin Gould was a gifted and meticulous astronomer. His very abilities, however, unfitted him for dealing with philanthropists or the citizens of Albany in general. Convivial and generous with his friends and scientific peers, he was often arrogant and petty in his relations with others. He tended to identify his personal fortunes with the integrity of science, and regarded those who questioned his judgment as enemies of human progress. Determined to make the Dudley Observatory "a place for careful, unostentatious investigation, rather than an exhibition of brilliant-looking instruments and curious contrivances," Gould arrived in Albany in September 1855.[48]

During the next two years a series of small incidents built a backlog of bitterness. The new instruments and the new emphasis upon research called for massive alterations in the observatory building. Gould ridiculed Mitchel's imposing edifice, and demanded changes which were scientifically efficient if architecturally disappointing. Gould's perfectionism, and the added costs it incurred, began to wear on the trustees' patience. "We fondly aimed at pre-eminence in all things," Thomas Olcott later declared, "and but too late discovered that Dr. Gould's superlative precision and transcendental exactness in ordinary matters, are in this respect allied to his determination of longitude; that the cost 'increases in more than cubic ratio with the degree of precision.' "[49] Moreover, Olcott discovered that Gould, while reiterating his allegiance to Albany, was simultaneously angling for a position in a proposed scientific school in New York City.[50] The trustees could not conceal their disappointment at the dedication ceremonies in August 1856. No instruments had yet been mounted; the observatory, surrounded by rubble from rebuilding operations, "had the appearance of a ruin."[51]

Nevertheless the dedication, timed to coincide with another AAAS meeting, was a success. Edward Everett's florid oration on "The Uses of Astronomy" captured the spirit of the occasion, and appropriately emphasized that in America science must depend not on government aid but on individual benevolence. Three weeks before the ceremony, the Scientific Council had advised Thomas Olcott that the observatory would require an annual budget of at least ten thousand dollars. Short of this "it would be decidedly advisable that the instruments should lie idle for a time." Such a suggestion was unthinkable. Olcott again visited Mrs. Dudley, and secured a fifty-thousand-dollar endowment "for the attainment of an object so rich in Scientific rewards and National glory." Her benevolence, reinforced by an active campaign for funds in New York City, prompted additional donations. Olcott himself added ten thousand dollars. William B. Astor, A. T. Stewart, and fifty-nine other New Yorkers contributed nearly twenty thousand more.[52]

After the momentary excitement of a full treasury had subsided, relations between the trustees and the Scientific Council began to deteriorate once more. Except for the participants' intransigence, the controversy began to take on the aspects of a comic opera. In the winter of 1857–58 Gould further antagonized Thomas Olcott by firing an assistant who had named a small, newly discovered comet in the banker's honor. The trustees censured Gould, and reinstated him only at the pleading of the Scientific Council. The following May, Gould bolted the observatory door in the face of several trustees, and soon after hired Albany's former chief of police to patrol the grounds and discourage visitors.[53] His action, declared trustee John Wilder, raised the question of "where the supremacy of this institution is vested. The time has gone when science or literature is sealed from the common people." It was time "to *get rid of Dr. Gould.*"[54]

The Scientific Council balked. Peirce, Henry, and Bache were Gould's closest friends, and also believed that he was technically correct in his specifications for the observatory and in his insistence that it be devoted to original research. Moreover, by a curious reading of the original agreement they had concluded that the Dudley Trustees were mere legal guardians while they, as the Scientific Council, actually controlled the observatory. The council "reviewed" the trustees' resolution to oust Dr. Gould, declaring it unwarranted and invalid. Specious law at best, this action confirmed the trustees' worst suspicions. "Having exhausted both their denunciations and advice," the council had proceeded "to exercise *squatter sovereignty* by taking the Observatory and its affairs into their own hands." On July 3, 1858, the trustees terminated all agreements with the Scientific Council, appointed O. M. Mitchel the new director, and threatened legal action unless Gould surrendered the observatory.[55]

Resolved to retain possession "until we are finally expelled by a process of law," as the council's representative Gould barricaded himself in the building and issued vindictive letters to the press. Meanwhile his three associates published a spirited *Defense of Dr. Gould.* For their part, Olcott and the trustees distributed more than 15,000 copies of a 173-page *Statement* impugning Gould's motives, moral character, and scientific competence. When this failed to dislodge the council, in January 1859 the trustees secured a court order, battered down the observatory door, and ejected Benjamin Gould into the snow. "Gould must get a good New York lawyer," raged Wolcott Gibbs from New York, "who is not under Albany influences & who don't care a d-m for Olcott & the whole boodle of wealthy and sanctimonious scoundrels with him."[56]

Gould did not go to law. Instead he published a *Reply to the Statement of the Trustees* which he had prepared during his voluntary imprisonment in the observatory. The *Reply* was characteristic of the man. In more than three hundred closely set pages Gould answered the trustees point by point. On a substantive level, he demonstrated conclusively that the trustees had quoted personal letters out of context and without permission, and in several cases had falsified documents in their attempt to discredit the members of the Scientific Council. But also, typically, Gould personalized the dispute. Protesting his good faith, he asserted that his "malignant and untiring persecutors" had employed "low cunning and insatiate meanness" to undermine his reputation. Constantly harried by Dr. Armsby, "the busy, untiring, gossiping, and wondrously meddlesome agent of Mr. Olcott for petty matters," Gould insisted that he had sacrificed untold time and expense to save a scientific institution from those to whom "unwitting legislation" had committed it. A victim of "deception, treachery and violated faith," he had given up only when "driven from my dwelling by a hired gang of rioters."[57]

The *Reply* could not go unanswered, and pamphlet followed pamphlet as Albany split into factions. The intensity of the conflict suggested a substratum of personal animosity whose sources never became public. Nor could any reader unravel and resolve the hopelessly contradictory statements issued by each camp. It was possible, however, to discern some substantive points of contention through the florid rhetoric. The trustees' legal position was secure, and they justifiably argued that they exercised ultimate control over the observatory. The Scientific Council was merely an advisory body, existing at their pleasure. The Scientific Council retorted that since they had invested their time, and above all, their professional reputations in the Dudley Observatory, they had a "moral right in equity" to manage its affairs.[58]

Much more was involved than the fate of a local astronomical observatory. All parties to the dispute understood that the overriding issue was the position of pure science (and its practitioners) in a republican culture. "However it may be in other countries," Thomas Olcott had written to Dallas Bache, "we cannot here erect a throne above the majisty [*sic*] of the people. If we depend on Royal favors we must respect majisty wherever it resides."[59] The council, and particularly Benjamin Gould, were reluctant to accommodate. Gould was convinced that "the success or failure of . . . science in America" rode on the outcome in Albany. As a well-known, well-endowed institution, the Dudley Observatory would set a disastrous precedent if it became "the empty dazzle of temporary show," where men of science were "interrupted by curious visitors, who suppose the establishment to be a sort of exhibition." Uncompromising in his devotion to science, Gould demanded that philanthropists share and subsidize his zeal, even though "the highest functions of a well-equipped and properly directed public observatory are precisely those which would be likely to meet with the least popular appreciation." It was a great deal to ask of ordinary people.[60]

The spectacle at Albany had attracted nationwide attention. In September 1858 the editor of the *Boston Advertiser* summarized public opinion, observing that the Scientific Council had "altogether outrun the limits not only of discretion but of propriety—we might almost say of honesty."[61] Soon influential friends began to urge caution, reminding Bache and Henry that the Smithsonian, the Coast Survey, and the scientific community at large could ill afford such adverse publicity. George W. Blunt, a New York merchant, urged Bache to abandon the field, "taking the ground that you are men of science not of 'war.' "[62]

Joseph Henry was the first to retreat, and in doing so he broke the united front of the Scientific Council. The Smithsonian Secretary would go to considerable lengths in the promotion of science, but the rancorous, personal tone of the Albany controversy had offended his sense of propriety from the start. "In his own quiet spirited way," reported his friend Jefferson Davis, "Henry . . . said he would give nothing more to friendship than he considered due to justice." But the secretary was also a realist, and his sense of politics told him it was time to call a halt. He reminded Bache, who insisted on pushing the controversy further, that "if we make a false move in this case, our means of doing good in the future will be greatly impared, if not entirely destroyed." A few months later Peirce too withdrew from the fight, protesting that Gould had been personally obnoxious and had "dishonored us in this affair."[63] By the summer of 1859 the controversy had subsided, and mounting sectional debate crowded Olcott and Gould and Blandina Dudley out of public consciousness. In subsequent years the observatory joined the ranks of respected, though minor, scientific institutions in the United States.

The Albany episode had been the scientific community's greatest tactical blunder thus far. In their enthusiasm Gould and his colleagues had, as Thomas Olcott charged, erected the throne of pure science too far above "the majisty of the people." When the reaction came it crippled a promising research institution and seriously undermined the common ground on which laymen and men of science had formerly met. "It will require years to bring again the same harmony that existed before," wrote James Hall, sadly, "and some at least of the present generation will die before the event can come."[64]

Although the Dudley Observatory debacle helped frustrate Albany's ambitions as a center of scientific excellence, astronomy still remained a popular philanthropic object in the country at large. The list of observatories and telescopes grew longer as the century progressed, as new communities and colleges pursued the higher learning. For in a society at once pious, practical, and sentimental, even "minds barely tinctured with scientific culture" could appreciate the study of the stars.[65] Few nineteenth-century Americans could long resist a science which so intimately linked the utilitarian with the sublime, and which so eloquently witnessed to their abiding faith in an orderly, beneficent universe.

3
The Personal Equation

Now I say the scientific man is wasting his time,
or is obliged to waste his time, when he is not provided with the appliances with which he can work
and by which he is capable of producing. And I hold
it is one of the duties of those who have the means,
to help those who have only their head, and who go
to work with an empty pocket.

Louis Agassiz, 1872

MORE than ordinary excitement greeted the arrival
of the Royal Mail Steamship *Hibernia* on October 3,
1846. Less than two weeks out of Liverpool, the packet
brought the latest foreign intelligence to Boston. The *Times*
had criticized President Polk's Mexican policy; the Spanish
Infanta would marry the Duke of Montpelier; American cotton was up a quarter cent on the Liverpool exchange. But on
this Saturday morning, a brief item on the *Hibernia* passenger
tally overshadowed commercial news and court gossip: "Liverpool to Boston—Agassie."[1] Jean Louis Rodolph Agassiz, the
epitome of European scientific culture, had arrived in America.
"He is a fine, pleasant fellow," remarked the Harvard botanist
Asa Gray when they met. "We shall take good care of him
here."[2] Gray's observation was both prophetic and ironic.
Americans did take good care of Agassiz, more lavishly than
they had ever previously supported an individual scientist.
Agassiz's ability to attract financial aid became legendary. His
achievements in this regard, contrasted to the modest accom-
plishments of Asa Gray, underscored the value of salesmanship
in scientific enterprise.

48

Agassiz was a man of boundless energy and ambition. "I wish to advance in the science," he had resolved as a youth of fourteen in his native Swiss village of Neuchatel, and henceforth his determination to excel in science had eclipsed all other concerns. For him all things seemed possible. Each grand project gave way to others still grander; a succession of monographs marked new stages of professional accomplishment. His *Recherches sur les poissons fossiles* (1833–44) and *Etudes sur les glaciers* (1840) demonstrated Agassiz's mastery of paleontology and geology, and brought international acclaim long before he had reached his fortieth year.[3]

In the early 1840's a new project beckoned, an expedition to the United States to study the natural history of North America. At the urging of Baron Alexander von Humboldt, Agassiz's mentor, the Prussian king agreed to subsidize the journey. Meanwhile, the English geologist, Sir Charles Lyell, prompted John Amory Lowell to invite Agassiz to deliver the Lowell Lectures in Boston during the winter of 1846. It was hard to determine who was more excited over the journey, the Swiss savant or American men of science. The Sillimans broadcast news of his coming through the pages of the *American Journal of Science*, assuring their readers that the famed naturalist would prove "a powerful auxiliary and fellow laborer in a common cause."[4] Agassiz was buoyant. "There is something intoxicating in the prodigious activity of the Americans which makes me enthusiastic," he wrote to an admiring Benjamin Silliman. "I already feel young through the anticipated contact with the men of your young and glorious republic."[5]

Neither Agassiz nor his American hosts were disappointed. Anxious to establish personal contacts with men he knew only through correspondence or reputation, Agassiz visited the major American scientific centers during the weeks before the start of the Lowell Lecture series in December. "How a nearer view changes the aspect of things!" he wrote to his parents. "I thought myself tolerably familiar with all that is doing in science in the United States, but I was far from anticipating so much that is interesting and important." Agassiz was impressed with the dedication and competence of American men of science, but he noted the lack of leisure for research that liberal patronage afforded their European counterparts. "I have never felt more forcibly what I owe to the king for enabling me to live for science alone, undisturbed by anxieties and distractions." In New Haven and Albany, Philadelphia and Washington he surveyed American collections and, to their delight, praised American investigators. His hosts considered him the personification of European science and culture, an engaging dinner companion who talked far into the night about the condition of science and the means of its pursuit.[6]

Agassiz returned to Boston in November and began his lectures on the "Plan of Creation in the Animal Kingdom." Bostonians had heard many scientific men from John Amory Lowell's podium, but they had never heard anyone quite like Agassiz. He had to repeat his lectures twice daily after crowds of five thousand filled the Tremont Temple to capacity. The sources of Agassiz's appeal stemmed in part from his own talents and in part from the culture in which he moved. The foreign professor was a popular curiosity in an age when the public lecture was a principal form of entertainment. Lecturing easily, Agassiz illustrated his remarks with skillful blackboard diagrams. His acknowledged scientific attainments, in and of themselves, guaranteed a ready audience in Boston. The lectures were popular science in the best sense, an entertaining exposition based upon sophisticated and original research. The "most intelligent people," reported Asa Gray, were "quite delighted and impressed."[7]

Quite apart from his showmanship, Agassiz struck the responsive chord of popular piety. Both his religious and social values harmonized with those of his Brahmin audience. Animate nature, he asserted with transcendental precision, was "a development of the thoughts of the Creator."[8] Buttressing the Argument from Design with the authority of paleontology and geology, Agassiz affirmed the comforting belief that God had fashioned an orderly universe according to His cosmic plan with man as the pinnacle of creation. "Man was not only the last creation up to the present time, but was intended to be the last. . . . No material progress is possible on that plan, but all progress to be expected within the limits of Mankind is improvement in intelligence and morals."[9] Learning, piety, progress, social reform: it was a familiar tune in the Boston of the 1840's.

"Never did the future look brighter to me than now," Agassiz wrote as he completed his course of lectures. He had captivated Boston and attracted invitations from other American cities. "If I could for a moment forget that I have a scientific mission to fulfill, . . . I could easily make more than enough by lectures . . . to put me completely at my ease hereafter."[10] Agassiz easily reconciled his dual role as investigator and popularizer. Americans were so eager for instruction that a very few performances would yield an adequate income and hardly interrupt research. In just six months he had earned upwards of six thousand dollars on the lecture circuit, enough to pay old debts and build a reserve for future studies. Europe, and his wife Cecile, seemed farther away than ever. Agassiz was too involved with America to turn back.

With other cities now vying with Boston for Agassiz's favor, Massachusetts men of wealth and men of science became understandably jealous. Anxious to affect a permanent alliance with their new-found cultural asset, John Amory Lowell urged Abbott Lawrence to make a permanent home for Agassiz in Harvard's new Lawrence Scientific School. Lawrence was as impressed with Agassiz as was Lowell, and in July 1847 the textile magnate and President Edward Everett made formal overtures. On October third, the first anniversary of his arrival in America, the Swiss naturalist committed his future and scientific reputation to the Lawrence Scientific School.

Soon Agassiz's union with the Boston-Cambridge community was cemented by marriage as well as by position. Cecile had died in Freiburg in 1848 while Agassiz was exploring the Lake Superior region with a party of Bostonians. Two years later his marriage to Elizabeth Cary drew the naturalist into a large family deeply involved in Boston's financial and cultural worlds. His father-in-law, Thomas G. Cary, was a former merchant who had turned to textile manufacturing at Lowell. Cornelius C. Felton, Agassiz's new brother-in-law, was a Harvard classics professor, an intimate of the Scientific Lazzaroni, a man who would serve as President of Harvard from 1860 to 1862. When news of the marriage reached Europe, Charles Lyell observed that Agassiz had forever turned his back on the old world. "He will be a New Englander for the rest of his life, and will be the founder of a school of zoology (for he has many pupils) of a high order. . . . His enthusiasm is catching, especially when he has a good soil to work on."[11]

Comfortably installed in the Scientific School, surrounded by a retinue of European assistants and American students, Agassiz felt driven toward greater things. He daily grew more conscious of his prominent position in American cultural life. He would create a research museum to rival those of Europe; he would publish his American researches.

Agassiz's interest in comparative studies of animal life, from present and past geological epochs, made a museum for the examination and preservation of specimens absolutely essential. In 1848 the Harvard Corporation yielded slightly to his demands by purchasing an old bathhouse on the Charles River as a makeshift warehouse and workroom.[12] Within five years barrels of pickled fish, boxes of fossils, and a menagerie of live animals crowded the bathhouse and threatened to drive the scientist and his family from their own home. The precarious state of college finances precluded any long-term support from that quarter. Abbott Lawrence, though willing to guarantee Agassiz's salary, was unwilling to found yet another scientific institution. In the summer of 1853 treasurer Samuel Eliot, a long-time Agassiz booster, took matters into his own hands. He easily raised $10,500 from wealthy Bostonians. The Corporation added $1,800 more, and Agassiz transferred his collections to Harvard. For less than two thousand dollars the university had acquired the nucleus of a great research museum. Yet the President and Fellows had invested more than they knew. Ownership implied responsibility, and though Agassiz had relinquished title to the specimens, he still had his own plans for natural history at Harvard. Agassiz, as his son Alexander later put it, was coming to understand the employment of "present means as a lever for further improvement." Early in 1855, in tacit recognition that the Lawrence Scientific School was no mere technological institute, the corporation turned over Engineer Hall to Agassiz and his students of comparative zoology.[13]

"I have now been eight years in America," wrote Agassiz in 1855, refusing an attractive professorship in his native Switzerland. America offered countless advantages, and there were great undertakings as yet uncompleted.[14] The immediate prospects for a great museum, though, seemed slight. Even resourceful Samuel Eliot could not squeeze additional funds from the college treasury, and no wealthy patron came forward to replace Abbott Lawrence. Undaunted, Agassiz was soon off on another tack. It was time that he show something for his eight years in America, so he shelved his museum plans for future reference and launched a publication scheme unprecedented in the annals of science in America. *The Contributions to the Natural History of the United States of America* would be his great gift to his adopted country and to world science. The boldness of the plan was in keeping with Agassiz's perception of his role as a statesman of science. "I am . . . aware how wide an influence I already exert upon this land of the future,—an influence which gains in extent and intensity with every year."[15] Comprehending the whole of American natural history within his own special system of classification, his lavishly illustrated volumes would at once put American zoology on a par with that of the old world, and set a standard of research technique and scientific publication for all subsequent investigators.

The *Contributions* would also be a monument to Agassiz the teacher. He took special pains to explain to European savants that the work was peculiarly American, in that it combined the increase of knowledge with its diffusion among the people. There was no distinct intellectual class in the United States as there was on the Continent. "I expect to see my book read by operatives, by fishermen, by farmers, quite as extensively as by the students in our colleges, or by the learned professions."[16]

Such a massive undertaking required both capital and a high degree of administrative skill. Agassiz found both in Francis Calley Gray. Trained in the law, and a sometime partner in his brother's iron works, Frank Gray had devoted most of his life to public service and to intellectual and moral uplift. A periodic contributor to the *North American Review,* in 1819 Gray had written an informed review of Cuvier's *Essay on the Theory of the Earth.* Later, as an advocate of common schooling, a member of the Harvard Corporation, and an expert on prison discipline, his name had turned up frequently in the lists of educational and social reform. Living easily on a fortune inherited from his merchant father, Frank Gray was in background and resources a fitting successor to Abbott Lawrence.[17]

Agassiz and Gray had met one another through the meetings of the American Academy of Arts and Sciences in Boston. When the professor mentioned the prohibitive cost of publishing his American researches, Gray responded enthusiastically to the challenge. He persuaded Little, Brown and Company to undertake publication if guaranteed five hundred subscribers for each twelve-dollar volume. In May 1855 the team of Gray, Agassiz, Harvard historian Jared Sparks, and C. C. Felton began a publicity campaign that constituted the first truly national appeal on behalf of science in the United States. Some ten thousand pieces of promotional literature, some of it distributed through the Smithsonian Institution, announced the project and called for a "liberal and extensive patronage . . . from the enlightened part of the community." It was doubtful that any New Englander, or any literate American escaped knowledge of the enterprise.[18]

The response exceeded even Agassiz's expectations. Subscriptions poured in from all thirty-one states, from Canada, Europe, South America, and the Philippines. By August the promoters had exceeded their quota of five hundred patrons, and with characteristic verve Agassiz enlarged the yet unpublished work to ten volumes. "I feel . . . no delicacy in pressing upon friends of science the claims of this undertaking," he explained. In the final tally twenty-five hundred people enrolled. It was unclear how many operatives, fishermen, and farmers remitted one hundred twenty dollars to Boston, but the twenty-seven–page subscription list read like a who's who of wealth and culture in the eastern states.[19]

Published in the autumn of 1857, the first volume contained Agassiz's famous "Essay on Classification," the last eloquent statement of pre-Darwinian zoology.[20] Wholly committed to the fixity of species, Agassiz insisted that different organisms were the product of successive Special Creations, not of adaptive evolution. It had to be so; otherwise natural history would not constitute "the analysis of the thoughts of the Creator of the universe, as manifested in the animal and vegetable kingdoms." The next three volumes of the *Contributions*, issued sporadically until 1862, presented a staggering compendium of the embryology, anatomy, physiology, and geographic distribution of North American turtles. Agassiz selected the *Testudinata* for good reason. He liked turtles. Furthermore, no other order better illustrated "the direct intervention of thought" in Creation, and the lowly creatures were common enough to be familiar to the ordinary Americans he hoped to instruct in the fine points of comparative zoology.[21]

Agassiz's genius lay in the conception of great undertakings; their execution was another matter. After four volumes of *Contributions* exhausted the turtles, the naturalist's interest waned. No more volumes ever appeared. The old dream of a grand museum, never far from his consciousness, once more began to dominate Agassiz's thoughts.

Francis Calley Gray had not lived to see even the first volume of *Contributions* off the press. Before he died in December 1856, however, he had promised that Agassiz would have an institution to rival the Parisian *Jardin des Plantes* and the British Museum. In his will Gray provided that two years after his death his executor and nephew, William Gray, would give fifty thousand dollars to Harvard "or such other institution as you see fit" for a museum of comparative zoology. The

institution was to be independent of any other faculty, responsible only to the corporation and overseers. The income from
the gift would go directly for research, not for real estate,
buildings, or salaries. Agassiz had dictated both the name and
the organizational scheme, insuring that the museum would
embody in concrete form the principles outlined in the "Essay
on Classification." And the fact that the Gray fund was limited
to research made the university and its benefactors responsible
for the physical plant and staff salaries. In his years in America
Agassiz had learned that the wealthy had to be guided in their
philanthropy, and that the best way to secure permanent institutional support was through tempting offerings of venture
capital.[22]

The Gray donation would become available in December
1858. Meanwhile Agassiz used the bequest to appeal to both
the university and the rich men of Boston. At this auspicious
moment a call from the French government to head its national
museum of natural history—a post befitting Cuvier's greatest
disciple—gave him an opportunity to reaffirm his devotion to
America. His well-publicized letter, rejecting all that European
science could offer, advertised the nation's debt to Agassiz.

He had already informed the Harvard Corporation of his
needs by the time William Gray formally presented his uncle's
bounty. He wanted a fire-proof museum building costing fifty
thousand dollars, salaries for a corps of assistants, and operating
revenue for research in addition to the Gray fund. In January
1859 he met with a group of leading citizens at the home of
Abbott Lawrence's brother James, where he organized a subscription drive. Before he returned home that evening, Governor Nathaniel Banks had promised to include an appeal for aid
in his annual message to the state legislature.[23]

The events of the following months demonstrated Agassiz's
ability to draw money like a magnet. Although he made fleet-
ing reference to the utility of zoological collections, the thrust
of his publicity campaign was a call for cultural independence
and scientific excellence. The aim was so to elevate American
natural history "that its students shall no longer be sent abroad

to be educated; nor its specimens to be examined . . . ; nor the papers of its ablest investigators to be appreciated and judged; but that we shall have schools of our own; collections of our own; our own scientific peerage."[24] Apparently Agassiz read the temper of the community aright. Charitable individuals, led by Nathaniel Thayer, who gave $5,000, came forward with $71,125. Harvard donated a plot of land. The Massachusetts legislature, in a rare show of generosity, allocated $100,000 to the museum from the sale of Back Bay lands.[25]

On November 13, 1860, accounts of the dedication crowded national political news from the Boston press. There was a "great deal more smoke than fire" in the secession threats anyway, declared the editor of the *Evening Transcript*. More exciting than the news from South Carolina was the procession of scientists, statesmen, and philanthropists filing into the First Church. More inspiring were the addresses of Governor Banks, President Felton, and Agassiz himself. Felton pointed out that the new museum stood facing the Harvard Divinity School, a mute symbol of the inseparable union of God's Word and His works. True to form, Agassiz used the occasion to lecture on America's responsibility to science and scientific men. Although much had been done, much remained to be done. "Raise your scientific institutions to a level with the foremost in Europe, that the American man of science may, like the American freeman, have the satisfaction of knowing, when visiting the Old World, that he is backed by the institutions he leaves at home."[26]

Until his death in 1873 Agassiz devoted most of his attention to the ever-growing museum. Private subscriptions for "Agassiz's Museum" became a yearly routine for New England's financial and cultural elite. At each session the legislature offered supplementary appropriations for operating expenses and additions to the building. Agassiz benefited from private philanthropy in other ways as well. In 1865 Nathaniel Thayer underwrote a sixteen-month journey to the Brazilian jungles, permitting Agassiz to convert a vacation cruise into a scientific expedition.[27] In 1871 Thayer again headed the list of patrons of

the Hassler Expedition, a combined Coast Survey and private
cruise to the Pacific in which Agassiz, in a last valiant effort to
check the rise of Darwinism, retraced the British naturalist's
Beagle voyage to satisfy the world (and himself) that Darwin
had misread the evidence of evolution.[28]

"I seem like the spoiled child of the country," Agassiz had
written to his mother in 1865. Since 1853, when Samuel Eliot
had arranged for Harvard to receive his collections, he had
secured more than a half million dollars from private and
public sources. For the development of science in America,
both as a systematic body of knowledge and as an honorable
professional pursuit, it had been money well spent. For if
Agassiz's critics galled at his idealistic philosophy of nature, at
his seemingly compulsive need to dominate whatever he encountered, no one ever doubted his genius as a grand strategist
of scientific enterprise. Years later Asa Gray would recall that
Agassiz had been a very fortunate man. "We all know how
almost everything he desired,—and he wanted nothing except
for science—was cheerfully supplied to his hand by admiring
givers."[29]

If there was a hint of envy in the botanist's words, there was
good reason. Asa Gray had welcomed Louis Agassiz to America as a co-worker in the task of institutionalizing the pursuit
of science, and then for two decades had lived under the
geologist's shadow. Gray had been the principal naturalist in
Cambridge before Agassiz's arrival. Though always excluded
from Benjamin Peirce's exclusive Lazzaroni Circle, he had
enjoyed the quiet authority that came with being the leading
(as well as the first) professional herbarium botanist in the
United States.

After several years of cordiality Gray began to have second
thoughts about the flamboyant Swiss. "A. and I always get on
perfectly well," he confided to his friend George Englemann
in 1849, "tho' perhaps we might not if we worked in the same
field."[30] Gray might have said the same community, for Cambridge was a small arena for two giants. Reserved, unassuming,
describing himself (unfairly) as a "closet botanist," Asa Gray

lacked the theatric flair that contributed so much to Agassiz's popularity. Agassiz's dominion over Boston and Cambridge social life was annoying; his warm associations with Emerson and Longfellow in the Saturday Club underscored the fact that Gray was an outsider; and the naturalist's almost hypnotic power over wealthy patrons made Gray's appeal for $3,800 to repair the botanic garden fence seem almost pathetic.[31]

Annoying, too, were Agassiz's ideas. He rejected the unity of the human races in favor of the idea of separate Special Creation. The matter was much more than an academic question for Americans in the 1850's. Agassiz, innocently enough, lent the weight of his scientific reputation to an argument justifying Negro slavery. In doing so he outraged Asa Gray's humanitarian as well as scientific sensibilities. Actually, the question of human types was only a small fissure in the intellectual chasm separating the two men. Agassiz remained faithful to the *natur-philosophie* he had absorbed as a student in Germany. Gray's own meticulous investigations prepared him for Charles Darwin's revolutionary hypothesis.[32]

The integrity of science and the easing of his own sense of social constraint made it imperative that Gray knock Agassiz from his pedestal. Skirmishing over the origin of species began in December 1858, a few months after Darwin had given Gray a preview of his forthcoming book. Gray had the better of the encounters, for by 1860 Agassiz's idealized conception of nature was outmoded, while the Darwinists spoke for the future. "I declare that you know my book as well as I do myself," Darwin wrote Gray from England, when he read of the disputations before the American Academy. "You ought to have been a lawyer. . . . Every single word seems weighed carefully, and tells like a 32-pound shot."[33]

Gray directed his attack solely against Agassiz's scientific concepts. He knew that Darwinian ammunition alone could not undermine the naturalist's social position, and outwardly the two men remained as friendly as the circumstances permitted. Perfectly aware of his adversary's overwhelming advantage in any popularity contest or campaign for institutional support, in the late 1850's Asa Gray temporarily surrendered any claims he might have had on local donors. For the present he had collections to organize, new plants to describe. Book royalties and his professorial salary brought in a small but satisfactory income. Convinced that he would defeat Agassiz in scientific debate (where, ultimately, it really mattered), Gray could afford to help in planting research institutions elsewhere. His own harvest would come in time.

In the middle years of the nineteenth century the trans-Mississippi West was a systematic botanist's paradise. Fifty years of government exploration and caravans of private collectors had only begun to chart the expanse of unexplored flora. Thousands of genera and species still awaited scientific description. St. Louis, Missouri, was the gateway to the region, both as a transportation hub and as the westernmost inland city with pretensions to real scientific culture. Asa Gray, whose study in Cambridge was the nerve center of an international network of botanical exchanges, had long cultivated contacts in the river city. Since 1840 Dr. George Englemann, a local physician and gifted botanist in his own right, had served as the Harvard professor's gate keeper to the vast domain where the plants had no Latin names.[34]

Englemann was a prominent member of the city's substantial German-American community. Born in Frankfort-am-Main in 1809, he had taken a medical degree at Würzburg in his twenty-third year, then went on to study at Heidelberg and Paris, where he was a classmate of Louis Agassiz. Reluctant to settle down at once to practice, Englemann had come to St. Louis in 1835 to look after the investments of an uncle who speculated in Illinois lands. He found a bustling community of sixteen thousand, peopled by numerous countrymen who had fled Prussian despotism at home. The young doctor quickly settled his uncle's affairs, opened a lucrative practice, and in his spare moments resumed his old avocation of taxonomic botany. In 1840 he sought out Asa Gray, then still living in New York with his botanical mentor, Dr. John Torrey. Englemann and Gray needed one another. The Missouri botanist, though skilled in his science, lacked the herbaria and library facilities to make final identifications; Gray, on the other hand, lacked a competent co-worker in the west. By 1856 Gray and Englemann had accumulated more than fifteen years experience as a working scientific team.[35] In April of that year, just as the excitement over Agassiz's *Contributions* was reaching a new pitch, Asa Gray must have been more than a little intrigued by a communiqué from St. Louis. "We have a very rich English man here," reported Englemann, "an old . . . bachelor who concluded to devote his time and fortune to the founding of a botanic garden and Collection, Kew in miniature, I suppose. . . . I hope something valuable and permanent will come of it."[36]

Englemann's Englishman was Henry Shaw, a cutlery merchant from Sheffield who in 1819 had arrived in St. Louis with a small store of kitchen goods. Parlaying his stock into a quarter million dollar fortune within two decades, Shaw had invested his money in real estate and retired at forty to live out his life as an English country squire in the middle west. During a trip back to England in the early fifties, Shaw had been struck with the beauty of well-kept English parks and estates, and by the internationally famous royal botanic gardens at Kew. "Why may I not have a garden too?" he reasoned. "I have enough land and money for something of the same sort in a smaller way."[37]

Soon the world of professional botany knew of Henry Shaw's desires. He corresponded with William J. Hooker at Kew, Asa Gray's friend and one of the greatest living botanists. He came to know George Englemann, and through Englemann and Hooker, Asa Gray. Each botanist reinforced the other. "I have not yet seen much of Shaw," wrote Englemann in May 1856, "and am unfortunately not the proper person in address & diplomacy etc to work on him—still I hope for the best; he seems very zealous. Get Hooker to encourage him."[38]

Encouragement from several fronts had its effect. In 1857–58 Shaw commissioned Englemann, who was taking his family on a European tour, to purchase books and negotiate for a forty-thousand-specimen herbarium available in Munich. While Englemann was abroad, Henry Shaw busily drew plans for his garden and forwarded them to Cambridge. As the design matured, it became apparent that Henry Shaw would require gentle but firm direction. His interest in botany was aesthetic, not scientific; he wanted attractive formal gardens like those of the English landed gentry. Englemann and Gray, on the other hand, pressed for a garden of exotic varieties to complement the real heart of a botanical establishment, its herbarium and library. The Munich herbarium was a beginning, and late in 1858 Shaw seemed willing to incorporate research facilities, albeit too small, into his plan. At the same time Englemann convinced him that "Missouri Botanical Garden" was a less pretentious alternative to the Englishman's own first choice, an awkwardly learned "Hort. Bot. Missouriensis." "I rejoice to hear that Mr. Shaw keeps up his zeal," wrote Asa Gray, certainly mindful that in two months Harvard would receive Francis Calley Gray's donation for the Agassiz museum.[39]

Suddenly it seemed that Henry Shaw's private affairs might wreck Gray's dream of a "Mississippian Kew." The wealthy gardener was "unapproachable at present," reported the astonished Englemann. "He has a breach of promise case at hand, damages laid at $100,000—probably a swindle; still there must be some cause for it."[40] Gray watched anxiously during the next few months as the harried bachelor went on with his garden plans, arranged to endow the institution at ten thousand dollars a year ("would he had more scientific education or taste," muttered Englemann), and consulted with his attorneys. Perhaps in an effort to keep Shaw's botanical concerns alive during that critical period, in March 1859 Gray published a glowing article on British herbaria in *Silliman's Journal.*[41]

"THE $100,000 CASE," as the St. Louis press headlined the breach-of-promise action, lasted more than a week. Judging from the reporters' appreciative descriptions, Miss Effie Catherine Carztang was sufficiently attractive to have invited Henry Shaw's attentions. No one disputed that he had called often at the boarding house she operated with her mother, or that he had taken her driving in his gardens at Tower Grove. Effie's attorneys charged that Shaw had promised marriage, that their client had been used unjustly by a rich old man, thirty years her senior. Henry Shaw's lawyers countered with the classic defense in such cases. A parade of knowledgeable witnesses affirmed that Miss Carztang had kept a similar boarding house in Charleston, South Carolina, a few years before. There she had been known far and wide as "Madame Carztang." However damaging such testimony, the jury awarded her one-hundred-thousand-dollar damages.[42]

"If he must pay, he may be crippled for a few years," wrote Englemann reassuringly, "but he tells us to go on nevertheless." The judge would probably set aside the verdict of a "partly bought, partly stupid jury" in any event. In consideration of procedural irregularities, and because he had produced additional testimony "against the morals of that woman," a year later Henry Shaw settled for $18,000, most of which went for legal fees. "What books etc could have been bought for that!" was George Englemann's only comment.[43]

As soon as Shaw had indicated that he might give his garden a permanent endowment, Gray had suggested that Englemann consider merging his personal herbarium with the Missouri Botanical Garden. "If I had one I could have free access to always," declared Gray, "I would not take the expense and trouble of keeping up and increasing one myself."[44] The physician replied that he had often considered the move, but saw no immediate prospects for a lasting alliance. "His establishment is 6 miles from here (no horse rail road either!) and with my time cut up by patients I must have everything around me, if I will work any."[45]

Gray and Englemann worked steadily to awaken an interest in research as the wealthy gardener continued to build his establishment. Both to create a position for his colleague and to insure the Garden's scientific value, Gray urged Englemann to cultivate Shaw more vigorously. Keep your own herbarium for the present if you must, he counseled, but adopt the

Garden's filing system and "look to an eventual combination, either in Shaw's lifetime or soon after." As botanist on the scene, only Englemann was in a position to fashion the formal gardens into an institution for botanical research. "This duty must devolve upon you, and when it does, with a decent salary, you could . . . throw physic to the dogs . . . and have time to do yourself justice in botany."[46]

George Englemann was hesitant. His position as a prominent physician had tangible advantages, and he was by no means anxious to assume the responsibilities of a scientific administrator. Neither did he relish his role as a middleman between private wealth and scientific research. "I do not understand the soft soaping as writers phrase it," he protested in April 1860. "A man who has no real scientific zeal nor knowledge who must be got to do things by diplomacy, I can not do much with. The proper way would be to get him interested in what interests us and seems important to us, but that I unfortunately do not understand."[47]

The physician-botanist undervalued his ability, though more than two decades would pass before American science realized the benefits. After the Carztang affair Henry Shaw had retired to the seclusion of his gardens. Englemann saw him occasionally, and continued independently to build his own reputation as the leading expert on American cacti. The Civil War intervened, throwing St. Louis into turmoil and demanding the full measure of the physician's medical skills. Finally in February 1884 George Englemann died, and two months later Henry Shaw, now in his mid-eighties, once again asked the advice of Asa Gray.

The old man looked back over thirty years of "building and planting and paying taxes." What had sustained him, he wrote, "was the pleasure of thinking that my plans would in some future time be appreciated, and the Natural Sciences attain to a high estimation among the future inhabitants of the Mississippi valley—as they do now in the more civilized countries of the world." The Garden had become a showplace, and Henry Shaw's real estate holdings, happily located in what was by now downtown St. Louis, brought in a "neat income." Shaw proposed to guarantee the Missouri Botanical Garden an annual income equal to that of the Smithsonian Institution. A number of his St. Louis friends had suggested that he deed the Garden to the thriving Washington University, but Shaw was hesitant lest his own creation be swallowed up in another institution. What should he do?[48]

That June, the Grays made a stop in St. Louis part of their summer tour to the West. Gray arrived wondering "whether all this was likely to be quite wasted, or was in condition to be turned to good account for botany and horticulture. I wished also to see that dear old Englemann's herbarium should be properly and permanently preserved." After several long interviews with the aging philanthropist, Gray left St. Louis convinced that his botanical colleague had not labored in vain. "If he follows my advice and mends some matters, there will be a great foundation laid."[49] Shaw commissioned Gray and William Trelease, the director of the Garden, to collect and publish all of Englemann's botanical papers in a beautifully illustrated memorial volume.[50] He also drew his will, all the while sending drafts to Cambridge for criticism, to satisfy both scientific and ornamental tastes. Shaw would leave the Garden proper as a public park for the enjoyment of the citizens of St. Louis. He would also endow a School of Botany, with an Asa Gray Professorship, at Washington University. St. Louis, announced a lead editorial in *Science* as soon as the provisions became public, would soon possess "much better facilities and larger means for botany than any other part of the country."[51]

The philanthropist died on August 25, 1889, surviving even Asa Gray by a year and a half. He left his estate as he and the Cambridge botanist had planned, except for a scattering of personal and charitable bequests. One of the latter, a perpetual trust to the Episcopal Bishop of St. Louis, revealed something of Henry Shaw's innermost beliefs and suggested that he too had been drawn to science by way of religion. Each year, read the will, a minister from the diocese was to pronounce a public sermon "on the wisdom and goodness of God as shown in the growth of flowers, fruits, and other products of the vegetable kingdom."[52]

During the years between the conception and realization of the St. Louis botanical establishment Asa Gray had received substantial support from the rich men of Massachusetts. The botanist's tactical retreat in the late 1850's laid the basis for new efforts a few years later. In part the new support stemmed from Gray's rising stature in world science, in part from the fact that the locus of power was shifting within the scientific community itself.

When Joseph Henry split with Dallas Bache over the Dudley Observatory affair in 1859, he had seriously weakened the Lazzaroni as a force in American science. Together with Bache in the Coast Survey, the secretary of the Smithsonian had been one pole of the Washington-Cambridge axis; without Henry's wholehearted support the Lazzaroni could not dictate the direction of American science. Furthermore, the group held sway during a critical but brief stage of development when they were virtually the only American investigators who combined technical talent with organizational ability, political influence, and the determination to make their calling a respectable profession. By the 1860's they were no longer alone. Though individual members like Henry and Wolcott Gibbs would continue to have a hand in shaping new scientific institutions, for all practical purposes the Lazzaroni ceased to be a vital power in 1867 with the death of their chief, Alexander Dallas Bache.

In Boston new alignments were visible in the patterns of institutional politics. In the early sixties William B. Rogers' upstart Massachusetts Institute of Technology and the agricultural college at Amherst beat out the Lawrence Scientific School in the scramble for the state's share of the Morrill Act bounty. At the same time a young Harvard chemistry professor named Charles W. Eliot scandalized Peirce and especially Agassiz by suggesting (with Asa Gray's vigorous nod) that Harvard integrate its semiautonomous scientific departments into a cohesive, modern university. The real test came in Boston's sovereign arbiter of science and culture, the American Academy of Arts and Sciences. In 1863 old Jacob Bigelow retired after sixteen years as president. To Agassiz's chagrin, the membership not only elected Asa Gray as the new president, but made William B. Rogers corresponding secretary and retained Gray's good friend, Josiah P. Cooke, as librarian.[53]

Asa Gray's resources grew with his emerging position as the dean of American botanists and patriarch of natural science in New England. As he had indicated to Englemann in 1859, Gray wanted to turn his herbarium and library over to Harvard provided the university would keep up the collections and contribute a fireproof building for their safekeeping. In the winter of 1863, while influential Bostonians were raising money for the United States Sanitary Commission, Nathaniel Thayer unexpectedly offered to supply the eleven thousand dollars required for the building. Gray hardly knew the Boston banker, who was making a second career out of donating money to Harvard.[54] With the herbarium building assured, two of Gray's friends raised a twelve-thousand-dollar subscription for a capital fund. Jacob Bigelow was former Rumford Professor at Harvard, past president of the American Academy, and a part-time botanist whose *Florula Bostoniensis* and *American Medical Botany* were both standard works. Dr. George B. Emerson held the triple distinction of having influenced Asa Gray's original appointment to the Harvard faculty, appointed Horace Mann to the Massachusetts State Board of Education, and published a respectable manual of the state's trees and shrubs. Together the two men "quietly circulated the paper among their well-to-do acquaintances in Boston" in the spring of 1864.[55]

Even if the Bigelow-Emerson operation lacked the fanfare of an Agassiz campaign, Asa Gray could rest assured that his 200,000 specimens and 2,200-volume library would be preserved to form the nucleus of one of America's principal herbaria. "My collections will be transferred to this their permanent home, to my great relief. My own donation is reckoned in money value at about $20,000."[56] When the new building opened early in 1865, John Amory Lowell donated 335 costly botanical works from his personal library. Lowell's offering was a significant index of Gray's standing in the community as well as a sign of the capitalist's own magnanimity. Five years earlier the gentleman botanist had taken Agassiz's side against Gray in the heated Darwinian debates. Gray, in turn, had criticized Lowell in the *Atlantic Monthly*, suggesting that his arguments against Darwin were so specious that their presentation involved a form of intellectual *"hari-kari."*[57]

Asa Gray was close enough to full research support to feel the lack of it acutely. Teaching duties and care of the botanic garden distressed him. "I envy you more and more in being able to devote yourself to systematic botany," he told an English friend in 1866, "without the distraction and sad consumption of time in professional and administrative duties . . . which make havoc of the opportunities for most botanists."[58] He yearned to complete his *Flora of North America*, a universal guide on which he had worked intermittently since he and John Torrey began the project in the 1830's. The only hope was to reorganize Harvard's botanical establishment, "get rid" of the hated garden by passing it on to a full-time curator, and find the funds to support his research.[59] It seemed for a time in 1866 that George Peabody, the Anglo-American businessman, might emerge as the long-awaited patron. Peabody's nephew, Othneil C. Marsh, however, channeled the millionaire's gifts into his own specialty of paleontology. "If I could get five hundred to one thousand more a year I would at once resign professorship and salary," vowed Asa Gray.[60]

Early in 1870 he toyed with plans for new buildings and hinted of coming financial support. James Arnold, a New Bedford merchant, had died the year before leaving his estate for agricultural, horticultural, or other philanthropic purposes. Dr. George B. Emerson was a principal trustee, and directed the vague bequest into an arboretum for Harvard at Jamaica Plain, situated on land donated earlier by another college benefactor. Gray intended to resign, but the inconvenient distance from the herbarium to Jamaica Plain dictated otherwise. He would stay on for another year.[61]

In 1871 the future seemed brighter. Gray met Horatio Hollis Hunnewell, "a man who is disposed to give money for . . . a much needed botanical lecture-room and laboratory for students."[62] Hunnewell was an immensely wealthy financier who had progressed from banking and foreign exchange to directorships in more than fifty railroad and manufacturing corporations. Casting about for an avocation to occupy his time, in the 1840's he had followed the advice of his cousin, Henry W. Sargent, and became a horticulturist. Like Henry Shaw of St. Louis, another gentleman gardener who loved beautiful flowers, Hunnewell converted his Wellesley, Massachusetts, estate into a regional showplace. But unlike his Missouri counterpart, Hunnewell developed considerable technical competence. He was a frequent contributor to horticultural journals, and made a specialty of collecting rhododendrons, azalias, and coniferous trees. Hunnewell determined to make his estate the most impressive and complete private garden in the region, if not in the nation. "It will be my aim," he noted in his diary in 1866, "to plant . . . every conifer, native and foreign, that will be found sufficiently hardy to thrive in our cold New England climate."[63]

Unknown circumstances united the Wellesley horticulturist and the Cambridge botanist. They were both members of the American Academy, but neither had previously indicated any acquaintance with the other. Nevertheless, in February 1871 Hunnewell agreed to build a twelve-thousand-dollar range of adjoining workrooms and laboratories, connecting Gray's house and herbarium with the conservatory 127 feet away. "A long affair, but don't imagine anything at all grand," wrote Gray of the new installation, where all phases of botanical research could be conveniently pursued under one roof. "A snake, of which our house is the head and the farthest wing of the conservatory the tail, will give you the best idea."[64]

In the autumn of 1872 Charles S. Sargent became director of

both the Harvard Botanical Garden and the Arnold Arboretum at Jamaica Plain. Asa Gray was at last freed of the garden. Even more important, Sargent cemented the bond between Gray and the Wellesley horticulturists. Charles had carried on the horticultural traditions of his relative Henry Sargent, and for years the Sargents and Hunnewells had carried on a good-natured rivalry over the beauty of their respective estates. Young Sargent was also a close friend of George Englemann's, and through him both Gray and the St. Louis botanist became frequent visitors to the Hunnewell gardens. In November 1872 Sargent induced Hunnewell and his own father, Ignatius Sargent, to provide Asa Gray with a permanent income of one thousand dollars per year, on the condition that he give himself wholly to completing *The Flora of North America*.[65] Asa Gray retired from teaching the following year. The Hunnewell-Sargent pension and his book royalties permitted Gray to spend his remaining dozen years comfortably, though not lavishly, pursuing the science to which he had devoted his life.

The careers of Louis Agassiz and Asa Gray demonstrated that until the support of research became institutionalized, solid scientific attainment often had to share the stage with the play of personality. Both Gray and Agassiz were brilliant men of science. Agassiz's stubborn adherence to a pre-Darwinian philosophy of nature should not obscure the fact that biology made great strides in the nineteenth century under the impulse of Germanic Idealism. In the larger community, it was Agassiz's personal flair that overwhelmed Gray and others for years. Had their roles been reversed, Gray might have attracted support for full-time research while he was still young enough to make the most of it; his *Flora of North America* might not have remained unfinished at his death in 1888. Agassiz, unlike Gray, was never frustrated for want of financial backing. The ability to attract such support would always affect the progress of science, but it would be crucial so long as the conduct of research depended primarily upon the uncertain patronage of individual men.

4

Science and
the Community Interest

The application of Science to the useful arts has
changed in the last half century the condition and
relations of the world. It seems to me that we have
been some what neglectful in the cultivation and encouragement of the scientific portion of our National
Economy.

Abbott Lawrence, 1847

IN 1846 Harvard and Yale each inaugurated a new president.
Neither Edward Everett nor Theodore Dwight Woolsey
was a reformer by temperament or experience; certainly neither entered his new office anticipating any substantial departure from tradition. Economic and social change, however,
soon swept the two presidents into the principal collegiate
reform of the day, an urgent effort to link higher education
more closely with the larger community interest. Contrary to
their expectations, Everett and Woolsey found themselves
overhauling old programs and creating new departments,
among them the Lawrence and the Sheffield scientific schools.
Both scientific schools were representative and revealing products of scientific progress and economic development, shaped
by local circumstance and tempered by individual personali-
ties.

Higher education had been one of New England's first
fruits. Since the third decade of the seventeenth century the
colleges had been a functional component of the social order,

preparing their graduates "in those branches of knowledge, of which no one destined to the higher walks of life ought to be ignorant."[1] Greek, Latin, mathematics, natural history, and natural philosophy were the standard fare, recitation from a text the approved pedagogical method. And though nineteenth-century critics ridiculed the old-style American college, it was the natural product of a traditional society where law, medicine, and divinity comprised the learned professions.

During the second quarter of the nineteenth century the industrial and transportation revolutions destroyed the traditional society and brought much of New England to a new stage of economic growth. First water, then steam power, and a regional talent for productive gadgetry sustained the manufacturing impulse. In the 1830's the railroad, full of power and promise, catapulted New England into the industrial age.[2] Only momentarily interrupted by the depression of 1837, economic development surged again in the early forties. The mills were humming, reported Hezekiah Niles's *Weekly Register*, "every spindle twirling, and *double sets of hands . . . engaged*, so as to work night and day."[3] Attracted by annual profits that averaged 10 per cent and often reached twice that figure, established merchants diversified their investments and became mill masters and railroad magnates. In 1845 the textile and shoe industries alone accounted for an estimated $36 million, one third of Massachusetts' total economic output. In that state one person in eight owed his livelihood directly to these phases of industrial production. When Harriet Beecher Stowe published *Oldtown Folks* in 1869, the society she depicted had long since vanished. In a single generation the old New England of "ante-railroad times, . . . a sort of half Hebrew theocracy, half ultrademocratic republic of little villages," had given way to Lynn, Lawrence, and Lowell.[4]

Economic and social change produced a crisis in American higher education. Rooted in the educational values and social needs of an earlier day, the colleges failed to keep pace with the times. By the 1840's industrialization, the spread of political democracy, and the advancement of learning itself had to a considerable degree "democratized the means and appliances of a higher life."[5] The release of social energy created new sources of and new outlets for individual talent, unsettling the old relations between the college and the community. "The College or University forms no integral and necessary part of the social system," complained Francis Wayland. "It plods on its weary way solitary and in darkness."[6] Few men perceived the problem more clearly than Wayland, who in 1827 had become president of Brown University. Like his counterparts at Harvard, Yale, and a dozen other institutions, Wayland faced flagging enrollments and a college treasury drained of tuition income. Throughout the forties Wayland analyzed the social and educational implications of economic development in a series of widely discussed reports and addresses. The most vigorous part of the community, he argued, followed avenues to wealth and prestige that proceeded with little reference to traditional patterns or traditional modes of schooling. "Steam, machinery and commerce have built up a class of society which formerly was only of secondary importance. The inducements to enter the learned professions have become far less, and those to enter upon the active professions, vastly greater."[7]

Higher education was losing its clientele to the "active professions." The colleges clung to the liberal arts when the movement of civilization was, in Wayland's words, "precisely in the line of the useful arts." They ministered to the vocational needs of a minority whose relative influence was on the wane. Comparative enrollment figures from Bowdoin, Waterville, Dartmouth, Middlebury, the University of Vermont, Williams, Amherst, Harvard, Brown, Trinity, Yale, and Wesleyan told of the consequences. Wayland showed that even though educational topics were matters of common conversation, college attendance was not keeping pace with an expanding population. In fact, the opposite was true. In 1830 one person in 13,650 had sought a degree; within two decades the percentage dropped to one in 14,080. "Our customers," wrote Wayland in an appropriately mercantile metaphor, "come from the smallest class in society. . . . We have produced an article for which the demand is diminishing. We sell it at less than cost, and the deficiency is made up by charity. We give it away, and still the demand diminishes."[8] Only immediate and substantial reform could save the colleges from financial ruin and restore to higher education its function in the social process. In 1846 Wayland incorporated part of his program in an elective English and Scientific Course at Brown, though a variety of internal complications prevented the wholesale implementation of his ideas.[9]

Francis Wayland's panacea was hardly original. His diagnosis and prescription for collegiate ills was, instead, a remarkable distillation of contemporary opinion. Other institutions, notably Thomas Jefferson's University of Virginia, Union College under Eliphalet Nott, and Harvard under George Ticknor, had previewed reform. And as Wayland drew on the useful arts to save his "struggling and sinking university" at Providence, fifty miles northward at Cambridge, Massachusetts, other reformers were applying the same ideas to create a thoroughgoing school of science.

Early in 1846 Henry Rogers, whose own educational dreams would finally materialize in the Massachusetts Institute of Technology, reported to his brother William that a new project was afoot at Harvard. "It has been Peirce's darling wish for a long time past," he wrote, "to reorganize the Scientific Corps of the Faculty. . . . They will make a sort of extra-faculty school of science for the use of young men who desire a scientific education without the diploma of the college and without the classics. . . . And they would place the Rumford Professor at the head, . . . and select him for his practical familiarity with the useful arts."[10]

Benjamin Peirce had hardly relaxed from his efforts at observatory promotion before launching a master plan for science at Harvard. He lost no time in approaching Harvard's new president, Edward Everett, who asked the mathematician to translate his "darling wish" into a concrete proposal. The result was a "Plan of a School of Practical and Theoretical

Science," submitted to the corporation less than two weeks after Everett's election. Meanwhile Samuel Eliot, Harvard's treasurer and a man who always seemed to be on the inside of new schemes, reminded the corporation that "men are devoting themselves, in a way which has been only recently known or required in this country, to various departments of science, as a means of honorable professional employment."[11]

The stated purpose of the proposed school was to "bring the University into more immediate and intimate connection with the community to which it belongs, by supplying the public demand for scientific eduction of various kinds." Specifically, the institution would be a professional school, offering students in science and technology advanced training equivalent "to that now enjoyed by students in law and medicine." Peirce expected the two-year course to attract four classes of students: college graduates bent on careers as men of science, engineers, astronomical observers, and industrial technicians of all kinds.[12]

The polytechnic school would incorporate most of the scientific talent already available in Cambridge. Peirce himself, William Cranch Bond, Asa Gray, the chemist John White Webster, and the physicist Joseph Lovering would all be present. Kingpin of the undertaking, the Rumford Professor on the Application of Science to the Useful Arts, had yet to be appointed. The chair had remained vacant since the resignation of Daniel Treadwell the year before.

With the Peirce "Plan" before him, Edward Everett prepared his inaugural discourse in the spring of 1846. On convocation day he ranged widely over the present condition and future expectations of the university. Proceeding to specific recommendations, Everett announced that Harvard must awaken to a new set of social obligations. A scientific school, he advised, would furnish men equipped "to explore and bring to light the inexhaustible natural resources of the country, and to guide its vast industrial energies in their rapid development." Though a few alumni and spectators grumbled at innovation, and Ralph Waldo Emerson shuddered at the prospect of science and "corpse-cold Unitarianism" loose in Harvard Yard, over-all President Everett's message pleased the community. It also gave notice to the Scientific Corps that they could expect support from the top.[13]

In November 1846 a corporation committee including James Walker, John Amory Lowell, and President Everett met to draw preliminary plans for a school of "Science and Literature." The main responsibility fell on Everett, who added a department of literature and philology in keeping with his own scholarly interests. Everett saw the school as the entering wedge for "a kind of German University" on the banks of the Charles. Such broad schemes for graduate education were, however, premature. For the present, Walker, Samuel Eliot, and the historian, Jared Sparks, joined forces to remind the president that "the school should be started on purely scientific grounds." On February 13, 1847, not quite a year after Peirce offered his proposal, the corporation approved Everett's revised plan for "the Scientific School of the University at Cambridge."[14]

The corporation had also appointed the Rumford Professor. There were a number of qualified candidates, but due to the combined influence of Everett and Peirce, there was never any real question about the selection of Eben N. Horsford, Peirce's choice for the chair. An engineering graduate of Rensselaer Polytechnic Institute, Horsford combined technical skill and experience with advanced scientific training. After service on the New York Geological Survey and a four-year interlude teaching natural philosophy in the Albany Female Academy, Horsford had traveled to Giessen in 1844 to study analytic chemistry in Justus von Liebig's famed laboratory. Returning to Cambridge in 1847 with Liebig's praise and an impressive list of published papers to his credit, Horsford began at once to sketch plans for a laboratory patterned on the best European models.[15]

As yet the scientific school was a paper organization. It had no funds and no facilities beyond whatever the university was willing to contribute. Since it was a semi-independent institution, an independent endowment was vital for survival. Early in June Edward Everett suggested that his old friend Abbott Lawrence might prove a willing patron. Samuel Eliot addressed a written appeal, Everett followed with personal visits. The president knew his man. On June 7, 1847, Lawrence agreed to contribute fifty thousand dollars toward placing the scientific school on a firm foundation.[16]

In many ways Abbott Lawrence typified New England's new commercial-industrial elite. He was born in 1792 on the family farm at Groton, Massachusetts; his formal education had ceased with graduation from that community's indifferent academy. In 1808 Lawrence left the farm for Boston, apprenticing himself to his elder brother Amos, a successful merchant in the British textile trade. Within six years he had risen to full partnership, then in 1831 became principal member of the firm when ill health forced Amos into retirement. During these years the domestic textile industry was booming, and the Lawrence brothers shifted easily from foreign imports to the products of American looms. Abbott soon moved into the circle of the Lowells, the Jacksons, and the Appletons, leading manufacturers who had established the Waltham Mills at Lowell during the War of 1812. He also became an early regional railroad promoter. In 1845 the seasoned entrepreneur founded the textile city of Lawrence, Massachusetts.[17]

Abbott Lawrence, however, was no ordinary cotton mill capitalist. Though schooled in commerce rather than college, he had close ties with New England intellectual life. Lawrence was a conspicuous inhabitant of that peculiar Boston environment which contributed so much to the flowering of New England culture in the pre–Civil War years. In 1841 Sir Charles Lyell had called attention to "the mingling of the professors, both literary and scientific, with the eminent lawyers, clergymen, physicians, and principal merchants of the place." Their mutual interaction, observed the great geologist, "forms a society of a superior kind."[18]

Over the years Abbott Lawrence had demonstrated a special interest in science and scientific men. The Sillimans had been welcome at tea since the 1830's. In 1843 he spearheaded the drive to secure a research observatory for Harvard. The next year he had contributed to a publication fund for the National Institute for the Promotion of Science. Considering his business interests, his great wealth, his previous support of science, and his friendship with Edward Everett, Abbott Lawrence was a tailor-made patron for a scientific school. He was one of those business leaders who, in the words of Freeman Hunt, a journalistic admirer, "trafficked in the busy world that they might endow professorships."[19]

Lawrence's letter of donation was a remarkable document. Its very length suggested that he took his philanthropy seriously, and its persuasive tone underlined the fact that applied science—the systematic employment of scientific discovery in industrial production—was still a novel proposition in New England. His thoughtful analysis of contemporary trends, moreover, marked Abbott Lawrence as a man of unusually acute social vision.

During the preceding half century, he wrote, science and technology had revolutionized social life. No longer were the traditional learned professions a sufficient outlet for the nation's best talent. "I believe the time has arrived when we should make an effort to diversify the occupations of our people, and develop more freely their strong mental and physical resources." Common schools already provided satisfactory elementary instruction. The academies and colleges answered well enough for the liberal arts. Existing professional schools prepared young men in theology, law, and medicine. Aspiring merchants turned to "the Counting House or the Ocean." But where, and how to train engineers, miners, mechanics? The problem was acute in Massachusetts. "For several years I have seen and felt the pressing want in our community (and in fact the whole Country) of an increased number of men educated in the practical sciences."[20]

The philanthropist's conception of what a "practical" education entailed was characteristic of his time. In the first instance this understanding was a function of the broadened range of vocational options available in the second quarter of the century. The old classical curriculum had been "practical" in the traditional society where law, medicine, and divinity encompassed the range of professional callings. But times had changed, as Samuel Eliot noted when he told the Harvard Corporation that now men pursued science "as a means of honorable professional employment." Practical training was utilitarian in a concrete, personal sense. It signified training for a career, whether that of preaching or merchandising, engineering or scientific research.[21]

Practicality carried another important connotation. The United States abounded in men of action, said Lawrence, "hard hands . . . ready to work upon our hard materials." But where were the "sagacious heads . . . to direct those hands?" For want of knowledge creative men laboriously rediscovered what was already known, while "ignorant men fight against the laws of nature with a vain energy, and purchase their experience at great cost." Here the industrialist joined the flight from Baconian empiricism. In Lawrence's view, a proper school of science would teach research, not shop practice. He would have agreed in principle with Dallas Bache's contention that "empiricism is the lowest form of knowledge. Science generalizes, and the scientific mechanic, instead of looking for separate solutions for every problem, solves many from one principle. It is easier to work down than up."[22]

As a manufacturer and financier, Lawrence had an understandable interest in engineering, mining (including metallurgy), and mechanics. He directed that these subjects receive primary attention in the scientific school. But he was too perceptive not to realize that such a curriculum necessarily rested on a solid foundation in the basic sciences involved. Doubtless Lawrence's close friend, Charles S. Storrow, the European-trained Chief Engineer of the Lawrence Mills, counseled the philanthropist on the proper relations between original discovery and its industrial applications.[23] Lawrence planned to invite business and industrial leaders to lecture periodically in the scientific school, but he stipulated that "none but *first rate* men" should constitute the regular faculty. "They should be men of comprehensive views with an enthusiastic devotion to the great interests of science. They should love their profession, and work in it day by day."[24]

All this would cost money. The businessman believed that professors' salaries should come out of student lecture fees—a simple method of insuring "exertion and fidelity" from the staff. He also wanted to be certain that the scientific school would not undercut other scientific enterprises. The Harvard Observatory already had a just claim on local liberality, and Asa Gray's botanical researches would certainly "present strong claims upon the public bounty." Consequently Lawrence allocated over half of his fifty thousand dollars for building construction and the purchase of apparatus. Only two new professorships were required to complete the scientific faculty, the Lawrence Chairs in geology and engineering. A complex fiscal system would equalize their salaries with the fifteen-hundred-dollar Rumford Professorship. The Scientific School now had a program and a patron. Lawrence and the corporation agreed, however, to postpone operations (except for Horsford's chemical department, temporarily billeted in Holden Chapel) until the new professors could be appointed.[25]

Lawrence probably had Louis Agassiz in mind when he established the geological chair. It mattered little that Agassiz's geological work was limited to glaciation studies, principally in Europe, or that a number of better qualified American geologists were eager for the post. The obvious fact he was "interested in applied science only to the degree that it might have a practical effect upon his future" seemed less important than insuring Agassiz's permanent connection with the Boston-Cambridge community. In the autumn of 1847 Agassiz joined the faculty of the newly named Lawrence Scientific School.[26]

Agassiz's appointment set a predictable course for the Scientific School. His grandiose research projects and cosmic expositions on the plan of creation left little time for lectures on mining and metallurgy, his official assignment. No matter in Agassiz's case—by all standards he met Abbott Lawrence's criteria for a *"first rate"* man. But the naturalist's devotion to research reinforced the predilections of Peirce, Lovering, and Jeffries Wyman, the promising new comparative anatomist.

There was still no professor of engineering in the spring of 1849. Treasurer Eliot, moreover, was finding it difficult to restrain the scientific corps. "I cannot lay down rules precise enough to hold these heedless professors, who seem to think they have a rich college, & a richer founder to spend for them as much as they want."[27] The founder was also perturbed. He was concerned about the substantive offerings of the Scientific School, but equally irritated by the arrogance of its faculty. Benjamin Peirce had annoyed him from the outset. When, during a conference in 1847, Samuel Eliot had dropped the impolitic (though accurate) observation that Peirce was really "the father of the Scientific School," Lawrence almost washed his hands of the enterprise. It required all of Edward Everett's diplomatic skill to sooth the ruffled philanthropist.[28] But by September 1849 the lack of an engineer, Peirce's personality, and Agassiz's tendency to plunge headlong into expensive projects caused Lawrence to rescind his original instructions concerning the Scientific School.

"Some of my expectations," he explained, "have proved erroneous." Horsford's chemical department was a success; he had a laboratory, a salary of fifteen hundred dollars from the Rumford endowment, and student fees would doubtless provide for other needs. Geology, on the other hand, had been so transformed under Agassiz that few students applied. Lawrence therefore abolished the geological chair, at the same time showing his personal devotion to Agassiz by promising him a fifteen-hundred-dollar annual income for the next five years. "The more immediately pressing call" involved engineering. Now placing engineering on an equal footing with chemistry, Lawrence re-directed twenty-five thousand dollars of the original gift into an endowment for the engineering chair. Voicing the convictions of a self-made businessman, he also expressed his dissent from "the views pretty distinctly intimated in the communications from the gentlemen of the Scientific Faculty

. . . that it is necessary, or important, or even desirable that the Scientific man should be raised above the necessity of taking care of himself, and his household, in order that he may devote his whole soul to scientific investigations. His mind is stimulated to more valuable effort," countered Lawrence, "by sharing with the rest of mankind, in a degree of uncertainty as to the future."[29]

By now, however, the Lawrence Scientific School had taken on a life of its own. The first graduating class of four (1851) was a fair sampling of the kind of "intelligent mechanics" who sought its offerings. William L. Jones would become a professor of natural science in his native state of Georgia; Joseph LeConte quickly became an eminent naturalist; David A. Wells, after a brief career in scientific journalism, turned to political economy; John D. Runkle subsequently rose to the presidency of the Massachusetts Institute of Technology.[30]

Lawrence's directive, written less than a week before he sailed for England as the new American Minister to the Court of St. James, had little lasting effect on the character of the Scientific School. His prodding did lead to the appointment of Henry L. Eustis to the engineering chair the following month, but the former West Point instructor was never able to build a strong department. He had to combat disinterest within the Scientific School and, after 1862, outside competition from the richly endowed Massachusetts Institute of Technology. Abbott Lawrence, meanwhile, was busy abroad with affairs of state, in no position to oppose the forces shaping his creation. Nor, in the final analysis, was he so inclined. Dazzled by Agassiz, committed to the general proposition that science was vital to an advancing society, Lawrence had ventured considerable capital on an educational experiment. At his death in August 1855, an additional bequest of fifty thousand dollars demonstrated that the financier was satisfied he had made a wise investment.

After Lawrence's death the Scientific School's chemistry offerings rapidly deteriorated. Eben Horsford took the title of his Rumford Chair, "on the Application of Science to the

Alexander Dallas Bache

Louis Agassiz

Benjamin Peirce

Joseph Henry

The Cincinnati Observatory

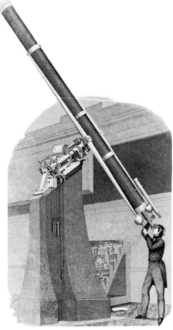

Ormsby MacKnight Mitchel   The Cincinnati Equatorial Telescope

The Dudley Observatory

George Engelmann

Abbott Lawrence

James Lick

Othniel C. Marsh

Edward D. Cope

George Peabody

Useful Arts," literally. Though he continued to offer instruction in the "solution of problems of research in experimental science," he found increasing satisfaction and reward outside Harvard as a manufacturing chemist. By 1863 the success of patent baking powder and Professor Horsford's Acid Phosphate, a reliable tonic for morning sickness, nervous prostration, and the "immediate ill effects of tobacco," led the Rumsford Professor to abandon academic life entirely for the management of his chemical works.[31] His replacement, Wolcott Gibbs, was an active Lazzaroni. Gibbs's own original research in organic chemistry infused new life into the program, and helped make the Lawrence School once again a center for professional chemical education.

As Horsford drifted away from the Scientific School, strange things were happening to chemistry in the college proper. John White Webster, the Erving Professor of Chemistry and Mineralogy, was waiting to mount the gallows in Leverett Street Jail. A physician-turned-chemist of no great ability, Webster had spent most of his years on the faculty entertaining lavishly and otherwise living beyond his means. Deeply in debt to a fellow physician, Dr. George Parkman (the uncle of the historian), Webster had balked at repayment until his relentless creditor badgered him in the presence of his students. Bankrupt, aggravated by Parkman's repeated dunning, publicly humiliated, in November 1849 Webster lured Dr. Parkman to his death in the laboratory of the Massachusetts Medical College. A week later a suspicious janitor broke through fresh masonry in the basement. Boston was horrified as a careful search of the building, and testimony during the subsequent trial, disclosed the lengths to which the physician-chemist had gone to hide his crime. John White Webster tendered his resignation from the faculty in July 1850, a month before he was hanged.[32]

By a fortunate coincidence, the day after Dr. Parkman disappeared the corporation had authorized Josiah P. Cooke, a young mathematics tutor with an interest in chemistry, to assume Professor Webster's freshman teaching duties. The following spring Cooke became an instructor, in reality the acting Erving Professor. Barely twenty-three, Cooke was an informed and enthusiastic teacher. Charles W. Eliot, chemist and reform president of Harvard, later recalled that as a student during Cooke's maiden term he "first learned what Chemistry was about, and what was the scientific method in observing and reasoning." In December 1850, Cooke's election as Erving Professor came as a surprise to no one.[33]

He brought two important qualifications to the chair. If Horsford's inferior in training, and Webster's in experience, Cooke was vastly more persistent than either in his determination to build a respectable chemistry department. Moreover, his friendship with Jared Sparks, extending from his undergraduate days at Harvard, assured the young professor a powerful ally on the corporation. Cooke had need of such a friend, for he faced a formidable task. Like his predecessor, he was obliged to deliver all the chemical and mineralogical lectures at Harvard as well as chemical lectures in the medical school. He had to purchase chemicals and apparatus out of his own pocket. Harvard provided a laboratory of sorts—the damp, ill-heated cellar of University Hall, already occupied by the college baker and uncomfortably close to the pit of the common college privy. Undaunted, Cooke petitioned for money and an expanded curriculum. By 1854 Harvard offered five laboratory courses where none had existed in 1850.[34]

In July 1856 Cooke pressed for a chemical laboratory for research and teaching. The cramped cellar prevented serious work, he explained to the corporation; the atmosphere ruined supplies and corroded apparatus. There was a serious fire hazard. "The effluvia and noxious fumes" constantly routed students and professors from the recitation rooms above. A separate building, to cost approximately ten thousand dollars, would solve these problems. Cooke realized that the college had no funds for such an enterprise; instead he based his hopes on "the well known liberality of the wealthy gentlemen of Boston." He only asked corporation endorsement for a private fund-raising venture.[35]

With official blessing, the enterprising chemist approached John E. Thayer, an immensely wealthy Boston broker. Thayer had contributed previously to the Harvard Observatory, and to Cooke's refurbishing of the old college mineralogical cabinet. Thayer's brother, Nathaniel, was a systematic patron of science at Harvard. Cooke shrewdly masked his appeal for funds as a request for counsel. "Immediately associated with the wealthy gentlemen of the vicinity," surely Thayer could suggest ways and means of raising ten thousand dollars, preferably from a single donor whose name would be perpetuated in the building. The chemist-promoter justified the new laboratory on practical and scientific grounds. There students "preparing . . . for any of the Scientific Professions, or for mercantile life" could gain invaluable laboratory experience. Recalling Abbott Lawrence's desire to educate the public on the value of technology, Cooke explained to Thayer that "the importance of discoveries in science and especially in Chemistry, which is so immediately associated with the manufacturing interest, is not apt to be understood in our community." The long-term return on the investment, however, would be the "extension of scientific knowledge by experimental investigations."[36]

Cooke delivered his letter and laboratory plans, then left Boston for a needed vacation. When he returned early in September, the chemist found that the financier had given the project considerable thought. Thayer immediately offered to assume one tenth of the total subscription. He also made a bold proposition. He informed Cooke that Ward N. Boylston had died in 1818, leaving a bequest to Harvard for an anatomical museum and a chemical laboratory. Under the provisions of the Boylston trust, the principal would accumulate until it reached thirty-five thousand dollars. At the moment it was twelve thousand dollars short of that figure. Why not increase the proposed subscription, add it to the old Boylston bequest, and build an even larger laboratory with the combined resources? Though delighted with the prospect, Cooke at first shrank from the banker's scheme to use a little money to realize more. Talks with Jeffries Wyman, Jared Sparks, and others soon convinced him that the plan was feasible. With Thayer's advice Cooke compiled a subscription list, printed a prospectus, and canvassed Boston's men of wealth. Professional scientific ambition and creative philanthropy formed a winning combination. Boylston Hall, dedicated in 1858, provided Harvard students with ample opportunities for first-hand laboratory work, and gave Cooke, Wyman, and their successors a place to advance as well as diffuse scientific knowledge.[37]

Harvard science developed in several parallel paths rather than along a solid front. Josiah Cooke went his way, the chemists in the Lawrence School went theirs. Benjamin Peirce dominated mathematics and astronomy, Louis Agassiz zoology, and Asa Gray botany. The emphasis was on the staff rather than the institution. That Joseph LeConte took a formal degree at the Lawrence School only as a favor to the professors, who wanted to make as large a showing as possible, was an indication of the loose organizational structure. "I had not given any thought to the Scientific School, or to any connection at all with Harvard," he later recalled. "I went to Harvard simply to study with Agassiz."[38] The easy organization of science at Harvard gave individual leadership free play, but also occasionally prevented concerted action. It remained for Charles W. Eliot to assume the presidency in 1869 and weld the fragments into a coherent university. In 1906 the Lawrence Scientific School ceased its separate existence and was absorbed into the total university structure.

For all its lack of system in the early years, the Lawrence School made an impressive contribution to American scientific endeavor. After the first class of four in 1851, nearly two hundred more bachelors of science graduated within the first two decades. Any institution could be proud of alumni like Simon Newcomb, Charles S. Peirce, Cleveland Abbe, Edward C. Pickering, Frank W. Clarke, and Frederic W. Putnam. Such men received their introduction to research because in mid-century Massachusetts the advancement of science became a community interest, guided by professional investigators and sustained by private liberality. However utilitarian their outlook, the generation of Abbott Lawrence and John E. Thayer understood that applied science presumed a body of scientific principles to apply. These entrepreneurs also knew that in a republic economic development, social change, and the advancement of learning had reciprocal effects which could not be ignored.

Like its sister institution at Cambridge, the Sheffield Scientific School at New Haven grew out of an interplay between academic science and community interest. But while the Lawrence School was conceived in an industrial environment, "Sheff" owed its inception to the conditions of Connecticut agriculture and its permanence to a unique network of family relationships.

Connecticut had lagged somewhat behind neighboring Massachusetts in the take-off toward industrialization. In the second quarter of the nineteenth century, manufactures centered in a few specialized lines, such as brass founding, ironware, textiles, clocks, and firearms. Even so, in 1845 a statewide economic survey revealed that Indian corn production outstripped brass products, that potatoes yielded more wealth than clocks. The hay crop exceeded the value of either cotton or woolen manufactures by more than a million dollars, a clear indication that livestock continued to bulk large in the Connecticut economy. As late as 1850 agricultural interests dominated more than 100 of the 148 towns in the land of steady habits.[39]

Though the economic balance swung toward the farm, the 1840's were a time of great stress and instability for Connecticut agriculture. The transition from farming for a living to farming for a profit had produced serious dislocations in economic and social life. A rapidly growing population crowded the land. Though New England factory towns and growing seaboard cities created a home market for enterprising commercial farmers, cheap agricultural products flowed eastward by rail and canal from the western states, more often than not undercutting the local producer. Enervated by the soil-sapping practices of traditional agriculture, rural Connecticut fell before the competition of eastern cities and western lands. Women and girls followed textiles from the family hearth to the milltown; young men sought success in urban centers or joined the Yankee exodus to the fertile lands beyond the Western Reserve. Rural relief became a matter for private concern and public action.[40]

Reinforced by the growing fear that urban depravity was about to corrupt the nation's rural virtue, hard economic calculations prompted a flurry of organizational activity in the 1840's. Connecticut agricultural societies and farm clubs proliferated, boosting the home state and propagandizing for agricultural reform.[41] Horace Bushnell's performance was broadly representative. Addressing the Hartford County Agricultural Society in October 1846, the minister and president of Middlebury College argued that modern tillage methods and enriched social life would hold people to the land. "Science and society," he declared, "are the great wants of agriculture." Moreover, farmers who deserted Connecticut for the "new world of the west" only deluded themselves. They exchanged material comforts, security, the blessings of organized religion, and the scenic New England countryside for the spirit-dulling monotony of life on the prairies. "The great west, which is now the Paradise of cheap land, will be known as a Paradise no longer, but rather as the great American corn-field, the Poland of the United States."[42]

While orators stumped from lecture hall to county fair proclaiming the horrors of the sod house frontier, recent advances in science held out a less grandiloquent but more realistic means of halting the flight from the farm. Organic chemistry was revealing, for the first time, something of the relations between plant nutrition and the composition of soils. Chemical analysis promised a substitute for folk wisdom, a way to explain crop failures and a means to secure higher yields through systematic fertilization. Science, as Bushnell had declared, would make rural life more attractive by making it more rewarding. "Chemical Farming" became the rage; Justus von

Liebig's pioneering handbook, *Organic Chemistry in Its Applications to Agriculture and Physiology* (1840), was quickly translated from the German and ran through three American editions in less than two years.[43]

Organic chemistry was in its infancy. Liebig had opened his laboratory to American students in 1826, and two decades later a practicing agricultural chemist was of necessity a professional investigator whose every experiment might contribute to the store of fundamental knowledge. Furthermore, only reliable analysis could combat the charlatans who peddled agricultural nostrums guaranteed to cure sick fields overnight and transform every barren tract into an Eden. Economic prosperity and the integrity of science both demanded competent workers in the field.[44]

Professional ambition acted as the catalyst in combining the advancement of chemical knowledge with the immediate social and economic needs of rural Connecticut. Since the first decade of the century Benjamin Silliman had been building a small but influential scientific establishment at New Haven. Though officially Yale science was less concerned with original investigation than with turning out pious and cultured graduates, Silliman's *American Journal of Science*, founded in 1818, had made the college a nerve center for American scientific activity.[45]

Benjamin Silliman, Jr., was in a position to build on his father's foundation. He had grown up as an accepted member of the Yale family. As associate editor of the *Journal* he came to know most American men of science, and was able to keep abreast of the latest work in Europe. A product of the last generation of natural philosophers, the younger Silliman belonged to the first generation of scientific men.

Yale was not prepared to follow the twenty-eight-year-old chemist and depart from the time-honored classical curriculum petrified in 1828 by the famous Yale Report.[46] Jeremiah Day, co-author of the report, still clung to the college presidency at seventy-one, still insisting that a college was no place for specialized training of any sort. In 1844 the younger Silliman grew impatient, announcing that he would offer private laboratory training in analytic chemistry, mineralogy, and geology. Though conducted under the shadow of the college, Silliman's "courses of Study and Physical Research" were an entirely independent undertaking. But as was often the case in the formative era of modern American scientific institutions, his personal enterprise served as an entering wedge.[47] In the summer of 1846 President Day announced his retirement. A change in administrations might mean a change in policy. In any case, as the elder Silliman noted in his diary, the transition period was marked by "much agitation of mind here & elsewhere" and offered an opportunity to work for a formal connection with the college.[48]

Equally important, John Pitkin Norton, the Sillimans' prize chemistry student, was back after two years advanced training abroad. Norton was the right man with the right training at the right time. His father, a wealthy Hudson Valley farmer, had educated his son in both the theory and practice of agriculture. Norton had spent his summers in the fields, his winters studying in Albany, New York, Boston, and New Haven. In 1841–42 and 1842–43 he had studied with the Sillimans, then at their suggestion had gone to Edinburgh to complete his training with Professor James F. W. Johnson, a pioneering agricultural chemist. Johnson combined systematic laboratory instruction with what later would be termed agricultural extension work, carrying the fruits of research directly to the working farmer. Obviously impressed with what he saw, Norton wrote glowing reports each month for publication in the principal New England farm journals. He returned from Europe a competent chemist and a zealous advocate of agricultural reform.[49]

With Norton in mind, in July 1846 the younger Silliman proposed that the Yale Corporation create a new professorship of Agricultural Chemistry and Vegetable and Animal Physiology. Presently, he explained, sounding the familiar call for cultural independence, training in these sciences could be obtained "only with great difficulty & expense, under the embarrassments of a European residence, & the inconvenience of a foreign tongue." It was also time that the college serve the state's agricultural interests. Most revealing, though, was Silliman's assertion that the new professorship would serve a new clientele. "The students having access to its advantages will be strictly professional & not academical."[50]

In August the corporation considered Silliman's proposal. As a special inducement to the penurious administration, John P. Norton's father, John T. Norton, anonymously offered five thousand dollars to support the new enterprise.[51] The corporation created two new chairs, one of agricultural chemistry and one of general chemistry for undergraduates, appointing Norton to the former and the younger Silliman to the latter. There were two important stipulations regarding the agricultural chemist. "Graduates and others not members of the undergraduate class" would constitute his students, and "the support of this professor is in no case to be chargeable to the existing funds or revenues of the College."[52]

The fiscal clause suggested the reluctance with which Yale welcomed the innovation. Perhaps in an effort to neutralize its scientific character, during the next few months the administration broadened the curriculum "to embrace philosophy, literature, history, the moral sciences other than law and theology, the natural sciences excepting medicine, and their application to the arts." On paper the new scheme resembled Edward Everett's initial plan for the Lawrence Scientific School. The corporation, which approved the program in August 1847, called it the Department of Philosophy and Arts.[53]

Conceived by scientific men, staffed by chemists, it was hardly surprising that the department fulfilled its promise only in the laboratory sciences. "Professors SILLIMAN and NORTON," announced the college *Catalogue* for 1847–48, "have opened a Laboratory on the College grounds." The two chemists had managed to rent President Day's former dwelling from the corporation, and had fitted it out as an analytic laboratory. The administration's willingness to have a laboratory "on the college grounds," even if it would not contribute to its support, was a measure of the forces of change at work. After guiding Yale along the straight and narrow path of classical education for years, old Jeremiah Day saw his own home converted into an enclave of aspiring professional scientists.[54]

The orphan had a home, but it still wanted for subsistence. Thrown on their own resources, Norton and Silliman paid for supplies out of their own pockets, then turned to commercial chemical analysis as a method of supplementing student fees and meeting expenses. They tested soils and fertilizers, well water and patent medicines. In 1849 Norton analyzed samples of India rubber for a young inventor named Charles Goodyear, who five years before had taken out his first patent on the vulcanization process. In 1852 Norton's assistant submitted a bill for eight dollars to the Rev. G. Bull with the terse report: "The samples of *tea* and *coffee* which you left at the laboratory . . . have been examined and found to contain a large quantity of *Mercury*, existing, in all probability, in the form of *Corrosive Sublimate*. The girl whom you suspect should be arrested immediately, if she has not been already." Such routine analytic work brought in needed revenue while it provided graduate students with opportunities to perfect their laboratory technique.[55]

John P. Norton aspired to make Yale the "leading chemical school of the country." The younger Silliman had been called to a chair in a Kentucky medical college, leaving Norton in full charge of the Department of Philosophy and Arts. "My intention," he told Wolcott Gibbs in the spring of 1849, "is after about a year of further experience to commence some movement for the building of a laboratory."[56] His rising professional consciousness was visible on several fronts. Norton joined with the Lazzaroni in planning the stillborn National University at Albany. At Yale he urged the awarding of a new degree, analogous to the German Ph.D., for graduates of his department. In the community at large he propagandized for excellence in research. "There is truth in science," he wrote in a prize-winning essay on scientific farming, "but it is not everyone who can draw it out." He treated the readers of Luther Tucker's influential farm journal, *The Cultivator*, to long essays extolling the man of science, the "true follower of patient, earnest, truth-seeking research."[57]

Overwork and failing health took their toll. John P. Norton died in the autumn of 1852, two months after his thirtieth birthday. "My apparatus and books in the laboratory," he said on his deathbed, "I wish given to the college, if the department shall be continued. I hope it will be kept up; it has cost me a great deal of labor."[58] Norton left a vigorous school of science, even if it shared in the precarious state of general college finance. Student enrollment had climbed steadily from eleven in 1847–48 to fifty-five in 1851–52. A permanent endowment was the only missing ingredient.[59]

Norton's successor was John A. Porter, another Silliman product. He graduated from Yale in 1842, and taught rhetoric in Delaware College before resigning to follow a career in chemistry. Returning in 1850 after three years with Liebig at Giessen, Porter had assisted Eben Horsford at Harvard, then went to Brown where Francis Wayland was pushing laboratory science into the curriculum. From Brown, Porter had come to New Haven, accompanied by William A. Norton, another former Brown professor, who added engineering to the Department of Philosophy and Arts. A paper merger between the engineering and chemical departments resulted in the formal establishment of the Yale Scientific School.[60]

For the future of science at Yale, Porter's private life was far more important than his Giessen training. Soon after his arrival he met Josephine Sheffield, whose father, Joseph, was a railroad magnate and leading New Haven citizen. Friendship grew into courtship. In July 1855 they were married. Though Joseph Sheffield had a legitimate interest in engineering and prided himself on his own grasp of precise technical information, family considerations overshadowed all others in turning his attention to science at Yale. He presented his first gift, six thousand dollars in railroad bonds, in August 1854.[61]

The next contribution to Yale science was also a response to family pressures, guided by an active faculty effort to put the Scientific School on a sound footing. In March 1856 Porter published an elaborate "Plan of an Agricultural School." Simultaneously the corporation (now more friendly toward the popular Department of Philosophy and Arts) hired Daniel Coit Gilman, a recent graduate just returned from Europe, as publicity agent for the campaign. Gilman's family ties with the Sillimans (his brother was Benjamin Silliman's son-in-law) brought him into close association with the geologist James Dwight Dana, another Silliman son-in-law. Together Gilman, Dana, and Porter organized public meetings, delivered speeches, and distributed pamphlets describing the "great Central School of Science" to be raised in New Haven.[62] The promoters emphasized the matter of scientific specialization, contrasting European achievement with American backwardness. "For any one man to be willing to 'profess' a knowledge of two such sciences as 'mining' and 'metallurgy,'" Gilman declared, "would in Germany be considered an indication of emptiness of mind or emptiness of purse." One of the first to respond was John P. Norton's father. Concerned for the institution his son had helped create, John T. Norton offered five thousand dollars provided others came forward with twenty thousand dollars more.[63]

Even without the ballyhoo, Joseph Sheffield could not easily have ignored the ongoing promotional activities of the scientific faculty. In April 1856 he purchased a mansion and grounds on Hillhouse Avenue, near the Scientific School, intending to donate the property and building for a *"scientific and agricultural* school."[64] Soon thereafter Joseph and Mrs. Sheffield left on an extended European tour. While abroad they apparently discussed their own plans and the future of the school in New Haven. Their daughter and son-in-law, the Sillimans, father and son, and the Danas all lived on Hillhouse Avenue. The Sheffields could renovate the recently purchased mansion and move into a congenial family, social, and scientific circle. A medical college occupied the adjoining corner lot. Mrs. Sheffield considered it an "insufferable objection" in the neighborhood, anyway, so why not eliminate the medical college and utilize the building for the Scientific School? From Italy Sheffield outlined the scheme to Porter and to the president of the medical college, offering to buy the grounds at a substantial figure. The physicians could move elsewhere and build a more suitable edifice, the Scientific School would have a new home, and, with the medical college out of the picture, so would Joseph and Maria Sheffield.[65]

The arrangements were completed before the Sheffields returned to New Haven in 1858. The philanthropist deeded the property to the corporation soon thereafter. Even though financial panic gripped the nation, Sheffield urged Yale to forge ahead in outfitting the new building. "In all probability those who have the means and the disposition to aid in such matters can do so as well at one time as another," he told his son-in-law, "while in such dull and disastrous times materials and labor may be had lower than ever, and what is more important, . . . employment to the poor laborer, even at low prices, . . . may save his family from want and himself from bad habits if not from crime."[66] Evidently other Connecticut men of wealth did not share his financial optimism or his sense of stewardship, for another statewide subscription campaign brought meager results.[67] Still another expected source of endowment dried up in February 1859 when President Buchanan vetoed Justin Morrill's land grant college bill.

Undaunted, John Porter and others convinced Joseph Sheffield of the *"absolute necessity"* of maintaining the institution himself. He rebuilt the old medical college, adding two wings for some thirty thousand dollars. In October 1860, as the building opened, he gave a fifty-thousand-dollar endowment for several professorships. The corporation celebrated the event by instituting one of John P. Norton's proposals of a decade before, becoming the first American institution of higher learning to award the doctorate of philosophy. In 1861, after repeated urging, Sheffield permitted the corporation to rename the Scientific School in his honor.[68]

"Sheff" continued to grow. As Sheffield put it, the college

"had an 'Elephant' on hand without any means, or rather means enough to feed him and keep him alive." The Scientific School did eventually receive Connecticut's share of the Morrill Act bounty, and in the late sixties a general campaign for endowment funds raised $47,800 in a little over two years. Joseph Sheffield demonstrated his continuing interest through repeated donations. In 1871 he built a new main building, Sheffield Hall, for more than $100,000. Before his death in 1882, the philanthropist had contributed more than $400,000 to the Scientific School. It was "a sum altogether greater than I had intended," he explained to his sons, "but for which timely aid, I am well assured by the board, and indeed am well satisfied myself, the institution could not have been sustained, with credit, and the Professors retained."[69]

In Joseph Sheffield's mind the Scientific School had become a family enterprise. It was more than symbolic that Sheffield Hall, the Sheffield mansion, the homes of the Porters, the Danas, the Sillimans, and of many other professors were strung along Hillhouse Avenue like an extended patriarchal settlement. "I had already given my children a very handsome —liberal 'setting out' in the world," wrote the philanthropist, reminiscing in his eighty-first year, "and . . . I felt that I should do no injustice to them—indeed cause lasting honor on the name—in sustaining an institution of so much value to the future youth of our country, to which my name, after repeated applications, has been given."[70] In his will he stipuated a variety of charitable bequests, then divided the residue of his estate into seven equal portions, one for each of his children and one for the Scientific School. He also bequeathed all his Hillhouse Avenue properties to the institution, assuring room for expansion in the years to come.[71]

Due in no small part to the success of the Scientific School, Yale became the first American university to put graduate training in science on a formal institutional basis. Of the first twenty doctorates awarded in the United States (all at Yale, 1861–71), fourteen were in the sciences.[72] Among them, in 1863, was that of Josiah Willard Gibbs, whose 1876–78 paper

"On the Equilibrium of Heterogeneous Substances" was the greatest contribution to scientific knowledge by an American since 1751, when Benjamin Franklin published his *Experiments and Observations on Electricity*. And though not a graduate, Daniel Coit Gilman later made good use of his Sheffield School experience when he launched The Johns Hopkins University in Baltimore.

In 1874 Benjamin Silliman, Jr., paused to look back at the years before the Civil War when the inchoate aspirations of his scientific generation first assumed institutional form. He recalled that economic growth and technological development had shattered the traditional society, imparting in the process an "almost convulsive shock . . . to the old-time system of education."[73] New material and intellectual needs had prompted Harvard and Yale to open the door to professional science education, but thirty years after the fact it was easy to forget their hesitance in doing so. Lawrence and Sheffield, and the proliferation of scientific and technical schools that followed their lead, were in essence extra-institutional and semi-independent; they developed alongside rather than within their parent institutions.[74] Yet their enforced autonomy had more advantages than disadvantages. If they were dependent on private financial support, they were also free to innovate, unfettered by the persistence of institutional inertia. Their fields of action extended to the limits of their patrons' vision and their promoters' zeal.

5

The New Astronomy

There apparently exists in the public mind a tendency to regard astronomical research with a feeling
of awe which is not accorded to other branches of
science. In its power of searching out mysterious
phenomena in the infinite regions of space a great
telescope seems to stand alone among the appliances
of an investigator. Partly because of this special ven-
eration for its principal instrument . . . astronomy
appears to command the interest of a great portion
of the human race.

George Ellery Hale, 1898

DURING the last three decades of the nineteenth century
the camera and the spectroscope revolutionized astronomical research. Traditionally the main work of an observatory had been mapping the sky with exquisite precision, the
preliminary step to reducing all celestial phenomena to New-
tonian law. Astronomers sought, in the words of Samuel P.
Langley, "to say *where* any heavenly body is, and not *what* it
is."[1] Stellar photography and spectrum analysis enabled Langley and other pioneers in the new astronomy of astrophysics
to go beyond celestial surveying and investigate the physical
and chemical composition of the universe. The observatory
became a physical laboratory, where the principal function of
a telescope was to gather stellar light so that it might be
subjected to analysis. A photographic plate could record pin-
points of light too faint to be detected by the human eye. The
spectrum of a distant star told its chemical composition and
many of its physical characteristics with laboratory precision.[2]

New tools of research stimulated astronomical investigation. But their full utilization had to wait upon specially designed instruments such as photographic telescopes, spectrographs, photometers, and spectroheliographs. The great telescopes of the 1840's, admirably suited to the old astronomy, gave only mediocre results when adapted to the new. To finance their new equipment and research the astrophysicists of the Gilded Age, like their predecessors, turned to private philanthropy. Some contributed to the growing literature of scientific mendicancy by writing "not for the professional reader, but with the hope of reaching a part of the educated public on whose support he is so often dependent for the means of extending the boundaries of knowledge."[3] Others, notably George Davidson, George Ellery Hale, and Edward C. Pickering, worked more directly. Partly by chance and partly by design they became active promoters as well as scientific investigators.

George Davidson combined technical competence with a concern for the social status of scientific research, both legacies from his Lazzaroni mentor, Alexander Dallas Bache. As a youth he had been Bache's student and scientific assistant at the Philadelphia High School Observatory, and subsequently had followed his chief into service with the United States Coast Survey. Directorship of the survey on the Pacific Coast brought him to San Francisco in the 1850's. Within a decade his official position made Davidson the principal organizer of West Coast scientific activity, which in turn led to his election as President of the California Academy of Sciences. Several trips to the high Sierras convinced the astronomer that mountain-top atmospheric conditions were ideal for astrophysical work. As early as 1869 he began agitating for an observatory in the Golden State. "I have been feeling the ground in this community among men likely to be interested about the establishment of a large observatory on this coast," reported Davidson to Benjamin Peirce.[4]

Nothing came of his probings until February 1873. Quite unexpectedly, James Lick offered the Academy of Sciences a valuable lot in downtown San Francisco on which to erect a museum and headquarters. The businessman's motives were obscure even at the time; contemporaries had long regarded him as eccentric, if not downright deranged. It was probable, however, that Joseph Henry and Louis Agassiz first acquainted Lick with "the wants of science." In 1871 the Smithsonian secretary had traveled to California for his health, and had stayed in San Francisco at the Lick House, one of the city's principal hotels. The disposal of his estate had been a topic of growing concern for the Californian, and he took advantage of Henry's visit to ask his advice. As America's elder statesman of science, Henry pointed out the benefits, both to humanity and to the reputation of the donor, that proceeded from the support of research. The story of James Smithson's bequest was a ready and telling example.[5]

Joseph Henry's introductory remarks were amplified in the autumn of 1872 when Louis Agassiz, ashore from the Hassler Expedition, addressed "a Large and Delighted Assemblage" at the Academy of Sciences. True to form, he reviewed his current research, then called for the support of local scientific men. Agassiz urged Californians to emulate the rich men of Massachusetts. "I know what they can do," he observed. It was particularly crucial, in a relatively new state, that the principal scientific society have the resources to sustain active scientific men. Otherwise an active tradition of research might never be established. The academy's presently cramped quarters and empty treasury, Agassiz declared, were a reproach to the state. "I hold it one of the duties of those who have the means, to help those who have only their head, and who go to work with an empty pocket." The next day San Francisco editors spread Agassiz's address on their front pages and called for action in their editorials. Coming four months later, James Lick's gift to the Academy of Sciences was too appropriate to have been entirely coincidental.[6]

George Davidson met the donor for the first time when he called to thank him on behalf of the academy. It was the first of many visits. Lick knew little about science and less about astronomy, but Davidson soon introduced him to the wonders of the heavens and hinted at the still greater discoveries that might be expected from proper instruments. In the meantime the California astronomer marshaled reserve forces in the East. "I know our people and thus beg for outside aid," he explained to Joseph Henry, requesting him to encourage the philanthropist by mail.[7] The Smithsonian secretary responded at once, praising Lick's "wisdom and enlightened sympathy" and reminding the aging millionaire of their conversations in 1871. "The study of abstract science without regard to its immediate application form an essential element in the advance of the world," Henry told Lick. There could be no more enduring or admirable monument than an institution for the advancement of knowledge.[8]

A memorial was James Lick's guiding concern. He had no near relative, save an illegitimate son in Pennsylvania, no assurance that he would be remembered. Deistically inclined, Lick felt that good works on this earth were a safer guarantee of immortality than the possibility of reward in the hereafter. He had first considered erecting an immense pyramid in downtown San Francisco. Next he contemplated a million dollars worth of statuary, of himself and his parents, believing that they would survive for future civilizations to admire as antiquities. At this junction Davidson and D. J. Staples, Lick's legal adviser, suggested that an astronomical observatory was at once a fitting monument and an active agency for the perpetual advancement of knowledge.[9]

When he announced the telescope gift before the academy in October 1873, George Davidson declared that he had been "deeply impressed with the breadth and practicality" of Lick's comprehension of "original research in cosmical physics."[10] In reality Lick understood no more than was reasonable to expect of a former piano maker. Moreover, his personal eccentricities were already trying Davidson's patience. Lick simply wanted the biggest telescope in the world, "as near a perfect instrument as the best Scientific Knowledge and skill and human workmanship can make." He did not appreciate the theoretical and practical problems involved in constructing such an instrument, nor did he at first understand that the telescope required an observatory building and a complement of accessories. His deed of trust stipulated only that the telescope was to be "superior to and more powerful than any telescope yet made."[11]

Alvan Clark of Cambridgeport, Massachusetts, was the only optician capable of grinding such a lens. Clark had just completed a thirty-inch refractor for the Imperial Russian Observatory at Pulkowa, and even he questioned whether it was possible to figure a larger one. Nevertheless, on the advice of leading astronomers Lick authorized Clark to attempt an objective with a clear aperture of thirty-six inches. Because the light-gathering power of a lens was a function of its area rather than diameter, the thirty-six inch would be fully one third more powerful than the thirty-inch Pulkowa refractor.[12]

Lick ordered the lens, but Davidson's difficulties were far from ended. The philanthropist persisted in viewing the huge telescope primarily as a monument rather than a precision research instrument. He wanted to erect the dome in the San Francisco business district where it would be visible to all, and surround the building with statuary groups featuring Francis Scott Key, Thomas Paine, and himself. Assuring Lick that harbor fog, city lights, and the vibration from passing vehicles would render the telescope useless in that locale, Davidson slowly guided the philanthropist toward a mountaintop observatory site. Relations were further complicated when Lick grew dissatisfied with his advisors, twice tore up his deed of trust, and three times appointed new trustees. Davidson insisted, after conferring with astronomers in the East, that a suitable astrophysical observatory would cost at least $1,200,000. Lick originally had contributed a half million, and had increased his gift to $700,000 only after repeated pleas. Because Lick refused to equip the observatory completely, because he settled upon the 4,200-foot Mount Hamilton site rather than Davidson's own choice in the high Sierras, in August 1874 the astronomer "declined further conference and responsibility" in the enterprise. Although Davidson had first

Bay. Berkeley and San Francisco dominated the state's cultural life. The prestigious Lick Observatory on nearby Mount Hamilton only heightened the imbalance. Just as the observatory neared completion an unprecedented land boom brought sudden wealth to the Los Angeles area. New communities and new millionaires sprang up overnight. Editorial writers proclaimed that prosperity had come to stay. "Not only rich men who wish to speculate and grow richer will come here in crowds, but our matchless climate will continue to attract for permanent residence the wealthy valetudinarians of the old states. Southern California is now recognized as the most efficacious sanitarium on the continent."[17]

At the peak of prosperity, in June 1887, Edward F. Spence announced that Southern California's regional pride demanded an observatory to dwarf Berkeley's thirty-six-inch Lick refractor. President of the First National Bank, President of the Board of Trustees of the University of Southern California, and a former mayor of Los Angeles, Spence had been one of the city's principal boosters. He could also afford to donate fifty thousand dollars to his own university as pump-priming for a telescope fund. During the succeeding weeks the press chronicled the numerous rallies and banquets that generated interest in the project.[18] Months of land boom had left Southern Californians giddy with speculative fever. The same sense of happy unreality colored their dreams of an astronomical research center atop Mount Wilson in nearby Pasadena. Railroad companies surveyed routes to the summit, enterprising realtors planned housing developments and grandiose hotels for the scientific staff and the hordes of visitors who surely would come on special rail excursions from the East. In January 1889 Edward Spence added a tract of valuable downtown real estate to his initial gift and appointed a board of trustees to oversee the enterprise. Alvan Clark came to Los Angeles, conferred with the trustees, and visited the Mount Wilson site. Four months later the trustees commissioned Clark to grind, if it were possible, a forty-inch objective. If French glassmakers could cast such large blanks, and if Clark could fashion them into lenses, publicity-conscious Southern Californians would forever possess the world's largest refractor. A forty-inch lens would reach the point of diminishing returns, where the increase in light from the larger diameter was offset by the decrease in light due to absorption as it passed through the thicker glass.[19]

After numerous failures, the Parisian manufacturer succeeded in casting satisfactory crown and flint glass disks. In 1890 they arrived in Cambridgeport, where Clark began the delicate process of grinding and figuring. Two years later, with the work partially completed and partially paid for, the Los Angeles land bubble burst. Edward Spence and other patrons retrenched. The University of Southern California was equally hard-hit, and could not in any case assume the financial burden alone. Joseph Widney, the President of USC, sensibly recommended that the trustees sell their interest in the lenses to the highest bidder and refinance a more modest observatory.

Edward Spence would have none of it, for regional and institutional pride were at stake. "I would not be satisfied," he asserted, "with any smaller glass in connection with the university." Spence's uncompromising, all-or-nothing stance made it impossible for the trustees to salvage anything from the enterprise. Reluctantly, in 1892 they defaulted on their contract with Alvan Clark. Shortly thereafter, in September, Edward Spence died, and with him passed whatever vital force still remained in the observatory movement.[20]

The Cambridgeport optician was understandably upset. His firm had invested sixteen thousand dollars in material and labor. The crowning achievement of his career lay unfinished in the shops. Luckily the nation's leading scientific men were then congregating in Rochester, New York, for the annual meeting of the American Association for the Advancement of Science. Clark hurried to the convention where, sitting on the hotel porch during the hot September evenings, he told his tale to the visiting scientists. It was their responsibility, he said, to see that some wealthy philanthropist buy the Spence trustees' interest in the refractor, complete the instrument, and present it to a worthy institution.

George Ellery Hale overheard Clark's story. Head Professor of Astrophysics in the newly planned University of Chicago, he had interrupted a fishing trip to attend the convention, unaware what fate held in store. A large telescope had occupied his thoughts, however, because his Chicago appointment had brought no promise from the university of instruments suitable for his investigations of the solar spectrum. Alvan Clark's unfinished lenses would tempt any astronomer, but they were irresistible to a brilliant and ambitious twenty-four-year-old just beginning his professional career. Whoever directed the great refractor would occupy a unique position among the world's astronomers. Its light-gathering power would open realms of investigation closed to all others. "It goes without saying that Clark's story gave me food for thought," Hale later recalled. "I returned to the Adirondacks, packed my fishing tackle, and hastened to Chicago."[21]

After several days of fruitless interviews with Chicago businessmen, Hale asked the advice of Charles Hutchinson, President of the Corn Exchange Bank and an influential trustee of the new university. Hutchinson knew his city's resources as well as the university's needs. "Why don't you try Mr. Yerkes?" he asked. "He has talked of the possibility of some gift to the University, and he might be attracted by this scheme."[22]

Charles Tyson Yerkes ruled Chicago's burgeoning traction system. After losing a fortune in Philadelphia, incidently serving a prison term for the misappropriation of public funds (he was pardoned after seven months), Yerkes had come to Chicago in the early eighties. His stated formula of business enterprise, "buy old junk, fix it up a little, and unload it upon other fellows," brought him immediate success.[23] Soon Yerkes controlled the city's lucrative street railways and, in the process, contributed measurably to Chicago's reputation as the "boodle Capital of the World." Yerkes served as the inspiration for

Frank Cowperthwait, the robber baron protagonist of Theodore Dreiser's *The Financier* and *The Titan.*

William Rainey Harper, the new president of the University of Chicago, was too engrossed with the problems of educational finance to inquire into the business morality of Chicago millionaires. He was launching a new university, and with the help of leading citizens such as Charles Hutchinson, Martin Ryerson, and Herman Kohlsaat, he had worked systematically down his list of wealthy Chicagoans. One by one they had succumbed to Harper's winning personality and to his appeals for help in building the city's reputation for culture and learning. Yerkes's name had come up first in January 1892. "As soon as Mr. [Sidney A.] Kent's case is settled," wrote Harper, refering to a pending $150,000 donation for a chemical laboratory, "we are to take hold of Mr. Yerkes." The traction magnate was down for a biological laboratory to complement Kent Chemical Hall.[24]

The educator and the financier met in New York on February 23, 1892. Yerkes had gone east on a pleasure trip; Harper and Herman Kohlsaat were on their way to Clark University to raid G. Stanley Hall's faculty. It was an exciting and promising meeting. The millionaire was interested. His wife, "the most gorgeously beautiful woman I have seen for years," was interested. "We worked with him the hardest we knew how. He gave us every chance. He did everything *but* say yes." Yerkes could not commit himself at the moment, but pledged that he soon would.[25] Weeks dragged by as Yerkes asked for more time on account of business reversals. Prospects brightened in April; Harper felt certain that the philanthropist would match Sidney Kent's $150,000. But suddenly in June he "backed out square." It was a serious blow, for not only was Harper unaccustomed to losing a philanthropist once he had bitten, but Yerkes's withdrawal might also discourage other donors already on the line.[26]

George Ellery Hale's story of the forty-inch telescope renewed hope of a gift from the traction king. The world's largest refractor might succeed where a biological laboratory had failed. President Harper was a shrewd judge of character. He knew that buying up old junk and unloading it upon other fellows had brought Yerkes social ostracism as well as great wealth. He knew that the millionaire, an avid and discriminating art collector, longed for acceptance by Chicago's cultural elite. Yerkes had, in fact, complained to Harper of being snubbed by the "great and good" members of the Civic Federation, who seemed to regard him as a malefactor bent on compromising the city's good name.[27]

At Harper's suggestion, George Ellery Hale drafted a long letter for Yerkes's eyes, recounting the history of the monster lens and presenting the case for its donation to the University of Chicago. The completed refractor would cost approximately $60,000, the mounting and dome, an additional $110,000. "If you will consider for a moment just what such a possession would mean to the University and the City of Chicago, you will agree that no effort should be spared to secure this prize." Hale also noted that $300,000 would build and completely equip the observatory and that an anonymous donor (in reality Hale's own father, a wealthy manufacturer) had promised one tenth of that amount as encouragement for other philanthropists. It was a unique opportunity, and Chicago must act quickly before other institutions learned the refractor was available. Such an observatory, Hale concluded, would rank first in the world, "a Mecca of thousands of science-loving pilgrims, as the Lick Observatory, even in its isolated position, is to-day. And the donor could have no more enduring monument."[28]

The letter turned the trick. During the first week in October Yerkes summoned Harper and Hale and agreed to build the observatory. Harper could hardly contain himself as they left the office: "I'd like to go on top of a hill and yell!"[29] He wrote Frederick T. Gates, Rockefeller's philanthropic adviser, that "the enterprise will cost Mr. Yerkes certainly half a million dollars. He is red hot and does not hesitate on any particular. It is a great pleasure to do business with such a man."[30]

Harper spoke too soon. The red-hot philanthropist cooled

noticeably over time. Construction did not begin until 1895. Selection of a site took months, as dozens of small midwestern towns vied for priority and Southern Californians offered the old Mount Wilson site. Yerkes added to the delay by accusing Hale of padding the budget with expensive and unnecessary apparatus. He also was suspicious lest other philanthropists detract from his glory by giving other instruments to be housed in the observatory. "While I do not ask to have them called the Yerkes telescopes . . . I certainly cannot permit other names to be used . . . and have the credit for the discoveries which might be made go into another channel." After many delays, in the spring of 1897 the observatory at Williams Bay, Wisconsin, neared completion.[31]

In the meantime Yerkes had grown increasingly testy and suspicious. His investment in philanthropy had not improved his reputation. No amount of charity could placate former partners and innocent investors on whom he had unloaded "old junk"; nor could patronage of the arts and sciences atone for the 382 people killed or injured in 1895 alone by poorly strung power lines along the streetcar tracks.[32] Moreover, since February 1897 Yerkes had attempted, in a particularly heavy-handed fashion, to bribe Illinois legislators into granting him perpetual traction franchises in the city of Chicago. The franchise question provided civic reformers with an excuse for an all-out municipal housecleaning. By April ordinary citizens had joined business leaders in a civic crusade to oust Charles T. Yerkes.[33] Outwardly he remained callous to the mass meetings and daily newspaper attacks. Inwardly he was embittered. When Harper requested seven thousand dollars to purchase vital instrumental accessories, Yerkes snapped that the university should ask elsewhere for further aid, perhaps from those "extremely good people" who wanted to see him ruined. He further demanded that guards patrol the observatory grounds to protect the great refractor from sabotage or mob violence. "I thoroughly believe," he wrote, "that there are many persons,—some of them high in the social scale,—who would even be pleased to see an accident happen to the telescope."[34]

On dedication day, October 21, 1897, anxiety and hatred were lost in a haze of rhetoric and good fellowship. Nearly eight hundred dignitaries crowded the special excursion trains to Williams Bay. Herman Kohlsaat's *Chicago Times-Herald* pronounced the occasion "an event without peer in the records of American things intellectual."[35] Under the great dome, Charles T. Yerkes sat on a raised platform canopied in white, seeming to blush at the standing ovations which punctuated the ceremony. In presenting the observatory to the university, he spoke of the motives that prompted men to support astronomical research. "One reason why the science of astronomy has not more helpers," he declared, "is on account of its being entirely uncommercial. There is nothing of moneyed value to be gained by the devotee of astronomy; there is nothing that he can sell." In response, William Rainey Harper lauded Yerkes's "sincerity and simplicity." Martin Ryerson, president of the trustees, added that the observatory would stand as a monument to spiritual values in a materialistic age, contributing "to the uplifting of men and upbuilding of character." The next day the reform-minded *Times-Herald* momentarily suspended its usual attacks on the Yerkes empire. "Whatever opinion we may hold of Mr. Yerkes in his relations with the people of Chicago," wrote editor Kohlsaat, "there can be only one opinion, and that extremely complimentary, of Mr. Yerkes as the founder of the Observatory at Lake Geneva."[36]

The philanthropist's fortunes deteriorated rapidly after the observatory dedication. As the most visible and flagrant example of municipal corruption, Yerkes's traction empire felt the full force of reform agitation. By 1898 the Citizens Independent Anti-Boodle League, a propaganda bureau established by civic reformers, systematically mobilized protest rallies throughout the city.[37] Hale and Harper had hoped that in time Yerkes would endow the observatory he had founded. But as his fortune dwindled his interest dwindled, and he contributed only a few hundred dollars each year toward supporting several assistants. In 1900 Yerkes left Chicago for New York, driven away from his palatial Michigan Avenue town house by

the Anti-Boodle League. In 1903 he stopped even token gifts to
the observatory. The next year he died, disgraced and nearly
penniless.[38]

A constellation of fortuitous circumstances had produced
the observatory at Williams Bay. Coincidence threw George
Ellery Hale, William Rainey Harper, and Charles T. Yerkes
together at a critical moment. Hale learned of the Spence
Observatory debacle by chance. Harper, on the verge of opening a new university, realized what an astrophysical observatory would mean to his fledgling institution, and was able to
produce a donor on demand. Yerkes, just then at the pinnacle
of financial power, was anxious and able to court public favor
through the support of science and the higher learning.

The timing of the Yerkes episode was all the more striking
in the light of Harvard's simultaneous efforts to obtain the
forty-inch refractor. The observatory at Cambridge had established a temporary station on Mount Wilson in 1887. Consequently Edward C. Pickering, Director of the Harvard Observatory, had become involved in the Spence promotion in an
advisory capacity. His interest quickened early in 1892 as the
land boom began to show signs of internal stress. If depression
hit Los Angeles, Harvard might be able to pick up the refractor and establish an observing station in the Southern Hemisphere. Most major observatories were clustered north of the
equator; a southern telescope would sweep virtually unexplored quadrants of the sky. Edward S. Holden kept Pickering
posted from California. "Why don't you try for the 40 inch
one?" he wrote in March, "the Los Angeles people will *never*
be able to pay for it."[39]

Pickering was primed for Alvan Clark at Rochester the
following September. By the time Hale had packed his fishing
tackle and returned to Chicago, Pickering had already issued a
circular from Cambridge urging someone to donate the refractor for a Harvard observatory in the Peruvian Andes.[40] Harvard had become the most richly endowed American observatory on the basis of such appeals; in time Pickering probably
would have located a patron. But because of the peculiar

situation in Chicago, time ran out before his circular could have any effect.

The unsuccessful contest with Chicago was only one incident in Edward Pickering's busy career as a promoter of scientific enterprises.[41] For nearly a quarter century he labored to bring order and reliability to the traditionally inchoate process of subsidizing research. Of all the sciences, astronomy was the most popular object of private support in the United States. Even so, contributions had been intermittent, and almost always in response to a specific request for major pieces of equipment. By the last decades of the century American astronomers were overstocked with instruments. What they needed were permanent endowment funds designated for research, publication, and salaries. The last was a particularly sore point. "A great telescope is of no use without a man at the end of it," declared Simon Newcomb.[42]

Edward Pickering believed that systematic management would eliminate inefficiency in the support of scientific research, benefiting investigators and donors alike. By pooling large and small contributions into a central endowment fund, he hoped to establish an international foundation for astronomical research. Aided by a committee of experts, he would advise philanthropists in their giving and assist in disbursing their bounty. "Like all schemes of this day," noted the editor of *Science* in 1886, when the Harvard professor first announced his Plan for the Extension of Astronomical Research, "Professor Pickering's is one of consolidation."[43]

It was understandable that American science shared certain characteristics of American life generally. In the 1880's business leaders were demonstrating, for better or worse, the efficiency of collective action. Pickering watched pools and trusts proliferate, marveling especially at the organizational genius of men like John D. Rockefeller and Andrew Carnegie. He saw himself doing for science what they had done for industry. "The same skill in organization, combination of existing appliances, and methodical study of detail, which in recent years has revolutionized many commercial industries," he explained, "should produce as great an advance in the physical sciences."[44]

Pickering's plan of 1886 called on philanthropists to contribute an initial capital fund of one hundred thousand dollars. From the income small grants (up to five hundred dollars) would be awarded annually for promising astronomical research. Pickering would receive and pass judgment upon applications.[45] The response to the plan was negligible, so in 1888 he turned temporarily to another pet project, a 24-inch telescope for photometric work. The fifty-thousand-dollar instrument would be the first large telescope designed solely for photographic rather than visual use.[46]

In June 1889 Catherine Wolfe Bruce, an elderly spinster in New York, wrote to Alvan Clark expressing her interest in subsidizing astronomical research. It was unclear whether she had seen Pickering's circulars, but within the month she had met with the astronomer and agreed to donate the photographic telescope to Harvard Observatory.[47] Moreover, in 1890 she offered to contribute to the 1886 endowment plan in the hope that a one-year trial might encourage others to increase the capital fund. She gave six thousand dollars, equivalent to a year's interest on one hundred thousand dollars. Eighty-four applicants responded to Pickering's notices in the principal scientific journals. The international character of the fund was apparent when Pickering announced the fifteen recipients of research grants. Eight were European, one Asian, one African, and five North American. The endowment scheme obviously worked. The grateful letters from recipients, furthermore, revealed what few resources were then available to overworked and underpaid academic scientists.[48]

Pickering's endowment scheme languished after the trial run in 1890. In 1901, in 1903, and again in 1904, he reiterated that the program "would serve as a valuable example to other sciences, and the moral effect of promoting uniformity of purpose, and friendly aid to one another, by astronomers of all countries, would encourage other donors." It was a noble dream, rational, well publicized, in harmony with other tendencies in American economic and social life. Yet Pickering's invitations to correspond with philanthropists, large or small, went unanswered.[49]

The master plan failed for several reasons. A number of extremely influential scientists resented Pickering's apparently monopolistic designs on the endowment field. In 1901 the trustees of the American and National Academies' research funds boycotted a joint meeting Pickering had called to coordinate their programs. "Only Pickering himself is to blame," commented Seth Chandler, editor of the *Astronomical Journal*, "that his claims & desires that every one should unselfishly cooperate with him & place him in charge of every thing as the wise & good dispenser of all things—are met with natural distrust."[50] Pickering, whose disinterested posture seemed genuine enough, never fully understood the rebuff from his scientific peers. "Who would object to a trust," he pleaded in 1906, "whose sole objects would be increased production, reduced cost to the public, and no profit to those forming it?"[51] Pickering forgot that in science, as well as industry, efficiency was not the sole standard of value. The same natural suspicions that led to trust-busting could block their formation in the first place. The Harvard astronomer also forgot that original research in science was far removed from the everyday life of most wealthy Americans. The pursuit of astrophysical truths might inspire a dedicated investigator, but it was too esoteric for the layman. Inconspicuous grants to little-known investigators in far-away places, however productive of discovery, made poor newspaper copy.

Catherine Wolfe Bruce came as close as any American to Pickering's conception of the ideal philanthropist. She was sympathetic, she was prompt, she asked nothing in return. Between 1889 and her death in 1900 she gave $174,275 for astronomical, principally astrophysical, research.[52] The mere amount of her giving could not raise Catherine Bruce above other moderately generous American philanthropists. But the nature of her giving earned her international gratitude as "one of the most sympathetic and generous patrons astronomy has ever known . . . aiding as perhaps no other . . . the progress of research."[53]

She was seventy-three years old in 1889. Unmarried, in feeble health for many years, she lived with her younger sister, Matilda, who often managed her affairs. Miss Bruce seldom left the house or received visitors. She achieved some public notice in 1887 when she donated a sixty-thousand-dollar public library to New York in memory of her father, George Bruce, one of America's pioneer typefounders and typographers.[54] But otherwise Catherine Bruce had lived in comfortable obscurity on the family fortune. The historical record revealed nothing of her educational background or the origins of her interest in astronomy.

Miss Bruce did read semipopular astronomical journals. In the February 1888 issue of the *Siderial Messenger* an article by Simon Newcomb profoundly upset her, and apparently prompted her decision to underwrite astronomical research. Newcomb was dean of the "old astronomers," those who computed the geometry of the heavens rather than the physical composition of the stars. By the end of the nineteenth century it appeared to Newcomb that the work begun by Isaac Newton was nearly complete. Two centuries of observation and mathematical refinement had made celestial mechanics the most elegant of sciences. "It would be too much to say with confidence that the age of great discoveries in any branch of science has passed by," he wrote, "yet, so far as astronomy is concerned, it must be confessed that we do appear to be fast reaching the limits of our knowledge."[55]

Newcomb's stagnation theory of discovery shocked Catherine Bruce. Soon after reading Newcomb's article she contacted Alvan Clark, and through him, Edward Pickering. The Bruce Photographic Telescope and sponsorship of the Endowment Fund brought her name before the international scientific community. Other astronomers soon found the frail old lady a willing dispenser of research grants. She favored the new astronomy, probably because the science was young and full of promise. "I think we are beginning," she told Simon Newcomb in 1890, criticizing his statements in the *Siderial Messenger*, "else why set to work [on] Photography, Spectroscopy, Chemistry and soon but perhaps not in this generation Electricity. Think of the great mechanical improvements—think of the double stars revolving round a common center, of the variable stars—of of—you laugh at being as it were lectured by me. The world is young."[56]

Fifty-four grants ranging from fifty to twenty-five thousand dollars showed her faith that science had not gone stale. Beginning in 1898, for five years she assumed responsibility for Professor Edwin Frost's salary at the Yerkes Observatory after the traction magnate had refused to endow his astrophysical chair.[57] Preferring lifetime giving to deathbed bequests, Catherine Bruce was an active rather than passive philanthropist. Though drawn in 1892 when astronomical research was on her mind (within the month she gave Lewis Boss twenty-five thousand dollars to re-equip the Dudley Observatory at Albany), her will contained only personal bequests.[58] Because a significant portion of the world's astrophysical research would be performed with Bruce instruments for years to come, the total effect of her aid to science was incalculable. She subsidized publications, purchased apparatus, and assisted promising investigators at critical stages in their careers. Edward E. Barnard put it simply in 1897: "I personally feel the deepest gratitude to Miss Bruce."[59]

In 1896 a popular journalist, commenting on "The Art of Large Giving," suggested that "monumentalism" explained the success of astronomy in attracting private funds for original research.[60] He was partially correct. Clearly, the promise of a monument drew James Lick to the science as it had, in a certain sense, drawn Charles T. Yerkes as well. But such an interpretation explained little about a Catherine Wolfe Bruce, or about the dozens of other Americans who subsidized the study of the stars in the Gilded Age. In the 1870's, for example, Leander McCormick, the younger brother of the farm machinery inventor, outfitted the University of Virginia with a twenty-six-inch Clark refractor. Benefiting their home state

was a McCormick family tradition, and it seemed to Leander
that a ranking observatory would contribute substantially to
the cultural reconstruction of the war-torn South.[61]

Still other examples illustrated the infinite diversity of mo-
tive and situation in the support of astronomical research. In
the 1880's Hubert H. Warner, a Rochester, New York, safe
salesman turned patent medicine magnate, gave his city a one-
hundred-thousand-dollar observatory. The building, a particularly garish example of Gilded Age Gothic, embodied the
donor's principal aims—attracting attention to himself and to
Warner's Safe Liver Pills.[62] Simultaneously William Thaw, a
Pittsburgh railroad executive, was underwriting far-reaching
astrophysical investigations at the Allegheny Observatory. An
amateur astronomer who lacked the ability to make fundamental discoveries himself, Thaw devoted a substantial part of his
fortune to the support of those who could. Samuel P. Langley,
James E. Keeler, and John Brashear all benefited from the
millionaire's bounty. "My appropriations to your enterprises,"
he explained to Brashear in the mid-eighties, "are primarily
contributions to original research in science. . . . It is not a
personal question in my estimation, but a public interest I am
serving in keeping you at your special work."[63] Finally, in the
1890's Percival Lowell, the grandson of Abbott Lawrence, left
a successful business career to build and direct a major observatory at Flagstaff, Arizona, where for years he labored to prove
that the so-called "canals" on Mars were evidence of extrater-
restrial life.[64]

From such varied causes, by 1902 American astronomers had
a complement of one hundred forty-two observatories, most of
which at least advertised a primary commitment to research
rather than instruction.[65] Yet the popularity of observatories as
philanthropic objects could be a curse as well as a blessing. At
the turn of the century it seemed to many astronomers that
their very successes had produced a lopsided astronomical
Establishment. Research required men as well as prestigious
buildings, endowment funds as well as periodic contributions.
"The first need of astronomy in this country," declared a

Carnegie Institution committee in 1902, "is not for more buildings and instruments as for more astronomical workers to use
the appliances . . . already provided."[66]

Edward C. Pickering had urged the systematic support of
research as early as the 1870's. In the tradition of Benjamin
Peirce he attempted, not entirely successfully, to divide his
time between original research and begging. But the demands
of science now called for more than part-time fund-raising. A
transitional figure, Pickering forecast the rise, in the next generation, of full-time foundation executives like former astronomer Henry S. Pritchett.

6

The Endowment of Research

We must exert our influence in developing the idea of the justice of systematic assistance. Pending that millenium, we must wrestle with the generous and the wealthy.

George Davidson, 1892

DURING the second week in October 1872, national politics was the principal topic of conversation. On Wednesday, the ninth, as late returns confirmed President Grant's victory over liberal reform, hardly anyone outside the scientific community noticed the arrival of Professor John Tyndall in New York. Invited by Joseph Henry and a committee of twenty-four other influential American scientists, the British scientist had come as a good-will ambassador in the cause of original research. He would tour the country, delivering a series of popular lectures designed to advertise the needs of the scientific community.[1]

No one since Louis Agassiz came better prepared to promote cordial relations "between science and the world outside of science."[2] Michael Faraday's successor as Superintendent of the Royal Institution of London, Tyndall was one of Great Britain's best-known men of science. Though his research had followed many paths, his principal discoveries dealt with the opacity of gases and vapors to various forms of radiant energy. But if skilled in the laboratory, he had even greater gifts as an expositor of scientific principles to laymen. Tyndall's widely read volume, *Heat As a Mode of Motion* (1863), was the first popular discussion of the mechanical theory of heat, and the

119

first of many books that had made him familiar to the American reading public.[3]

Tyndall's very popularity, in fact, worried some American scientists, who like Benjamin Peirce questioned the desirability, if not the possibility, of simplifying complex physical concepts. Their striving for professional respectability had left them hypercritical of "scientific dabblers," and other popularizers who sometimes distorted science in the press and on the platform.[4] But regarding Tyndall, most investigators sided with Peter Lesley, Secretary of the American Philosophical Society. "I quite comprehend your views & feelings about inviting Tyndall," he had told Peirce in the autumn of 1871, "but nevertheless I cannot see why we should not use tools when they lie around loose and we have hard locks to pick. The hardest lock I am acquainted with is the soul of man. Tyndall is not primus inter pares . . . but he is certainly one of the best illustrators of physics in the world, and these are our leaders among the common people. They prepare the way for that acceptance of the necessity for accurate & abstract Science which Society is so loth to yield."[5]

Tyndall arrived with two assistants and trunks of demonstration apparatus. He had decided to lecture on the physical and optical properties of light. The subject was intellectually stimulating and, equally important, the interplay of light, darkness, and color made for impressive displays in large lecture halls. He inaugurated the first series of six lectures in Boston at the Lowell Institute. After his Boston triumph, a little reminiscent of the reception Louis Agassiz had received a quarter century before, the British physicist repeated the series in Philadelphia, Washington, New York, and Brooklyn. He gave three lectures in Baltimore, two in New Haven, and declined innumerable invitations to visit cities in the West. Though tickets for the lectures were relatively expensive, Tyndall usually spoke to a packed house. Invariably, dutiful newspaper reporters transcribed his remarks in full for the next day's editions.[6]

The lectures were didactic in a double sense. Tyndall hoped

to teach something about light waves and their behavior. But basically, his exposition on light was an extended illustration of the nature and dynamics of scientific discovery. The first five performances, replete with sputtering arc lights, whirling apparatus, and flashing spectra, were a come-on for the sixth and concluding lecture. There, assured of an attentive audience, Tyndall presented his case for the support of original scientific research.[7]

He drew his image of American society partly from Alexis de Tocqueville, who four decades before had sought to explain "why the Americans are more addicted to practical than to theoretical science." The Frenchman had concluded that the "universal tumult" of democratic society would never allow the calm and meditation necessary for profound scientific thought. Tyndall agreed that historically the Americans had been less concerned with theory than with practice, but he explained it as the natural condition of a frontier culture. The democratic temperament was not, as Tocqueville believed, inimical to the pursuit of science for its own sake; it was simply that "the newcomers had to build their houses, to chasten the earth into cultivation, and to take care of their souls." Even now, declared Tyndall, in the Far West "hardy pioneers stand face to face with stubborn Nature."[8]

Gentlemen in the eastern seaboard cities, on the other hand, had their houses, and their dinners were secure. "They have, in fact . . . reached that maturity, as possessors of wealth and leisure, when the investigator of natural truth, for the truth's own sake, ought to find among them promoters and protectors." They would prove Tocqueville right or wrong. "Your most difficult problem will not be to build institutions, but to make men. . . . Keep your eye upon the originator of knowledge. Give him the freedom necessary for his researches, not overloading him either with the duties of tuition or of administration, not demanding from him so-called practical results— above all things, avoid that question which ignorance so often addresses to genius, 'What is the use of your work?' "[9]

"I was as plain with them as I could be," Tyndall later

reported to an English friend. "I took to pieces the claims of their practical men."[10] At the conclusion of his visit, in February 1874, his hosts staged a farewell banquet at Delmonico's in New York. Its objects, said Joseph Henry, were to honor the physicist and "to advocate the claims of abstract science, to higher appreciation and more liberal support."[11] After dinner Tyndall rose to make a final appeal to the two hundred business and professional leaders assembled in the hall. Again quoting liberally from Tocqueville's text, Tyndall hammered at what he saw as a serious imbalance between the status of applied science and science itself. Americans had been lavish in their support of education, he observed, but "hitherto their efforts have been directed to the practical side of science, and this is why I sought in my lectures to show the dependence of practice upon principles." Professional investigators understood the problem; they were ready with advice. "I think, as regards physical science, they are likely to assure you that it is not what I may call the statical element of *buildings* that you require so much as the dynamical element of *brains*."[12]

Tyndall reinforced his rhetoric with action. The net proceeds from his lecture tour totaled slightly more than thirteen thousand dollars. Independently wealthy and driven by missionary zeal in the cause of science, the Englishman had intended from the first to contribute any surplus over expenses to a worthy scientific cause in America. While still in England he had decided to donate the money to the scientific community in Chicago, then rebuilding after the Great Fire of October 1871. "The calamity there has been overwhelming," he explained to Joseph Henry, "and many needs will have to be looked to before Scientific ones are considered. Therefore I think that good may be done by helping Chicago to get upon its scientific legs."[13]

A first-hand acquaintance with science in America, and conversations with Joseph Henry and Edward L. Youmans, editor of the *Popular Science Monthly*, convinced Tyndall that professional scientific training should receive priority over disaster relief. As his contribution to the promotion of original research in physics in the United States, Tyndall established a fund to assist promising American students who sought graduate degrees in European, and especially German universities. The gift of a European, the Tyndall Fund was one of the very first postgraduate fellowship programs earmarked for American men of science. It was somehow appropriate that the first recipient of a Tyndall grant, Michael Pupin, was himself a recent European immigrant.[14]

The Tyndall Fund itself was the most tangible result of John Tyndall's mission to America. Though his lectures were well attended and well publicized, apparently he failed to pick the lock of private patronage. Partly to blame was the physicist's often belligerent agnosticism, which scandalized pious Americans and no doubt detracted from his effectiveness in generating sympathy for science. General economic conditions also worked against him, for the uneasy period before the Panic of '73 was no time to beg money for any purpose.[15]

Tyndall's words, however, reverberated for a quarter century and his ideas provided the framework in which American scientists perceived the changing relationships of their craft to the larger society. When Tocqueville had visited the United States in the 1830's, the distinction he drew between basic and applied science was more imagined than real. In the mid-twentieth century the triumph of "research and development" would again blur such nice distinctions. But during the last quarter of the nineteenth century, Tocqueville's analysis seemed particularly timely. The very success of applied science, especially telegraphy and steam engineering, threatened to eclipse science itself. "Such applications, especially on this continent," Tyndall had noted, "are so astounding—they spread themselves so largely and umbrageously before the public eye—as to shut out from view those workers who are engaged in the quieter and profounder business of original investigation."[16] Ultimately science would profit, both because technology derived from scientific discovery, and because industrial enterprise produced pools of surplus capital that could be drained into scientific channels. But in the short run (and like other men, scientists generally lived in the short run), the imbalance between applied science and original discovery made it imperative that the latter received added support.[17]

Working men of science had long acted as their own business managers, and many had shown initiative and imagination in capitalizing upon the contingent and the unforeseen. But as science grew more complex and research more expensive, the old, informal mechanics of private patronage no longer served. Philanthropists were always few and far between, often erratic, and generally most attracted by objects within their own range of experience. Removed from common view and hidden away in the laboratory, original discovery could not expect the same gratuitous and continuing interest that more obvious social institutions received as a matter of course. Increasingly, scientists reiterated the need for "enduring and universal" rather than "local and transitory" assistance.[18] Robert H. Thurston, an engineer, put it plainly to the American Association for the Advancement of Science in 1878. "The Endowment of Research has formed no part of a complete scheme for the advancement of science, or, at least, it has never had the attention and the time given to its procurement that it should have had."[19]

Until late in the century there were very few endowment funds on which to draw. The multitude of local and national scientific societies gave little tangible assistance to research. Like the venerable American Philosophical Society, whose "long and distinguished career of honorable penury" was not relieved until the 1930's, most scientific societies lacked the means to subsidize original work.[20] Instead they generally devoted their meager assets to publishing memoirs and bolstering professional morale by awarding medals and cash premiums for valuable discoveries. One minor exception was the twenty-five thousand dollar Augustus E. Jessup Fund administered by the Academy of Natural Sciences of Philadelphia. Jessup had served as mineralogist and geologist on the Long Expedition to the Rocky Mountains in 1819, then devoted his energies to business and the affairs of the academy. After his death in 1859,

Jessup's children established the fund in his behalf, to be devoted to the support of "deserving poor young . . . men . . . who may desire to devote the whole of . . . their time and energies to the study of any of the Natural Sciences."[21]

The research endowments available before the 1870's came almost exclusively from within the scientific community. Personally involved in the complex and expensive business of discovery, they understood the relative value of before-the-fact and after-the-fact encouragement. The first, risking capital on the unknown, made advancement possible. The second merely rewarded success. Benjamin Thompson, Count Rumford, had launched the first permanent fund in 1796 when he gave the American Academy of Arts and Sciences five thousand dollars in trust for a biennial premium and medal for significant research into the nature of light and heat. The fund accumulated more rapidly than it could be spent, quadrupling in value by the 1830's. Frustrated by the precise wording of Rumford's trust but anxious to carry out his general purpose of encouraging scientific research, in 1832 the academy secured an important ruling from the Massachusetts Supreme Court. Henceforth, ran the decision, the academy could devote the yearly residue of the Rumford Fund to research.[22] Light and heat were sufficiently inclusive categories to cover the purchase of apparatus for the Harvard Observatory, photometric and spectroscopic research by Wolcott Gibbs and Edward C. Pickering, Samuel P. Langley's investigations of radiant energy, and Henry A. Rowland's new determination of the mechanical equivalent of heat. By 1900 the American Academy had awarded more than eighty grants from the Rumford Fund, with a cumulative value of $28,765.[23]

Save for the Smithsonian Institution, founded in 1846, the Rumford Fund stood alone in its field until 1867. In that year Alexander Dallas Bache died, leaving the National Academy of Sciences (founded in 1863) $50,000 for general purposes and, more important, the residue of his estate in trust for "the prosecution of researches in Physical and Natural Science by assisting experimentalists and observers." The estate, turned over to the academy in 1871, amounted to $40,515. Within the next two decades the academy distributed more than $38,000 from the Bache fund.[24]

Initially there was some question whether the academy, a creature of the federal government, could legally receive and administer private trust funds. The Incorporating Act of 1863 was silent on the matter. An enabling clause was added to the agency's constitution in 1872, but the organic act still contained no specific provision. Finally in June 1884, Congress authorized the National Academy to receive bequests and donations "to be applied by the said Academy in aid of scientific investigations and according to the will of the donors."[25] The delay had been a function of lethargy rather than encountered difficulties. Similar provisions subsequently became standard in the organic acts of many government scientific and social service bureaus, a pointed reminder that the lines between public and private revenue were often badly blurred.

Without waiting for the resolution of legal technicalities, a number of individuals had followed the example of Dallas Bache and added to the National Academy's research endowment. In 1878 three of Joseph Henry's close friends, businessman Joseph Patterson, engineer Fairman Rogers, and publisher George W. Childs, raised forty thousand dollars as a personal tribute to the physicist. Thirty-seven American business leaders joined in expressing to Henry their "respect and esteem for your personal virtues, their sense of the great value of your life's devotion to science . . . and your constant labors to increase and diffuse knowledge and promote the welfare of mankind." Aware of Henry's sense of propriety, his admirers knew he would never accept the money if it were offered solely as a personal gift. Accordingly they established a trust fund. Henry and his family would receive the annual income as long as they lived. After the death of his survivors, the principal would revert to the National Academy as the Joseph Henry Fund "to assist meritorious investigations in natural science."[26]

The Henry Fund was not available until 1903, but meantime

John C. Watson, O. C. Marsh, Wolcott Gibbs, the widows of Henry Draper and J. Lawrence Smith, and Benjamin A. Gould's daughter had all contributed substantial sums to the academy's resources for research.[27] By 1895 the aggregate principal amounted to ninety-four thousand dollars, making the National Academy easily the most important single source of scientific research grants in the United States.[28]

Surprisingly, so far as research was concerned, the American Association for the Advancement of Science was penniless throughout its first twenty-five years. Although the nation's largest and most active scientific organization, the AAAS traditionally had operated from year to year solely on membership dues. Indeed, when in the 1850's Benjamin A. Gould had raised the question of a permanent research fund, similar to that administered by the British Association, the AAAS had concluded that its function was social, not financial, and that such a fund would be "both undesirable and futile to attempt."

In 1873 Elizabeth Thompson became the association's first Patron by donating one thousand dollars for the promotion and publication of original research. The wealthy and eccentric New York philanthropist also intimated that additional gifts might be forthcoming.[29] It was unclear why she singled out the AAAS, though Mrs. Thompson frequently took the initiative in seeking out worthy causes. In this case she claimed an awareness of the "financial difficulties which beset those noble men of science who labor more for the truth than for profit's sake."[30]

"She is a lady of wealth interested in the promotion of science and in the intellectual and moral improvement of the human family," wrote Joseph Henry in 1877.[31] Childless, widowed in 1869, an invalid in her old age, Elizabeth Thompson found a rewarding outlet in a wide range of charities. Her husband, Thomas Thompson, a Boston art collector, had inherited a fortune and in turn left her an annual income of sixty thousand dollars. One of her earliest concerns had been temperance reform, to which cause she contributed not only financial support but a widely circulated statistical tract on drunkenness titled *The Figures of Hell.* She also gave liberally to the Women's Free Medical College in New York, subsidized homesteaders in Kansas and Colorado, and helped innumerable individuals complete their educations or launch business careers.[32] In 1878, during a serious yellow fever epidemic in the southern states, she underwrote the investigations of a United States Public Health Service commission after Congress had refused to appropriate public funds for the purpose.[33]

Elizabeth Thompson's personal religion seemed to reinforce her sense of social obligation. She repudiated formal creeds for a theistic natural theology. "The truths of the Bible appeal to me," she told a *New York Tribune* reporter, "but not more than the wonderful revelations in Nature, written by God's own hand. Every new discovery in science, every invention in mechanics, awakens in me always the deepest interest. If only a small part of the money spent every year for intoxicating liquors could be devoted to the workers in these fields, what glorious results would be seen!"[34]

In 1884 Elizabeth Thompson made her second and most significant contribution for the support of science. For some time Charles S. Minot of the Harvard Medical School had been promoting an International Scientific Congress under the joint auspices of the AAAS and its British counterpart. The scheme appealed to the philanthropist, for she had long been a disciple of George J. Holyoake, an English social reformer who advocated a world government directed by an intellectual elite.[35] In her view, an international scientific congress was the ideal agency to administer a research endowment. In September 1884 she told Minot that she would give five thousand dollars for an international research fund, add five thousand more the following year, and still another five thousand if other donors would contribute a total of ten thousand dollars.[36] The following year, however, when the proposed congress failed to materialize, Mrs. Thompson transferred the five thousand dollars to an independent Board of Trustees and added twenty thousand dollars to constitute the Elizabeth Thompson Science Fund. Allowing the trustees full discretion over administration and the selection of recipients, she stipulated only that the annual income "be devoted to the advancement and prosecution of scientific research in its broadest sense."[37] Elizabeth Thompson set an important example. Her initial gift to the AAAS (devoted to the publication of S. Horace Scudder's memoir on *Fossil Butterflies*), awakened the organization to the possibilty of a permanent research fund. Hitherto an unincorporated society without legal existence, in 1874 the association hurriedly secured a formal charter from the Commonwealth of Massachusetts. The AAAS also instituted life memberships, the proceeds to accumulate in a fund for research. In 1891 the association established a permanent committee to solicit endowments "from friends of scientific investigation."[38]

Establishing a research endowment when such funds were rare, Elizabeth Thompson also had the unusual foresight to trust her trustees, and to free her gift of hampering restrictions. "It is certainly very remarkable," said Charles S. Minot, "that a person not especially versed in science . . . should be induced by a desire to benefit her fellows, not to give for some temporary need, but with exceptional insight, to give for the development of the very sources of progress."[39] She might have done even more for science had bad health not intervened. Though she lived until July 1899, a paralytic stroke in December 1888 ended Elizabeth Thompson's philanthropic career.[40]

During the 1890's the problems surrounding the support of a biological station in Naples, Italy, aptly illustrated how discontinuous support prevented American scientists from making the best use of existing research opportunities. In 1874 Anton Dohrn, a young and wealthy German biologist, had opened the world's first marine zoological station at Naples.[41] The rich variety of marine life in nearby waters had attracted Dohrn to the Bay of Naples during his student days, and he determined to make its special advantages available to scientists of all countries. Investing his own fortune in the project, Dohrn had secured land from Naples and financial assistance from the

German government and from a group of English naturalists led by Charles Darwin and Thomas Huxley.[42]

Conceived and operated exclusively as a research institution, the station maintained extensive aquaria, collecting boats and crews, experimental apparatus, a large scientific library, and dozens of small, individual laboratories called "tables."[43] Scientific societies or governments leased tables at five hundred dollars per year, and selected the occupants. The Naples Station supplied the research facilities and, more important, whatever living specimens the visiting scientist required. "It is the ideal that every laboratory man in zoology . . . looks forward to," exclaimed Harry Russell, an American bacteriologist who worked at Naples in 1891. "As a scientific station this far transcends any other sea-side laboratory in the world."[44]

Ever since Charles O. Whitman spent the winter of 1881–82 as Dohrn's guest, a continuing stream of American scientists had visited the Naples Station.[45] Williams College and the University of Pennsylvania supported tables in 1883 and 1885, respectively. But despite pointed suggestions from Anton Dohrn, no American scientific society, much less the federal government, leased a table on a permanent basis. Instead, Americans depended on the generosity of Germany and England, who maintained several tables, or on Dohrn's own hospitality. The situation was doubly embarrassing. For want of an "American Table" many competent scientists had to forego the advantages of a summer at the Naples Station. Those who did go, moreover, "had the very doubtful pleasure of seeing every civilized nation present in its representatives except their own."[46]

In 1891 Major Alexander Henry Davis, a foot-loose Civil War veteran and Syracuse, New York, businessman, visited Naples in the course of a European tour. Its imposing Italian marble edifice and great aquaria made the station a favorite tourist attraction, and in the first instance probably attracted Davis to Anton Dohrn. The "amiable long haired Teuton" and the "typical Yankee cultured traveler," as Harry Russell described them, quickly became close friends.[47] Davis was shocked that there was no American table. At once he leased a table for a year, subsequently endowing it till 1895. Davis also gave Dohrn substantial sums for the station itself and, in an effort to force further American support, asked Dohrn to close European tables to American investigators.[48]

The action touched off a flury of activity in American scientific circles. Professional periodicals shamed Americans for their parasitic dependence upon foreign generosity. In August 1891 Charles W. Stiles, a government zoologist, brought the matter before the AAAS. He secured one hundred dollars from the association, and with official association sanction raised the remaining four hundred dollars from the University of Indiana, the Association of American Naturalists, Professor Charles O. Whitman, and Alexander Henry Davis.[49] Stiles, backed by a petition bearing the signitures of nearly two hundred American scientists, also prompted the Smithsonian Institution to lease another table in 1893. At the same time Alexander Agassiz, who had made millions in Michigan copper mines, secured a table for Harvard, while William E. Dodge, a steady patron of Columbia University, helped reserve one for that institution.[50] In 1898 a group of academic women, led by Dr. Ida H. Hyde, a Cornell biologist who had worked at Naples, joined in leasing a table for American women scientists. Their organization, subsequently called the Association to Aid Scientific Research by Women, continued to support a "Women's Table" into the 1930's.[51] After 1903, thanks to funds provided by the newly established Carnegie Institution of Washington, American scientists were always assured a place at the Naples Zoological Station.[52]

The Naples Station problem dramatized the limitations and embarrassment of haphazard finance, doing so in a period when the mounting pace and complexity of American life were already prompting a general search for operational efficiency. Businessmen sought security through cooperation and integration; "scientific" social workers pondered the mechanics of Charity Organization; scientists appealed for research endowments.[53] The Elizabeth Thompson Science Fund, the AAAS Research Fund, and the various funds administered by the American and National academies were part of that quest.

John Tyndall's American visit in 1872–73 had dramatized the needs of the scientific community. By the last quarter of the nineteenth century private giving had become something of an American national trait, but original investigation in science shared comparatively little of the bounty. The contrast in value between research endowments and endowments for higher education told the relative popularity of the increase and the diffusion of knowledge. There was no shortage of surplus capital in America. The gross national product more than doubled between 1869 and 1901; by 1892, according to a generally reliable *New York Tribune* survey, there were at least 4,047 millionaires in the United States.[54] Between 1875 and 1902 these and other wealthy Americans added nearly $153 million to the endowment of higher education. During the latter year alone, benefactions totaled more than $17 million.[55] On the other hand, endowments specifically earmarked for scientific research amounted to less than $3 million by 1903. Furthermore, the bulk of the science endowments were concentrated in only three agencies, Harvard University, the Smithsonian Institution, and the National Academy of Sciences. As a consequence of its continuing hold on the public imagination, astronomy claimed nearly half of the available funds.[56]

Two decades after John Tyndall's mission to the United States, American scientists were still begging for assistance. But increasingly their appeals showed a shift in strategy, a change in emphasis. Financial support, as such, was no longer enough. Because of the mounting cost and complexity of original investigation, its support had to be continuing, not intermittent, systematic, not haphazard. "Wrestling with the generous and wealthy," as George Davidson put it in 1892, might have served in the past, but all working men of science knew that piecemeal patronage could not meet the needs of the twentieth century.[57]

7

Fossils
and Free Enterprisers

In wandering through the "Mauvaises terres," or
"Bad Lands," it requires but little stretch of the
imagination to think oneself in the streets of some
vast ruined and deserted city. On ascending the butte
to the east of our camp, I found before me another
valley, a treeless barren plain, probably ten miles in
width. From the far side of this valley butte after
butte arose and grouped themselves along the horizon, and looked together in the distance like the huge
fortified city of an ancient race. The utter desolation
of the scene, the dried-up water-courses, and absence
of any moving object, and the profound silence
which prevailed, produced a feeling that was posi-
tively oppressive. When I then thought of the buttes
beneath my feet, with their entombed remains of
multitudes of animals forever extinct, and reflected
upon the time when the country teemed with life,
I truly felt that I was standing on the wreck of a
former world.

Joseph Leidy, 1873

ONE summer day in 1868 the Union Pacific made an un-
scheduled stop at Antelope Station, a tiny dot on the
rolling Nebraska prairies, just east of the Wyoming line. A
dapper, obviously Eastern gentleman leapt from a parlor car
and began searching through a mound of dirt beside a recently
dug well. Othniel C. Marsh, a Yale paleontologist, had come in
response to newspaper reports of fossil human bones unearthed

by a well digger. He failed to find fragments of early man, but what he did find excited him hardly less. For scattered over the ground were remains of many animals, among them a diminutive horse which Marsh subsequently identified as an important link in the evolutionary chain. He left the scene only after the impatient conductor had flagged the train ahead, leaving the preoccupied scientist to run after the last car. "I could only wonder," Marsh later recalled, "if such scientific truths as I had now obtained were concealed in a single well, what untold treasures must there be in the whole Rocky Mountain region. This thought promised rich rewards to the enthusiastic explorer in this new field, and thus my own life work seemed laid out before me."[1]

During the next three decades enthusiastic explorers, notably Joseph Leidy, Marsh himself, and Edward Drinker Cope, unearthed an extinct fauna of unimagined richness and variety. Before the three entered the field there were fewer than one hundred species of fossil vertebrates known in America. By the end of the century they had dug more than two thousand new species from the fossil cemetaries of the Great Plains. In the process they assembled impressive support for Darwinism, laid the foundations of modern paleonotology in the United States, and became embroiled in one of the bitterest scientific and political controversies of the late nineteenth century.

Gilded Age paleontologists were not, of course, the first to exploit the scientific resources of the frontier. The man of science had marched in the westward procession of civilization since it left the Atlantic seaboard in the seventeenth century. Cotton Mather had reported the discovery of fossils near the backwoods town of Albany, mastedon bones which the Puritan divine naturally mistook for the antediluvian giant mentioned in Genesis.[2] Later in the eighteenth century Thomas Jefferson had contributed to the literature on American monsters by describing a fossil "quadruped of the clawed kind," which he named *Megalonyx*, or Great-Claw, and likened to a lion. The *Megalonyx* (actually a large but placid ground-sloth), the mammoth, and the mastedon were of particular interest in Jefferson's day because of the prevailing belief that living forms had been fixed for all time in the Creation. The admission of an extinct species, like the admission of a rebellious planet disobeying Newton's laws, would have rendered the natural world unintelligible. "If one link in nature's chain might be lost," explained Jefferson, "another and another might be lost, till this whole system of things should evanish by piece-meal."[3]

The fossil monsters raised immediately practical problems as well. The bones proved empirically that the animals had existed. The theory said they must therefore still exist. Perhaps they were, as one of Jefferson's contemporaries warned the American Philosophical Society, "yet stalking through the western wilderness." Surely if there was room enough in the vast interior for Americans "to the hundredth and thousandth generation," there was also room enough for elephants and lions, mammoths and megalonyxes.[4]

As Jeffersonians searched for old bones and pondered their meaning, European naturalists were at work laying the basis for modern vertebrate paleontology. Through painstaking comparative anatomy, Georges Cuvier in France and Richard Owen in England demonstrated the correlation of parts and functions in animal organisms. Long legs implied a long neck to reach the ground; the feet and teeth of grazing animals were characteristically different from those of carnivors who ran down their prey. The comparative method (and a great deal of luck) enabled an anatomist to infer an entire animal, his habits, and much of his habitat from a few fragments of fossil bone.[5]

Americans were slow to incorporate the comparative method, for want of both museum specimens and competent investigators. In the 1850's, however, the Smithsonian Institution sent a box of western fossils to Dr. Joseph Leidy of Philadelphia. One of the last of the universal naturalists, Leidy was also a recognized specialist in several fields. His study of *The Ancient Fauna of Nebraska* (1854), published as one of the prestigious Smithsonian Contributions to Knowledge, announced the end of the monster school and the beginning of modern fossil study in the United States.

For more than a decade Leidy virtually monopolized the field, piecing together the fragments of former life shipped east by collectors, army officers, and frontiersmen. Although not a theorist by temperament, a decade before Darwin he was groping toward evolution almost in spite of himself. The fossils from the west made it clear that successive species had come and gone before the advent of man; it was only a matter of tracing the genealogy in the rocks. "We no longer doubt our power to unveil the past," he wrote, "even to the period when the encrinite, the trilobite, and the brachiopod, were the sole representatives of life upon our planet."[6]

But unveiling the past in the geological record was easier said than done, as Charles Darwin was the first to admit. Thus far fossil strata simply had not displayed the "finely graduated organic chain" demanded by Darwin's theory. Instead of orderly evolution, in fact, the rocks showed complex organisms suddenly appearing and disappearing without a trace of either ancestor or descendant. The evidence seemed to favor Progressionism, the respectable doctrine of Genesis and geology championed by Louis Agassiz. Undaunted, Darwin and the Darwinists had plunged ahead, blaming the missing links on the imperfection of the geological record. Fossilization only occurred under rare circumstances, they argued, and in any case only a fraction of the globe had been explored. The geological record was, in short, "a history of the world imperfectly kept, and written in a changing dialect," a book of which whole chapters had been lost, or never imprinted in the sediments of primeval seas.[7]

The fossil strata of the Great Plains held many of Darwin's missing chapters. Fortunately for the scientific community the territory was just now becoming accessible, as westward expansion gained momentum after the Civil War. Soldiers and miners, cattlemen and homesteaders all quickly discovered the practical utility of a careful scientific reconnaissance of the public domain. Their practical needs plus natural curiosity added up to political pressure, so that by the late 1860's the federal government had launched elaborate scientific surveys of the western territories. Prior to the establishment of the United States Geological Survey in 1879, six overlapping surveys were at work. The Coast and Geodetic Survey extended westward the meticulous geodesy begun decades before by Hassler and Bache. The General Land Office parceled out the public domain. Ferdinand V. Hayden's Survey of the Territories was a comprehensive if occasionally haphazard investigation of natural history. Clarence King's Geological Exploration of the Fortieth Parallel surveyed a hundred mile strip along the route of the transcontinental railroad, and brought new standards of sophistication to government geology. John Wesley Powell's ambitious Geographical and Geological Survey of the Rocky Mountain Region added to the store of data, and brought national publicity to the heroic, one-armed explorer of the Colorado. Lieutenant George M. Wheeler's Military Reconnaissance West of the Hundredth Meridian was prompted by fears in military circles that the new civilian surveys would leave the Corps of Topographical Engineers with nothing to do.[8]

Thanks to vague enabling legislation, each survey was virtually autonomous, and often acted less like a government agency than a private exploring expedition. Hayden, King, Powell, and Wheeler, each jealous of his prerogatives, made little if any attempt to coordinate their work. The result was administrative chaos in Washington and a duplication of effort in the field which even friendly critics estimated at 25 per cent. This bureaucratic snarl worked to the advantage of the fossil hunters, however, for the confusion bred more employment, offered more opportunities for field training and collecting, and opened more avenues for publication. They cared little that old bones were of only marginal interest to cattlemen looking for water or miners looking for gold.

Joseph Leidy was the first to benefit. F. V. Hayden was a close friend as well as a colleague in the University of Pennsylvania, where Leidy taught anatomy. This personal association, plus Leidy's stature in the field, made him the obvious person to work up the fossil vertebrates from the Hayden Survey. Much of the Philadelphian's lasting reputation, in fact, would rest on his reports and monographs issued under survey auspices. Leidy a man of modest means, probably could not have undertaken the research otherwise. The special problems of frontier life made research there doubly expensive. Self-sufficient expeditions had to be outfitted with everything from bacon to bowie knives, tons of bone-bearing rock had to be hauled overland to the rail head, hostile Indians had to be bribed or repulsed. Moreover, only a heavily subsidized or independently wealthy scientist could contemplate the publication of elaborate, illustrated scientific memoirs.[9]

Just such a lack of capital, plus his own retiring disposition, eventually forced Joseph Leidy from the western fossil fields. From the 1870's on O. C. Marsh and E. D. Cope contested for supremacy in vertebrate paleontology. Had the two men lived in different eras, each would undoubtedly have had a less controversial career. While Joseph Leidy seemed to value peace at any price, Marsh and Cope were prepared for war at any cost. Both were independently wealthy, scientific robber barons, fitting contemporaries of Daniel Drew and Commodore Vanderbilt. Joseph Leidy was forced to surrender, a casualty in the Cope-Marsh war. "Professors Marsh and Cope, with long purses, offer money for what used to come to me for nothing, and in that respect I cannot compete with them. So now . . . I have gone back to my microscope and my Rhizopods and make myself busy and happy with them."[10]

Marsh owed his long purse—indeed much of his scientific career—to his uncle, George Peabody, a self-made man who had amassed a fortune in Anglo-American trade and finance. Like most nineteenth-century American merchants, Peabody recoiled from the tooth and claw version of business enterprise popularly labeled Social Darwinism. He preferred to picture a benign social order governed by a benevolent God, in which wealth came to the virtuous and industrious almost as a matter of course. Since wealth came from society, Peabody believed that a millionaire was obliged to return it to the source. Long before Andrew Carnegie coined the term and elaborated the doctrine, Peabody practiced the Gospel of Wealth. Acutely aware of his own lack of formal schooling, he was particularly attracted to education, which he came to consider "a debt due from present to future generations." He would be best remembered for the Peabody Education Fund, which attempted broad-gauge educational and social reconstruction in the former Confederate States. But hardly less significant was Peabody's more than half-million-dollar investment in science.[11]

Peabody was a doting bachelor uncle, who paid special attention to the education and well-being of his nieces and nephews. Routine family philanthropy prompted him to see O. C. Marsh through preparatory school and Yale, through two years graduate work in the Sheffield Scientific School, plus three more years of study abroad.[12] Marsh set his sights on a professorship of paleontology at Yale. His mentors, James Dwight Dana and the younger Silliman, had also schooled him in the logistics of scientific enterprise, so that by 1862 Marsh was prepared to combine his request for further personal subsidy with a general plea for science at Yale. Marsh reported that Peabody had strong commitments to Harvard, and that he had already promised Edward Everett $100,000 for astronomy, or perhaps art. Still, there was hope. "As I have at present no interest in any institution except Yale," he assured Silliman, "I shall use all my influence with Mr. P. in her favor."[13]

Silliman and Dana had long since envisioned a grand natural history museum and research center to fill out the Scientific School. Their protégé was to be the living bond between the plan and the patron. By May 1863 Marsh had secured a $100,000 Peabody legacy for Yale science. Three more years of complicated revision converted the legacy into a lifetime donation, and increased the amount to $150,000. In the meantime Marsh had also helped the Cambridge scientific corps redirect Peabody's proposed Harvard gift from a school of design to a museum of archeology and ethnology, and in the interest of institutional parity, had convinced his uncle to make equal gifts to the two universities.[14]

George Peabody drew the formal trust deed in October 1866, establishing a museum specializing in zoology, geology, and mineralogy. It was, for all practical purposes, his nephew's private research institute. Several months before the grateful Yale Corporation had invited Marsh to fill a full professorship of paleontology created for the occasion. He had agreed to serve without salary (Uncle George provided a substantial allowance, and at his death in 1869 would leave him $100,000), so that the university could not demand that he teach undergraduate courses. Moreover, as a legal trustee of the museum as well as its director, Marsh could dictate research policy, control the collections, and publish his research at institutional expense. It was an enviable position for a fledgling scientist of thirty-five.

Under Marsh's direction the Peabody Museum quickly gained prominence. In the summer of 1870 he launched the first of a series of annual wild west fossil hunts. The Yale expeditions were technically private affairs, funded by the museum, but their familiarity with the government surveys, and their constant use of army facilities and personnel, clothed them at least partially in the public interest. The expeditions provided field training, augmented Marsh's collections, won him national publicity, and, at least to his own satisfaction, established squatter sovereignty over the fossil fields of the Great Plains.[15]

In 1871 Edward Drinker Cope trespassed on Marsh's self-proclaimed preserve. "I am now in a territory which interests me greatly," he reported from Kansas. "The prospects are that I will be able to do something in my favorite line of Vertebrate Paleontology. . . . Marsh has been doing a great deal I find, but has left more for me."[16] Cope had only recently committed himself to a full-time career in science. His wealthy Quaker father had intended that he become a farmer, and in the interests of scientific agriculture had provided Cope with a comprehensive if unorthodox scientific education at home and abroad. But Cope hated farming, and found the teaching of zoology at Haverford College little better. He had attached himself to the Hayden (and later the Wheeler) Survey, and began with a certain malicious enthusiasm to compete with Marsh for priority of discovery and publication. If Marsh had entrée to *Silliman's Journal* in New Haven, Cope had the Government Printing Office. "Hayden has fathered my Paleontological Bulletins. . . . A disagreeable pill for the Yale College People."[17]

For the next twenty years the Cope-Marsh conflict sputtered intermittently, much to the embarrassment of the scientific community at large. It proved in the long run to be a war of attrition in which Marsh countered Cope's brilliant but erratic forays with a less spectacular but relentless marshaling of financial, personal, and institutional support. The turning point came in 1878, when Marsh succeeded Joseph Henry as President of the National Academy of Sciences. Marsh's commanding position in the academy carried prestige and power. But even more significant in 1878 was the fact that Congress had recently asked the academy, as official science advisor to the government, to recommend a unified scheme for the scientific surveys which would "secure the best results for the least possible cost."[18] Fate had placed Marsh in a position to cut off his rival's source of support.

Several factors had prompted the economy move. The spiraling expenses of several competing surveys had irritated the cost-conscious for years. Reform-minded congressmen also saw the surveys as enclaves of scientific spoilsmen left over from the days of Ulysses Grant. But the most important impetus for reform, though few congressmen realized it, came from a survey itself. For some time Clarence King had been cultivating alliances in the political underworld of government science, looking ahead to the day when "the feudal period" would end and the rival scientific agencies would be consolidated under strong central authority.[19] King's charisma had made him the talk of Washington society. "One Clarence King only existed in the world," wrote an admiring Henry Adams.

"Whatever prize he wanted lay ready for him—scientific, social, literary, political,—and he knew how to take them in turn."[20] Speaking through such congressional friends as Abram S. Hewitt and James A. Garfield, in 1878 King called for reform, the first maneuver in his campaign for control of the western surveys.

The practical outcome was quickly told. Marsh's National Academy report (adopted with the sole dissent of E. D. Cope, who understood that reform would in effect freeze him out), urged a scheme which would have provided for geodesy, the systematic disposition of public lands, and theoretical and practical geology.[21] Congress, in keeping with the general tenor of the Gilded Age, ignored all but the latter when it authorized the creation of a new United States Geological Survey. After all, said Congressman Hewitt, "the science of geology and the science of wealth are indissolubly linked." Nations became great only as they developed "a genius for grasping the forces and materials of nature within their reach and converting them into a steady flowing stream of wealth and comfort."[22] The Hayden and Powell surveys, once work in progress had been completed, were to be either absorbed or abolished. With Marsh's help Clarence King emerged as director of the new survey, only to be replaced by John Wesley Powell, when King left government service the following year. Largely in return for past favors, in 1882 Powell appointed Marsh official paleontologist of the Geological Survey. E. D. Cope, cut off from federal patronage, could only bewail his dwindling fortune, appeal for congressional and private support, and rage at his enemies, who he charged had created "a gigantic politico-scientific monopoly next in importance to Tammany Hall."[23]

More was at stake than a personal feud and bureaucratic empire building. The survey reorganization of 1878–79 was of lasting significance as the beginning of a ten year debate over the proper relationship between science and the federal government. Except in special circumstances, notably Joseph Henry's Smithsonian battle of the 1850's, heretofore government science had been neither costly nor controversial enough to attract searching congressional criticism. But by the late 1870's it had grown too big to ignore, and politicians began to understand what years of salutory neglect had wrought.

Because Gilded Age Americans thought themselves wedded to the doctrines of limited government and laissez-faire, the rise of large-scale government science posed broad questions of social theory and public policy. The Union armies had settled the issue of national sovereignty at Appomattox Courthouse, but the issue of national responsibility still remained. Republicans who favored emancipation, protective tariffs, and railroad subsidies were not necessarily convinced that the increase of knowledge fell within the limits of the general welfare clause. Clarence King's strategists, alive to congressional fears, had even turned the bogy of socialized science to good account as a rationale for a consolidated scientific survey. In spite of the fact that he was fast becoming the most powerful scientist-administrator in Washington, John Wesley Powell had urged that federal patronage be "very limited and scrupulously confined," lest centralized control thwart scientific genius.[24] James A. Garfield went even further, warning his colleagues that the government had already gone too far. In the West federal science was the rival of individual enterprise, "a formidable and crushing competitor of private students of science."[25] Garfield was not entirely convincing in his argument that a strong, consolidated survey would halt the trend.

The difficulty was not merely that government scientists and their friends were employing the shibboleth of laissez-faire as political propaganda. Even under the best of circumstances self-made science, like self-made manhood, had always been a matter of degree. Like many enterprises in the Gilded Age, the scientific surveys were in fact a productive partnership between public and private, corporate and individual effort. Their dual nature was often disguised by formal labels, but in practice nice distinctions were impossible so long as the personal fortunes of a Marsh or Cope were so freely mingled with federal appropriations, or when private research was published as a public document.

The confusion could not be clarified by piecemeal administrative reform. In the mid-1880's the debate began once more when Grover Cleveland's Democracy attempted to bring "business principles to public affairs."[26] Government scientists had good reason to be apprehensive over the new administration. Cleveland had vetoed a state geological survey when Governor of New York, and there were fears that he opposed government science in principle.[27] Furthermore, the scientific bureaus did have their share of graft and spoilsmanship, favoritism and boodle. But most important, John Wesley Powell had violated the spirit if not the letter of the 1879 congressional directive by building the Geological Survey into a wide-ranging research agency.

In December 1884 a six-member congressional commission launched an investigation, determined to introduce "greater efficiency and economy" into the scientific surveys. Although Senator William B. Allison was chairman, Representative Hilary A. Herbert of Alabama was clearly the driving force behind the inquiry, and the only member who addressed himself directly to the larger issues of public policy at stake.[28]

The former Confederate colonel was not personally hostile toward either science or scientists. He was, however, a disciple of classical laissez-faire, and it seemed clear to him that Powell and the Geological Survey had gotten out of hand. "I am radically Democratic in my views," he explained to O. C. Marsh. "I believe in as little government as possible—that Government should keep its hands off and allow the individual fair play. This is the doctrine I learned from Adam Smith & Buckle, from Jefferson, Benton and Calhoun, and from this standpoint I believe we have too much to do (the Gov't) with pure science."[29]

Forced to justify his administration, Director Powell now shifted from his position of 1878, and argued that federal patronage of science was a positive good. There was no limit to the unknown. Therefore activity in one sector could only serve to stimulate work in another. "Science feeds upon itself and grows."[30]

Most American scientists agreed with Powell that the source of research support was less important than the amount. Even the dissenters seemed prepared to tolerate in practice what they condemned in theory. In his voluminous essays in political economy, for example, Simon Newcomb argued that government should always be guided by the "let-alone principle." His advocacy of laissez-faire did not, however, prevent him from serving as Superintendent of the Naval Observatory, nor did it curtail his lobbying activities in behalf of the observatory, the Coast Survey, and other agencies in which he had a personal or professional interest.[31]

Alexander Agassiz presented an even more striking mixture of principle, propriety, self-interest, and envy. His own experience had convinced him that in America self-made wealth was within easy reach, and that consequently a scientist without his own research funds had only himself to blame. Growing up in his father's household had, of course, provided an exceptional scientific education in itself. Agassiz then studied at the Lawrence Scientific School, and assumed directorship of his father's Museum of Comparative Zoology. Even so, family heritage and educational advantage could not overcome the fact that scientific research was not self-supporting. "I want to make money," he told President Eliot of Harvard. "It is impossible to be a productive naturalist in this country without money. I am going to get some money if I can and then I will be a naturalist."[32] In 1867 he left for upper Michigan, where unusually rich veins of copper were attracting eastern investors. With Boston backing he reorganized a mining company, and with considerable technological and business acumen began to expand its operations across the peninsula. Agassiz returned just a year later, bored with business enterprise but secure in the knowledge that he now had the financial base necessary for a life in science. By the end of the century his Hecla Calumet mines had paid Agassiz and the other investors total dividends in excess of one hundred million dollars.[33]

Alexander Agassiz lived in a world of Horatio Alger heroes come true. Like another self-effacive millionaire of the Gilded Age, Andrew Carnegie, Agassiz had every reason to believe that fame and fortune waited on any man with initiative and integrity.[34] His faith in the general benevolence of the social order made him forget that only the talented and the lucky found acres of diamonds at every hand. It also made him oppose what he termed "the general and unlimited government coddling of science," which was undesirable because unnecessary. It was also dangerous, for in the end federal patronage would produce an official clique in Washington. Commanding respect or buying allegiance, "political scientists" would manipulate American science for selfish ends.[35]

Their intrigues had already compromised the Coast Survey, the one scientific agency Agassiz thought deserving of massive support. In this case conscience took a back seat to interest, for the Agassiz family had enjoyed a favored relationship with the Coast Survey since the days of Alexander Dallas Bache. Like his father before him, Agassiz had gained the use of specially outfitted research vessels under a cost-sharing plan with the survey.[36] In 1885, he had even been offered the superintendency, but declined, claiming a low tolerance for red tape and a disdain for bureaucratic etiquette. Had Agassiz followed his first inclination and accepted the post, he would have then been in a position to reform from within. Instead, he condemned himself to the less effective, more frustrating role of outside critic.[37]

Agassiz found an ally in Hilary Herbert. As the Allison Commission gathered testimony, he fed information and opinions to the congressman, wrote polemic articles for the press, and appealed personally to President Cleveland. Herbert had singled out paleontology as the least practical, hence most vulnerable activity of the Geological Survey. When he asked Agassiz "where to draw a line that would lop off some of this sort of work," the biologist replied in a manner that revealed his personal antagonism to O. C. Marsh. Envy as well as principle lay behind his assertion that paleontology was "just one of the things which private individuals and learned societies can do just as well as the government."[38]

Although Agassiz often appeared austere, stoically self-reliant, impervious to either criticism or praise, he was in fact as sensitive as any man. Marsh had gained a national reputation for his personal investments in research; he had not. Marsh had merely spent George Peabody's money; he had made his own. Marsh had published at government expense; he had scrupulously published his Coast Survey researches himself. "Marsh of New Haven appears before the country as a great patron of science," he complained. "We have had quite enough of this posing as benefactors of science by men whose support of science was paid for by the government." Curtailing the Geological Survey might serve the public interest. It would sooth the private hurt.[39]

Thanks to Agassiz's coaching, Hilary Herbert was ready to act before most members of the Allison Commission had digested their findings. Appearing to speak for the entire commission, in April 1886 he introduced a bill emasculating the Geological Survey. The Herbert Bill lopped off paleontology entirely, except for the collection and storage of fossils. It cut the elaborate publication program back to a brief annual report. Drastic measures were necessary, he wrote, in order to suppress a government monopoly and restore open competition in scientific discovery. Otherwise America was doomed to repeat the tragic experience of France under Louis XIV where, according to the historian Buckle, court subsidies had perverted science into mere jobbery.[40]

Within a few days it became clear that Herbert had spoken only for himself, for his fellow Alabaman John T. Morgan, and for Alexander Agassiz. Herbert's wholesale attack had rallied the scientific community behind John Wesley Powell, who again defended the Geological Survey as an economic benefit and a stimulus to science in the private sector. Powell admitted Herbert's theoretical objection to a government monopoly of science, but he doubted it was a practical threat. "The laws of political economy do not belong to the economics of science and intellectual progress," he asserted, rejecting Herbert's easy analogy between business enterprise and scientific discovery. "The learning of one man does not subtract from the learning of another, as if there were a limited quantity of unknown truth. . . . Scholarship breeds scholarship, wisdom breeds wisdom, discovery breeds discovery."[41]

Powell also turned on Alexander Agassiz. He denounced his anti-Geological Survey, but pro-Coast Survey stance as hypocritical. He implied that Agassiz was merely jealous of government science, for he dreamed of using his great wealth to make the Agassiz Museum "the American center for scientific research, and the agency which should create, control, and diffuse the increasing knowledge of the New World." Agassiz was also an aristocrat, incapable of understanding the vital interest ordinary people had in the pursuit of knowledge. Should the "genius of only the wealthy be employed in advancing the boundaries of human knowledge, and does great wealth invariably inspire its possessors with love for research, insight into Nature's laws, and patience in long labor?"[42]

Powell's counterattack, plus his influence in both scientific and political circles, carried the day. The majority of the Allison Commission repudiated Hilary Herbert's retrenchment policy. At the same time, however, the commission also rejected a National Academy proposal for a highly centralized, cabinet-level Department of Science.[43] In essence the commission voted for the *status quo*, recommending only that in the future Major Powell submit detailed budgets instead of lump-sum requests for funds. Their implied criticism of Powell's administration scarcely diminished his victory. Herbert explained to Agassiz that they had been out-politicked by patronage and "scientific demagogism."[44]

The congressman had long since learned to accept defeat as part of the political process. The scientist took it personally. Powell had impugned his motives, insulted his family name, hurt his feelings. "This is the kind of thing which will sicken any honest man and disgust them with Washington methods," he wrote, the day he read Powell's attack. He would not reply. "I don't propose to discuss a subject with people whose only weapon is abuse."[45] Except for a brief period in 1892 when he joined forces with Hilary Herbert and E. C. Cope in the last skirmish of the Marsh-Cope feud, Alexander Agassiz never again ventured into the political arena. He sought sanctuary in marine biology, and devoted his remaining years to the study of the evolution of coral reefs. "No man with any self respect," he explained, "can be expected to dirty his skirts again."[46]

On the institutional level, the final result of the long and bitter controversy over the western surveys was to affirm that scientific research was indeed a legitimate function of the national government. By virtue of its inaction the Allison Commission accepted John Wesley Powell's conception of a modern, multipurpose scientific bureau, and thus cleared the way for twentieth-century government science. Yet by rejecting a centralized Department of Science, they agreed that although such a scheme might appear efficient on paper, in operation a certain amount of institutional rivalry was a spur to progress. In government science as in the government itself, the conflicting claims of authority and independence, nationalism and federalism, were best resolved through compromise.[47]

On the ideological level, the controversy showed some of the difficult adjustments which rapid economic and social change forced upon traditional modes of thinking. In Gilded Age America both government and corporate business enterprise were expanding their functions at a bewildering rate, inevitably encroaching upon traditional spheres of individual activity in the process. The resulting tensions were bound to distort the familiar boundaries between the public and the private sectors, rendering discourse and policy confused at best and self-contradictory at worst. The situation was little better in Victorian England, where the pace of change had also widened the gap between social theory and social practice. A decade before the Allison Commission, its British equivalent had covered similar ground, trying to determine whether public research grants tended to "chill private enterprise."[48]

It was this very confusion, this paradoxical quality, that made Gilded Age science so much a part of Gilded Age society at large. Americans wanted to believe in self-reliant science, just as they wanted to believe in self-made manhood. Yet it was obvious that rags to riches was the exception, not the rule, just as it was obvious that intellectual distinction could not rest solely on a foundation of "private cupidity and the law of supply and demand."[49] Thus when scientists paid lip service to rugged individualism one moment and lobbied for federal subsidies the next, they were merely being true to their time. They were no more, or less hypocritical than the transcontinental railroad magnates of their day. It was simply that the Gilded Age reading of laissez-faire said that government might legitimately help, but must never hinder private enterprise. Except for a few austere individualists like Hilary Herbert, William Graham Sumner, and, to some extent, Alexander Agassiz, the issue was not government intervention. It was merely government favoritism.

8

Science and
the Higher Learning

> Whatever expedients of decorative real-estate, spec-
> tacular pageantry, bureaucratic magnificence, elu-
> sive statistics, vocational training, genteel solemnities
> and sweat-shop instruction, may be imposed by the
> exigencies of a competitive business policy, the uni-
> versity is after all a seat of learning, devoted to the
> cult of idle curiosity,—otherwise called the scientific
> spirit.
>
> *Thorstein Veblen, 1918*

T HE University of Chicago celebrated its tenth anniversary
in 1903. At the decennial Convocation, Daniel Coit Gilman
reviewed the formative decade and called attention to the
university's distinctive characteristics. In his address, appropriately entitled "Research," Gilman told how the encouragement
of original investigation had made Chicago "the most suggestive, the most comprehensive, the most successful, and the
most hopeful of many new foundations among us for the
advancement of higher education." The massive *Decennial
Publications* gave substance to Gilman's hyperbolic praise, and
demonstrated the truth of President William Rainey Harper's
claim that from the beginning the university had emphasized
"pure science."[1]

Harper had assembled one of the nation's most distinguished
science faculties, selected, as he put it, "not because of their
ability to teach or lecture, but rather on the ground of their
ability to investigate."[2] The general educational climate, influenced by the achievements of The Johns Hopkins and Clark

universities, favored such a policy.[3] The founder, John D. Rockefeller, believed that investigation was as sound an investment as instruction. The president, an educational entrepreneur of incredible energy and imagination, instilled an enthusiasm for the institution which, in Rockefeller's words, "was so great that no vision of its future seemed too large." Together, these elements made Chicago the foremost symbol of the higher learning at the close of the nineteenth century.

John D. Rockefeller's gifts, totaling nearly thirty-five million dollars, dwarfed all other Chicago benefactions in amount and notoriety. The familiar story of his bounty, in fact, obscured the contributions of others to the over-all development of the university.[4] Rockefeller supplied money for general endowment and construction; others supplied Chicago with laboratories, with the world's finest refracting telescope, with a ranking school of science. The circumstances surrounding these benefactions afforded an inside view of how the abstract research ideal achieved concrete institutional expression.

Daniel Coit Gilman once remarked that six things were needed to launch a university: an idea, capital, a plan, an able staff, books and apparatus, and students.[5] In the case of Chicago the sources of the idea were remote, rooted in the general context of academic reform, in the aspirations of the American Baptist Education Society to revitalize denominational education in the Middle West, and in the sanguine dreams of William Rainey Harper. In May 1889 Rockefeller (on the condition that the Baptist Education Society raise four hundred thousand dollars more) offered the initial capital of six hundred thousand dollars for what was then to be a Baptist college. In September 1890 he subscribed a million more, an inducement for Harper to leave his biblical studies at Cornell and assume the presidency.

Harper's creative imagination transformed Rockefeller's Baptist college into a ranking university. "On my way from Chicago the whole thing outlined itself in my mind," he told Rockefeller, "and I have a plan which is at the same time unique and comprehensive, which I am persuaded will revolutionize university study in this country; nor is this only *my* opinion."[6] Harper's enthusiasm infected the university trustees, who enlarged the original site from seventeen to twenty-three acres to accommodate the new design. It was an extraordinarily optimistic step. The university had no president, for Harper did not formally accept until the following month. It had no staff, no students, and would not open for at least two more years. The Panic of '93 already loomed on the financial horizon. Moreover, grandiose expansionism ran counter to Rockefeller's ingrained habit of "feeling his way along" with limited and conditional gifts. Still, Harper plunged ahead. "Invariably and against his own experience," wrote Frederick T. Gates, Harper "both overestimated resources and underestimated expenditures. . . . His resistance was small and his temptations great."[7]

Help came from an unexpected quarter, confirming Harper in his plans to make original research a Chicago trademark. From New York, Leighton and Mornay Williams had watched the developments in Chicago with considerable interest. The Williams brothers were both attorneys, both active Baptists. From 1880 to 1887 they had practiced in partnership, specializing in trusts and estates. Leighton then had given up formal practice to fill his father's old pulpit at the Amity Baptist Church, and to join with his friend, Walter Rauschenbusch, in preaching the social gospel. Meanwhile Mornay had become one of New York's leading experts on the intricate law of charitable trusts, and a prominent advocate of Charity Organization.[8] During the first week of January 1891, President Harper received an intriguing letter, his first, from Rev. Leighton Williams. It began like many other letters that praised "the work" at Chicago. But, Leighton continued, "I write chiefly to ask if you can appoint a time to meet here at my brother's office a gentleman . . . who takes a strong interest in the new University to confer in reference the possibility of an endowment on certain terms for Scientific Studies."[9]

Harper was on the New York train within the week. He was walking into a vastly complicated situation, as Williams explained on the way to meet Andrew H. Green, the gentleman in question. Green, a prominent lawyer and civic leader, was the principal executor of the William B. Ogden estate.[10] Ogden had been an early Chicago settler and the city's first mayor, a patron of the arts and sciences who had succeeded Stephen A. Douglas as President of the Board of Trustees of the old University of Chicago. Illinois real estate and Wisconsin timber lands had made him a multimillionaire. Retiring to New York after the Chicago Fire of 1871, he had lived his remaining five years in a villa on Fordham Heights. He left an estate valued at six to seven million dollars and a will so involved that Green had called in Mornay Williams as personal counsel. Ogden left 37/40ths of the estate to his widow, his brother-in-law, and eighteen collateral relatives. His trustees were to distribute the income from the remaining 3/40ths among charities of their choice. Over the years they had distributed some $450,000 to a variety of causes.[11] Green, now seventy-one, in failing health, and about to leave for Europe, wanted to dispose of the estate while he was still able. Two of the five trustees had already died. In December 1890 several of Ogden's nieces and nephews had added to the confusion, and to Green's concern, by contesting the will on the technicality that the charitable clause was too indefinite. The New York courts were simultaneously declaring Samuel J. Tilden's four-million-dollar library bequest to the city of New York void on similar grounds. Andrew Green, also Tilden's executor, was involved in that litigation and understandably wanted to save Ogden's benefactions from a similar fate.[12]

Green had selected Chicago and science for several reasons. Ogden's own patronage of the old university and the Chicago Academy of Sciences made such a designation appropriate. Most of the Ogden estate properties were located in Illinois, safe from the restrictive doctrines of New York charity law. Mornay and Leighton Williams, his closest advisors, had a strong denominational interest in Chicago. Mornay in particular was playing the uneasy (and somewhat unethical) dual role of disinterested counsel and active middle-man.[13]

In the first instance, Green probably turned to science out of deference to William Ogden's evident interests. He might have been encouraged to specify original investigation by the current efforts of his friend, Seth Low, to reform Columbia University. President Low, though a businessman with no scientific training, had embraced the research ideal. His "central pet idea," reported an admiring Columbia physicist in 1890, "is the University and original research by professors and advanced students. This he perpetually talks of, in season and out . . . and some of our fossils are greatly scandalized."[14]

Andrew Green confirmed his conversation with President Harper in a letter dated January 12. Would Chicago accept a three-hundred-thousand- to five-hundred-thousand-dollar endowment for a school of science, he asked, a school "exclusively for advanced scientific work, either in the support of well known specialists or in the encouragement of original investigation among graduate students of proved ability?" Might the donors name the school and have a voice in its management? Would Baptist sponsorship of the University impose religious tests on faculty or students? Would Harper submit plans for a school meeting Chicago's needs and the donor's stipulations?[15]

Sketching bold and detailed programs was Harper's special talent. A week later he returned an outline for a school "devoted mainly to furnishing the best facilities possible for scientific investigation." Men with creative ability in science, he wrote, often lacked the resources to pursue their work. The school would incorporate all the university's graduate work and research in science. The denominational complexion of the board would not curtail academic freedom. With an administrator's natural dread of binding commitments, however, Harper hedged, graciously, on the question of assigning the Ogden executors a seat on the University Board of Trustees.[16]

Four months of on-again, off-again negotiations dragged by after the initial exchange. The lawsuit brought by the Ogden heirs was still pending. Andrew Green's failing health, and his increasing irritation with the other trustees, who had a personal interest in endowing a homeopathic hospital, hindered agreement on the Chicago designation. "We have been pushing all we can," reported Leighton Williams. "I am as anxious as you can be," added Mornay early in June, "but . . . I have been at a loss for any way in which to expedite the matter, though every reason seems to me to make haste imperative."[17] By mid-June Harper could stand the uncertainty no longer. An expeditious journey to New York and a long talk with Andrew Green prompted immediate action.[18] On June 30 Green wrote that Chicago would receive 70 per cent of the Ogden bounty for the Ogden School of Science. The remainder would be divided between miscellaneous charities and a memorial hospital at Elmira, New York, Mrs. Ogden's birthplace. Because of the "unfortunate litigation" still pending Green was unable to indicate the amount of the gift, though he was confident that it would be no less than three hundred thousand dollars and might exceed a half million.[19] On June 11 he and Mrs. Ogden signed the formal agreement, confident that the courts would decide the case in their favor. Elated, the Chicago trustees pledged themselves "to lift the school up into the highest excellence and the greatest fame."[20]

Legal snarls and personal disputes delayed the actual transfer of funds. The Williams brothers were piqued when, after all their efforts on behalf of his university, Rockefeller refused their application for financial aid in church work.[21] The New York Supreme Court ruled Ogden's bequest void for uncertainty, even though the decision had no real effect on the Chicago benefaction. The adverse ruling affected only Ogden properties in New York; the real estate comprising the Chicago gift was located in Illinois, safely beyond the Court's jurisdiction.[22] Andrew Green insisted that his brother be appointed a university trustee, and only after considerable discussion accepted Leighton Williams as a substitute. The end result, however, a six-hundred-thousand-dollar school of science, was well worth the months of tedious negotiations.[23]

In accepting the Ogden benefaction the trustees had bound themselves to original scientific work and to an enlarged view of the university's future. Driven by Harper's quest for the "highest excellence and the greatest fame," they resolved in November 1891 to raise an additional million for general expansion. Meanwhile the president was devoting all his energies to supplying the third ingredient in Daniel Coit Gilman's university formula: a distinguished faculty. The first few months brought only crushing disappointment. He sought established scholars and experimenters; only to discover that such men were rare and usually hard to move, especially to a "Standard Oil" university still in the planning stage. "We have not a head professor after nine months of constant work," he wrote Frederick Gates the day after Christmas. "I am in despair. . . . The only thing that I can see is nine hundred and ninety-nine unfinished deals."[24]

By a fortunate coincidence Clark University, the purest American expression of European university ideals, was then on the verge of collapse. Jonas Clark, a Worcester, Massachusetts, businessman, had founded Clark in 1888 intending it to be a college for poor and virtuous youths. Under President G. Stanley Hall, formerly of The Johns Hopkins, it matured "quite uncontaminated with undergraduate work."[25] After several years, conflicting aims and personal animosities had alienated the founder from the president.[26] Hall, in turn, had antagonized the staff. Henry Donaldson, a Clark neurologist, a former Hall student, and one of the psychologist's friendlier critics, remembered him as "a man of unusual mental gifts and the most suggestive and stimulating person with whom I ever came in contact—but untrustworthy. . . . His wisdom was more serpentine than admirable."[27]

In January 1892 a majority of the disgruntled Clark faculty resigned in bloc. A few days later William Rainey Harper, who had heard of the troubles at Worcester, swooped down on the crippled university. He came, recalled Hall, "like . . . the eagle who robbed the fishhawk of his prey." Hall brooded while Harper wooed his faculty with princely salaries of seven thousand dollars and promises of richly endowed research laboratories. Charles O. Whitman, John V. Nef, A. A. Michelson, Henry Donaldson, and eleven others followed Harper in the "great hegira" to Chicago. The move prostrated Clark, but as Hall later observed in his autobiography, it made Chicago's reputation overnight. It gave notice that "the new institution by the lake would not be Chautauquaean but would have a solid scientific nucleus."[28]

The financial picture began to brighten as well. In January 1892 Sidney Kent, a Chicago meat packer, agreed to give a $150,000 chemical laboratory. Charles T. Yerkes seemed ready to donate a comparable laboratory for biology, which was Head Professor Whitman's price for quitting Clark.[29] On February 23 Rockefeller gave a second million in endowment "as a special thank offering to Almighty God for returning health."[30] In April, department-store owner Marshall Field promised $100,000 if $1,000,000 was raised in sixty (later ninety) days, an incentive for Chicagoans to match Rockefeller's latest benefaction. During the next three frenzied months, local philanthropists met Field's stipulation. George C. Walker, a businessman, university trustee, and long-time patron of local scientific associations, contributed more than $100,000 for a museum. Martin Ryerson, the president of the trustees, gave $150,000 for a physics laboratory. Ryerson had intended to build a dormitory, but quickly substituted the laboratory when Harper pointed out the needs of the new Head Professor of Physics, A. A. Michelson. Michelson set out to make the Ryerson Laboratory "one of the finest and best in the world." His 1907 Nobel Prize, the first awarded to an American in any field, was a measure of his success.[31]

The Ogden School of Science, the Kent and Ryerson laboratories, the Walker Museum, and the Yerkes Observatory gave Chicago a commanding lead in the physical sciences. The life sciences, however, were still without a patron when the university opened its doors in October 1892. Two years later the biologists were still waiting, and their patience was exhausted. Donaldson and Whitman complained of cramped quarters and insufficient funds for research. "I'm not angry," said Whitman, "only upset because of the state of biology. We ought not to wait another year for a building. I really feel humiliated at the present state of our departments, as compared with what we had planned, and were promised." In 1895 he delivered an ultimatum: "What I want to know is not what the future holds, but what I can depend upon now, if I remain."[32]

On his way to Clark in 1892, President Harper had met with Charles Yerkes in New York and secured a tentative pledge of a biology building from the traction magnate. Later Yerkes had backed down, still later he had given the great observatory. Ever since Yerkes's refusal Harper had tried in vain to find a substitute benefactor for biology. He redoubled his efforts under mounting faculty pressure. At the Summer Convocation in 1894 he plead for a biological laboratory, "the greatest need of the University today." He reiterated the appeal at each succeeding convocation until the winter of 1896, when the long-sought benefactor appeared.[33]

At sixty-three Miss Helen Culver was a remarkable woman, a shrewd business executive in an era when woman's proper place was still the home. Born and educated in New York state, she had joined the great migration to the Old Northwest in the 1850's, determined to bring culture to the frontier. She established a short-lived academy at Sycamore, Illinois, then moved to Chicago, where from 1854 to 1861 she taught and served as a principal in the city's schools. She lived with her cousin, Charles J. Hull, then amassing a fortune from real estate in the booming city. At Mrs. Hull's death in 1861, Helen Culver gave up teaching to rear her cousin's children. In 1868 she became his business associate as well. At Hull's death in 1889 she inherited and carried on his multimillion dollar business.[34]

Charles J. Hull had made a second career of philanthropy. He visited jails and slum neighborhoods, working to rehabilitate social outcasts. His guiding principle, a complement to his business interests, was that "land is the natural wealth of a nation and when it is not distributed discontent and revolution will come."[35] In Chicago, in Baltimore, and in several other southern cities he distributed (for a fair price, since Hull believed that outright charity only pauperized the recipient) unoccupied land to the poor. Neither religion nor ordinary philanthropy, he explained to Miss Culver in 1874, could "counterbalance the mischievous results of concentrating the wealth of the country in a comparatively few families. If this process of concentration goes on extensively the poor will join in riot (their revolution) and level down from the top, by destroying the property of the rich. Our idea is to *level up from the bottom*, by giving the poor a fair chance to rise."[36]

Helen Culver carried on Hull's philanthropy as she carried on his business. She continued the land distribution scheme. In 1889 she gave the old family homestead to a young reformer named Jane Addams, who soon made Hull House world-famous as a social settlement.[37]

At the dedication of the Hull Biological Laboratories William Rainey Harper spoke of the unexpected and unsolicited nature of Helen Culver's million-dollar gift to the University of Chicago. In a sense she had taken the initiative, but her action was preconditioned by circumstances which neither she nor President Harper ever made public. In contrast to the lifeless official rhetoric of the dedication ceremony, Harper's confidential account of the Culver benefaction was a rich and revealing account of the human side of philanthropic giving.

"The story of the Culver gift is almost a romance," he began. "Three years ago I learned that Miss Culver had made a will, giving all her property to a niece, the wife of a professor in Oberlin. Strangely enough, the husband and the niece were not on the best of terms. . . . I discovered a gentleman who had a large influence with the niece, and he was found to be a man of very great ability. He came to Chicago at that time as a fellow in the Dept. of Sociology."[38] The niece promised the persuasive sociologist, William I. Thomas, that if she inherited Helen Culver's fortune she would turn it over to Chicago as an endowment fund for sociology. She also introduced him to her aunt.[39] Thomas "acquainted Miss Culver with all the inside of the University . . . giving her the information without in any way seeming to be prejudiced. He has reported to me every month or so during these three years."[40]

Late in November 1895 Professor Thomas reported that Miss Culver had decided to give her fortune to some permanent institution instead of to her niece. Thomas mentioned the university, but she replied that she disapproved of the ways in which John D. Rockefeller made his money. "This of course troubled us," commented Harper, "but we took courage, and went to work. It was impossible for me, under the circumstances, to visit her. She was very shy of all outsiders." Quite to Harper's surprise, on December 3 Miss Culver asked him to call. She wanted to devote part of her fortune to a public purpose, and had selected the university as the most fitting and reliable agency. "This was the culmination of three years work, and you can understand how amazed, and at the same time delighted I was."[41]

Harper called at Miss Culver's Ashland Boulevard town house on December 6. "I found that she had made up her mind on two points: (1) that the money should be used on the West Side and (2) (would you believe it?) that it should be used for an Art School and a Picture Gallery. I held my breath, but concluded that there must be some change of arrangement." An hour's conversation disposed of art. "Then she proposed music, for she was determined that it should be used for something which would refine." Harper again objected, countering with sociology, with medicine, with pedagogy, but none seemed to strike a response. Finally he suggested biology. "I found she had read carefully the Convocation statements, and was well posted on the whole matter, and in ten minutes it was agreed that it should be either Music or Biology. This was the first interview, which lasted four hours and forty minutes. It included dinner."[42]

When Harper called again on the tenth Miss Culver had made up her mind. She had rejected the arts for science, and presented him with an inventory of 480 Chicago tenements, worth a million and then yielding a net annual income of fifty thousand dollars. She asked him to prepare a letter of donation for her signature. She also pledged an additional six hundred thousand dollars as a future gift or possibly as a bequest. "She is perfectly happy over the gift, and while a woman of very great reserve and strength of character, is almost beside herself with pleasure and satisfaction over what she has done. Of course it means everything for Biology in this country, and will put us on a level with any European institution."[43]

Helen Culver disclaimed all credit for the benefaction, and refused to have her name associated with the four zoology, anatomy, physiology, and botany laboratories that made up the Hull Quadrangle. Charles Hull was the real donor; he had amassed the fortune and instilled the philanthropic impulse. She was merely his agent. "It is by an accident merely that I was left at last to designate the object, and sign the papers." At the dedication ceremony in July 1897 she explained that since Hull had survived his children, she had a family responsibility "to leave in concrete form a definite resultant of the life here and to give it such direction that it may move on as a continuation of personal effort. . . . To you," she told Harper and the trustees, "I pass the name, which no son or daughter is left to wear." Later in the ceremony she added a revealing statement of personal belief which, if sincere, partly explained her decision to endow the life sciences instead of the arts: "I have believed," she said, "that moral evils would grow less as knowledge of their relation to physical life prevails—and that science, which is knowing, knowing the truth, is a foundation of pure religion."[44]

In 1889, the same year that John D. Rockefeller agreed to found a university at Chicago, Charles S. Peirce had defined a university for the new *Century Dictionary*. A university, declared the scientist and logician, was "an association of men for the purpose of study . . . that the theoretical problems which present themselves to the development of civilization may be resolved." A little baffled, his editors wrote that they understood a university to be an educational institution. Peirce replied, bluntly, that they were "grievously mistaken, that a university had not and never had had anything to do with instruction and that until we got over this idea we should not have any university in this country."[45]

Only a few champions of the higher learning, like Thorstein Veblen, would have demanded such an uncompromising statement of the research ideal. The representative American university was no copy-book replica of the German university, nor could it be, given the healthy heterogeneity of American life.[46] Most ranking universities developed, by accident or design, along the lines laid down by Ezra Cornell—institutions where any person might find instruction in any study. Even Chicago became what campus wits labeled a "Harper's Bazaar." Nevertheless, Peirce's classic definition embodied a long-standing commitment to original inquiry that had dominated the thinking of American scientific men, and that came to distinguish such institutions as Chicago from the traditional American college.

From the 1840's onward, American men of science had striven for the recognition of research in institutions of higher learning. At first discouraged in their efforts to reform the old-style colleges from within, they had resorted to independently endowed scientific schools and entertained recurring visions of a so-called National University.[47] Introducing research as an integral university function, however, involved sweeping changes in personnel and organization. "You know as well as I do," wrote Louis Agassiz in the late 1860's, advancing a frank appraisal of the current academic scene, "what [a] deep struggle is going on in scientific circles among us, and how deeply the future prospect of science in the U.S. is involved in the contest, though the community at large knows nothing about it." There were two kinds of professors, the vast majority "whose chief claim to success lies in their familiarity with what others have done to advance science," and a "small band which by original independent research contribute to the advancement of science." Only the latter, asserted Agassiz, could "place our country on a level with the most progressive nations."[48]

The research ideal demanded institutional reorientations as well as scientific personnel. America had no shortage of degree-granting institutions, 375 by 1875, but few that billed themselves as universities really warranted the appellation. "Some have little more than a name, a charter, and a bias," complained Daniel Coit Gilman.[49] Working scientists, especially those personally exposed to the German university system, deplored the proliferation of small, weak institutions. Too much money had been wasted already in needless duplication, too many promising young investigators had been lost, "ground through the mill of an unendowed country college professorship."[50]

The research idea nevertheless gained momentum during the last three decades of the century. The German influence, everywhere evident after the 1870's, reinforced the tendency toward fewer, stronger universities with a firm research commitment. The rise of great entrepreneurial fortunes provided a source of capital for new educational ventures, as in the case of Cornell, The Johns Hopkins, Clark, Stanford, and Chicago. In 1883 it seemed to the editor of *Science* that the time "when every American professor will be expected to be also an investigator" was still in the future. But by 1896 William Trelease, a prominent botanist, sensed a decisive change. "The feeling is growing among men able to foster such enterprises that research is a thing worthy of being promoted, and we have before our eyes the spectacle of a gradually unfolding class of institutions in which investigation is not only tolerated but expected."[51]

That gradual unfolding was the result of the dreams, and often the schemes of imaginative scientific men and educational administrators. Men like William Rainey Harper, whom Veblen called a "captain of erudition," were quite able to cope with captains of industry in the Gilded Age. The organization of scientific research at the University of Chicago, though outstanding in its success, was broadly representative in the character of its inspiration and support. John D. Rockefeller, William Rainey Harper, Leighton and Mornay Williams, Andrew Green, Charles Yerkes, Sidney Kent, Martin Ryerson, and Helen Culver had little in common in other respects, but together they gave Chicago a lasting claim as a center of scientific discovery. Old John D. Rockefeller understood better than most the larger significance of their effort. "An individual institution of learning," he wrote, "can have only a narrow sphere. It can only reach a limited number of people. But every new fact discovered, every widening of the boundaries of human knowledge by research, becomes universally known . . . a benefaction at once to the whole race."[52]

9

A University in Which There Are No Students

In recent years there has been no more striking
social phenomenon than cooperation in industrial enterprises. Whatever may be thought about certain
aspects of such cooperation, there is no question that
from the point of view of abundant, cheaply manu-
factured products, industrial cooperation has been
of tremendous advantage. Science has reached a stage
in its development in which cooperation is as essential as cooperation in business. . . . The independent advance of science . . . left unoccupied great
intermediate fields.

Charles R. Van Hise, 1903

AFTER my book, 'The Gospel of Wealth,' was published," recalled Andrew Carnegie in his autobiography,
"it was inevitable that I should live up to its teachings by
ceasing to struggle for more wealth . . . and begin the infi-
nitely more serious and difficult task of wise distribution."[1]
The Gospel of Wealth and Other Timely Essays appeared in
1900. Within a year Carnegie, motivated by business considerations as well as by his sense of stewardship, sold out to J. P.
Morgan for $492 million and retired to preach the gospel of
wealth by example. His early benefactions covered a wide
range, including welfare funds for steelworkers and their families, numerous public libraries, a ten-million-dollar endowment
fund for Scottish universities, and the ten-million-dollar Carnegie Institution of Washington. Through the latter, chartered in

January 1902, Carnegie hoped to relieve America's "National Poverty in Science" and win for his adopted country a commanding position "in the domain of discovery."[2]

The founding of the Carnegie Institution marked an epoch in the organization of scientific research in the United States. Its antecedents, the dream of a national university, the example of the Royal Institution of London, the perennial attempts of scientific men to coordinate university and government science, and the benefactions of James Smithson and others, were characteristic nineteenth-century solutions to the problem of financing research. Its final form and function, on the other hand, distinguished the Carnegie Institution from its predecessors and made it (along with the Rockefeller Institute for Medical Research, founded in 1901), the prototype of the twentieth-century research foundation.

There had been periodic agitation for a national university since the 1790's, when George Washington urged congressional action and bequeathed a tract of land on which to locate the institution. Never an actuality, over the years the national university became a conveniently formless ideal whose character changed with changing conditions. Washington had believed that a national university would unify national culture, acting as a potent antidote to the provincialism that bred political faction. Later John Quincy Adams revived the project in the hope that it might counteract anti-intellectualism in American political life. In the 1850's research-oriented men of science thought of a national university as a means of institutionalizing their calling outside the existing framework of collegiate education. Immediately after the Civil War, the National Education Association and other groups proposed a national university as a means of reuniting North and South.[3]

During the last three decades of the nineteenth century, John W. Hoyt emerged as the most ardent proponent of a national university. An educator and one-time territorial governor of Wyoming, Hoyt rallied the National Education Association behind his cause and organized a pressure group of four hundred prominent citizens who bombarded Congress with a steady stream of petitions. Hoyt pressed for federal action on educational and patriotic grounds. Without an all-inclusive national university of the highest grade, specializing in graduate work, the American educational system would remain a "truncated pyramid." Furthermore, he argued, America's standing as a civilized nation, and a patriotic respect for Washington's memory demanded such an institution.[4]

Beginning in the 1880's a number of prominent scientists and educators, notably U.S. Geological Survey Director Charles D. Walcott, Andrew Dixon White, Simon Newcomb, Daniel Coit Gilman, and Nicholas Murray Butler, also began to urge that Washington, D.C., become the nation's cultural, as well as political, capital.[5] They shared many of John Hoyt's ideals, but were less optimistic that a public institution was the answer. "There is nothing in the tendencies of modern politics," wrote Gilman in 1886, two years after the scurrilous Blaine-Cleveland campaign, "to show that the representatives of the people, as they are in these days elected, would have the wisdom to mark out the pathway of a great university."[6]

Nor were they convinced that a super-university, at least as envisioned by Hoyt, was really necessary. Cornell, The Johns Hopkins, Clark, and a host of aggressive land grant state universities already provided the nation with an impressive, if decentralized educational plant. What was needed was some way of coordinating research activities among the existing universities, of consolidating the growing scientific activities of the federal government, of opening the vast resources of government science to private investigators. In 1898, in an effort to gain these goals, Walcott, Newcomb, and a number of other government scientists organized the Washington Academy of Sciences, the latest in a long succession of informal coordinating groups.[7]

The parallel movements to make Washington a cultural capital received added impetus in 1899 on the hundredth anniversary of George Washington's death. To honor the occasion a group of patriotic ladies banded together to promote a Washington Memorial University.[8] The Washington Centenary also prompted John W. Hoyt to approach Andrew Carnegie, whose *Triumphant Democracy* (1886) had documented the millionaire's patriotic devotion and whose recent library benefactions had revealed him as an open-handed philanthropist.

Hoyt arrived at Carnegie's New York mansion in the midst of a February blizzard. "It was so cold, with a driving storm of sleet so dense, that the row of houses on the other side of the street scarcely made a shadow." Hoyt presented his card, and much to his surprise was immediately welcomed into the library, where Carnegie sat before the hearth pouring over the day's stack of begging letters.[9]

"Come in, Sir," said the millionaire, motioning Hoyt to a seat before the fire. "I assume that you have come to talk to me of the National University movement. . . . I have heard something of it, but really know very little from any reliable source. Now be good enough to enlighten me fully." Overjoyed at the warm reception, Hoyt outlined his scheme for an hour. Carnegie reacted in characteristic fashion. He listened attentively, seldom interrupting, but when Hoyt had finished he subjected him to more than an hour's searching cross-examination. A great national university, the capstone of American education, appealed to Carnegie's patriotism and to his love of the dramatic and unusual. "Well, Sir," he replied when Hoyt at last asked for financial aid, "this is a magnificent enterprise. It moves me profoundly. But," he added quickly, "it will require many millions, very many, to carry it to a fitting consumation; and you will have to wait a while for me. . . . Just now . . . I have library on the brain."[10]

Although Carnegie refused to commit himself to a national university, John Hoyt did set him thinking about the problems of higher education on a national scale. In the spring of 1901, when Carnegie's friend, Andrew Dixon White, also suggested that he endow a university in the nation's capital, Carnegie already had mature views on the subject. "You suggested National University at Washington, Washington's desire," he wrote White. "Several have; but while this does, as you say, ensure immortality to the Founder, it has hitherto seemed to me not needed, and this puts immortality under foot." Carnegie advanced a countersuggestion. Recently Daniel Coit Gilman had mentioned that The Johns Hopkins had outgrown its original site and was searching for a new location near Baltimore. It seemed unnecessary to have two great universities forty miles apart: why not combine The Johns Hopkins with a new Washington institution somewhere between the two cities? "Don't care two cents about future 'glory,' " added the millionaire, true to his gospel of wealth. "I must be satisfied that I am doing good wise beneficial work in my day."[11]

Carnegie's concern for doing good works in his own time made him an active, creative philanthropist. He had many advisers, but his decisions were his own. He spent the summer of 1901 at Skibo, his Scottish castle retreat, pondering the needs of higher education. He exchanged a steady stream of letters with Andrew White, then serving as American Minister in Berlin. He invited White, Daniel Coit Gilman, and John Shaw Billings to Scotland to confer on the proposed Hopkins-Washington merger. White was excited at the prospect. "Let me hear from you fully," he advised Gilman. "It is a chance for us to render to education and to our country the culminating service of our lives; and I am ready to throw down everything in order to do my part in presenting the matter."[12]

Meanwhile Carnegie had presented the Scottish universities with a ten-million-dollar endowment fund. In May Arthur James Balfour, First Lord of the Treasury and soon-to-be Prime Minister, wrote thanking him for the gift. "According to my views (which I think you share)," he told Carnegie, "we ought to regard our Universities not merely as places where the best kind of knowledge already attained is imparted, but as places where the stock of the world's knowledge may be augmented. One discovery . . . may do far more for mankind than the most excellent teaching of what is already known, absolutely necessary to national welfare as this latter is."[13] The implications for America were too obvious to miss. Furthermore, Carnegie's broad intellectual interests and business experience had given him an unusual appreciation of the value of research. In the 1870's, when most iron-masters still relied upon industrial folk wisdom, Carnegie had made himself the object of ridicule by hiring a metallurgical chemist to supervise his blast furnace operations. His competitors laughed at his university-trained expert—until Carnegie's mounting profits convinced them that "nine tenths of all the uncertainties of pig-iron making" were indeed "dispelled under the burning sun of chemical knowledge."[14]

Just a month after Balfour's letter, Carnegie learned of important new developments in Washington. Charles D. Walcott and other organizers of the Washington Academy of Sciences had joined forces with the patriotic George Washington Memorial Association. The joint body, incorporated in the District of Columbia as the Washington Memorial Institution, had a two-fold program. Though a private agency, relying solely upon private support, its close ties with government science would enable the Memorial Institution to sponsor private investigators in government laboratories. It would, moreover, coordinate the research work of individuals, universities, and learned societies with that of the federal government. The Memorial Institution, explained Charles Walcott, its chief architect, aimed at becoming "the federated head and clearing-house of all the higher education interests of the country."[15] Daniel Coit Gilman, recently retired from the presidency of The Johns Hopkins University, was a prestigious choice as director. "There are no funds, buildings, regulations, only *ideas* to be worked out," he reported to Andrew White. "The movement . . . can, I think, be brought into great service, but just how I do not yet see." White was more sanguine as he passed the news on to Carnegie in Scotland. "This seems to me a very happy coincidence;—indeed, I doubt not but that a majority of good, sturdy Scotchmen would call it 'providential.' "[16]

Providential or planned, the Memorial Institution idea supplanted Carnegie's original scheme for a Hopkins-Washington merger. Late in November, after his return from Skibo,

Carnegie summoned Gilman and John Shaw Billings (Andrew White was still abroad) to his New York mansion. The philanthropist was in a thoughtful mood. "How is it that knowledge is increased?" he asked. "How can rare intellects be discovered in the undeveloped stages? Where is the exceptional man to be found?" Would existing universities regard a new institution as a threat? Who would manage it, and for what precise ends? Finally Carnegie announced that he was prepared to give ten million dollars for an institution whose purpose was "the advancement of knowledge." It was clear that Carnegie had abandoned the idea of a university, at least in the ordinary sense of an institution for higher education.[17] He had concluded that the rise of American universities in recent years had rendered Washington's old dream obsolete. Moreover, these very universities might regard a national university as an unwanted competitor. It was better to strengthen existing universities than to create another. In any case, Carnegie was less concerned with institutions than with men. His fundamental intent in November, as Gilman later recalled the conference, was "to help out men of extraordinary talent; not necessarily of extraordinary poverty . . . if by any process such men can be discovered."[18]

Out of the November meeting came the first concrete plan for the Carnegie Institution of Washington. The Draft Plan outlined six basic objectives. The first was "to increase the efficiencies of universities & other institutions . . . by seeking to utilize & add to their existing facilities & to aid their teachers in experimental work." The second, "to discover the invaluable and exceptional man in every department of study whenever and wherever found, and make the work for which he seems specially designed his life work." The third, "to promote original research, paying great attention thereto." The fourth, to increase facilities for higher education. The fifth, to make government scientific institutions more available to students who came to Washington. And sixth, to subsidize scientific publications. The plan showed the influence of the Washington Memorial Institution. Its prime mover, Charles D. Walcott, now joined White, Gilman, and John Shaw Billings as Carnegie's principal advisers.[19]

On December 10 the newspapers released the story: "CARNEGIE MILLIONS FOR A UNIVERSITY." John Hoyt wired his thanks under the mistaken impression that Carnegie had acted on his plea for a national university. Because of the word "university" in the press release, the general public remained confused for some time about the nature and purpose of the new endowment.[20] Even those close to Carnegie soon discovered that the philanthropist had no intention of holding to the November outline.

"Suggestions and counter suggestions were made," reported Gilman to White after a meeting with Carnegie on December 27. "Not everything has gone on as you would prefer, nor as others would prefer, but on the whole I am delighted with the plan."[21] On January 4, 1902, the Carnegie Institution was incorporated "to conduct, endow, and assist investigation in any department of science, literature, or art, and to this end to cooperate with governments, universities, colleges, technical schools, learned societies, and individuals."[22] What this meant in actual operation became clear in Carnegie's deed of trust, dated January 28. In the November organizational scheme, the first aim of the institution had been to assist universities, the third to promote original research. Now the university clause was relegated to fourth place. The first objective was "to promote original research, paying great attention thereto as one of the most important of all departments."[23]

An article in the January number of the *North American Review* had triggered Carnegie's decision to reshape the still plastic institution. "I read last night an interesting article . . . which sums up our National Poverty in Science," he wrote Simon Newcomb on January 3. "To change our position among the Nations is the Aim I have in view—We should succeed."[24] In the article Carl Snyder, a free-lance science journalist and editorial writer for the Washington *Post*, had presented a dreary picture of "America's Inferior Position in the Scientific World." Snyder suggested that much of the

vigor of European scientific research came from its solid institutional base. America had nothing to compare with research
centers like the College de France, the Pasteur Institute, or the
Royal Institution of London. Snyder concluded his article
with an open appeal for such an institution "in the chief city of
the New World."[25] Later, when Henry S. Pritchett recommended the Snyder article to Carnegie, he remarked that it was
"a rather curious thing" that the writer should have prophesied
an agency "so nearly like the one you are about to found."
The circumstances were "curious" in the same way that the
organization of the Washington Memorial Institution had been
"providential." Although there was no clear evidence that Carl
Snyder had planted the article for an interested party, its
strategic placement in Carnegie's favorite magazine and its
obvious appeals to cultural nationalism were too timely to have
been entirely coincidental.[26]

The newly chartered institution was unusual in several respects. Unlike many philanthropists, Carnegie had no illusions
about his ability to predict the future. He gave the trustees full
authority to re-direct the trust if its original design became
outmoded through the passage of time. Free of his "dead
hand," the Carnegie Institution would remain, in Carnegie's
words, "an active force working by proper modes for useful
ends."[27]

The trustees showed unusual foresight themselves. Taking
the broad view that "the limits of research are bounded only
by the knowable," they realized that the best way to implement their program was first to seek expert advice. Consequently they set aside the eight-month period between their
first meeting in January and the second in November, 1902, for
a systematic study of the problems of scientific investigation.[28]
Under the able direction of Charles Walcott, now Secretary of
the Institution, an Executive Committee consisting of Gilman,
Billings, Abram S. Hewitt, Weir Mitchell, Elihu Root, and
Carroll D. Wright appointed advisory committees of specialists
in each discipline. They sent circular letters to nearly one
thousand educators and others asking for suggestions, commis-

sioned James McKeen Cattell to prepare a comprehensive biographical directory of American scientists, and compiled a detailed checklist of existing research endowments in America. No final decisions would be made, declared Gilman, whom Carnegie had made President of the Institution, until the trustees understood "what is now going forward in every department of science in any part of the country."[29]

During the eight-month fact-finding period the Carnegie endowment was a principal topic of conversation within the scientific community. The policy of prior consultation won uniform praise. "Mr. Carnegie has erected a supremely worthy monument and inscribed it 'to the man who knows,'" exclaimed Joseph Jastrow, a leading psychologist. He added that "such conspicuous recognition of learning as an expert art of national consequences" was unusual in the United States.[30] In a similar vein Simon Newcomb identified the Carnegie Institution as a coming agency of reform, correcting many of the "Conditions which Discourage Scientific Work in America."[31] The sincerest note of gratitude came from Elihu Root. Root, himself an enthusiastic promoter of scientific enterprises, still retained vivid memories of his father's frustrations as a professor of mathematics at Hamilton College in the 1840's. "To any one brought up as I was, in an atmosphere of scientific inquiry, hampered and hindered by poverty, the tremendous possibilities of what you are about to do seem almost to belong in a fairy tale."[32]

One of the most comprehensive discussions of the Carnegie Institution appeared in *Science*, the weekly voice of the American Association for the Advancement of Science. In September 1902 editor-in-chief J. McKeen Cattell invited his readers to join in a public discussion of how research endowments in general, and the Carnegie Institution in particular, might best serve the advancement of science. The forty-four men who accepted the invitation represented a cross section of the American scientific community. Their contributions ranged from unabashed begging letters to thoughtful essays on the logistics of scientific investigation. Over-all, however, the discussion in *Science* polarized around two questions of continuing significance for the Carnegie Institution.[33]

Andrew Carnegie had abandoned the plan for a national university because he feared that it might prove a competitor rather than an adjunct to existing institutions. The writers in *Science* feared a collateral problem: a disbursing agency like the Carnegie Institution might dry up local sources of financial support. America was not Germany, where the traditions of political and social organization made centralized support of science appropriate. Even at the expense of temporary inefficiency, argued Hugo Münsterberg, senior psychologist at Harvard, a broadly based public sentiment was "more wholesome, more educative, more adjustable, more American." He added that "every cent from Washington which disburdens the local officials is an opiate for this feeling of responsibility."[34]

The second area of discussion concerned the best means of discovering and assisting the exceptional man. A few contributors, among them Henry S. Pritchett and Charles Bessey, the botany editor of *Science*, urged the creation of a great research center in Washington. Otherwise, as Bessey put it, the endowment would be frittered away in "ineffectual dribblets."[35] But the vast majority agreed with Edward S. Holden, former director of the Lick Observatory, that institutions were only appendages to men. "First of all let the man of science be free. Then assist him if you can."[36] Since the 1840's men of science had struggled to gain recognition, and their efforts had always been distinguished by an intensely personal focus. Stanford geologist John C. Branner admitted that grants to individuals required more time, more investigation, and more judgment than blanket allocations for research projects or institutions. "The perpetual-motion man is bound to turn up, and he will have to be turned down." But between the crank and the established researcher there were many little-known but promising scientists. In this group, Branner insisted, the Carnegie Institution would find its exceptional men.[37]

By November the executive committee had read through the *Science* discussion and digested the mountainous reports of the advisory committees. Two lines of action seemed open: to make a large number of small grants to independent investigators, or to sustain a few large research projects. The latter received priority. "In the field of research," read the first policy statement, "the function of the Institution is organization. . . . Hitherto, with few exceptions, research has been a matter of individual enterprise, each man taking up that problem which chance or taste led him to and treating it in his own way." But today science and American society were too complex to rely on the automatic appearance of the scientific genius. "The most effective way to find and develop the exceptional man is to put promising men at work at research, under proper . . . supervision. The men who can not fulfill their promise will soon drop out, and by the survival of the fittest the capable, exceptional man will appear."[38]

The policy statement showed the hand of Charles Walcott, now emerging as the chief architect of institutional policy. Like Henry S. Pritchett, another scientist turned foundation executive, Walcott believed that modern science, like modern business, demanded "strong, effective direction from a central office." He argued that creative scientists were "very much like other human beings" in that they had to be "looked after if waste of time, energy, and money is to be avoided."[39] Walcott's contention ran counter to the ideal of the unfettered genius seeking knowledge in his own way, one of the most cherished traditions in the scientific community. It seemed to older scientists like astronomer Lewis Boss that such "machine-like organization" might be the preliminary step toward a "scientific dictatorship."[40]

Machine-like or not, organization in science was as inevitable in a modern industrial society as was organization in business. In the 1840's science had undergone a rapid transformation at the hands of young scientific men. Now at the beginning of the twentieth century a new generation of scientists was witnessing another organizational revolution. Walcott offered Andrew Carnegie an unusually keen analysis of the process. There were two basic approaches to discovery, he explained in January 1903: Individualism, "the old view that one man can develop and carry forward any line of research," and Collectivism, "the modern idea of cooperation and community of effort." Walcott explained that most of the younger American scientists, thirty-five to fifty years old, were thoroughgoing collectivists, while their elders still remained loyal to the individualistic traditions of an earlier day. "In my opinion," he advised the philanthropist, "we might as well try to make a great research institution of the C. I. by pure individualism, as to expect success in great industrial enterprises by the individualism of 1850 to 1870."[41] Walcott's analysis fitted nicely with Carnegie's own assessment of the social process. A man untroubled by inconsistencies, Carnegie was at once a celebrant of self-made manhood and an exponent of collective, corporate organization. Like John D. Rockefeller, Carnegie believed that rugged individualism was a passing phase in the nation's development. In the world of business "the day of small concerns within the means of many able men seems to be over, never to return."[42] Bigness was not a curse, but a blessing, for the aggregation of capital and the pooling of effort worked for the general welfare. In Carnegie's view, consolidated scientific enterprise had the same advantages over isolated research as the department store had over the small shopkeeper. The "bigger system grows bigger men," declared Carnegie in 1900, "and it is by the big men that the standard of the race is raised. . . . Dealing with petty affairs tends to make small men; dealing with larger affairs broadens and strengthens character."[43]

During the succeeding years the Carnegie Institution evolved slowly, but decisively, along "collectivist" lines. Institution President Robert S. Woodward likened the process "to the struggle of an organism which is trying at once to discover its proper functions and to adjust itself to the conditions of its environment."[44] The most obvious external condition was the fact that the universities had become "the chief centers of research" in the United States. Initially the institution followed the old plan of the Washington Memorial Institution, assisting college and university scientists with small research grants. But this mode of operation produced more problems than benefits. "We are learning," wrote President Woodward in 1906, "how the giving of aid by one institution to another, even indirectly, tends to sap the independence and diminish the available income of both."[45] Instead the Carnegie Institution concentrated on a program of scientific publication reminiscent of the Smithsonian Institution, and developed its own independent research departments where teams of investigators tackled major scientific problems. It became, in Woodward's phrase, "a university in which there are no students."[46]

During the first decade the Carnegie Institution established ten research departments. The trustees expended a total of $5,500,000, of which nearly $4,000,000 had gone directly for research.[47] Three of the major research projects were particularly noteworthy. At Cold Spring Harbor, New York, the Department of Experimental Evolution became the fountainhead of the American eugenics movement.[48] Under the auspices of the Department of Terrestrial Magnetism the nonmagnetic brigantine *Carnegie* crisscrossed the oceans surveying the earth's magnetic field, discovering in the process that most of the existing nautical charts were dangerously in error because of earlier and less precise surveys of magnetic declination. The institution also established a Solar Observatory on Mount Wilson in California, breathing new life into a project which had lain dormant since the Spence Observatory debacle of the late 1880's.

The Mount Wilson Observatory was one more product of George Ellery Hale's fertile imagination. The great forty-inch Yerkes refractor had been in place only a few years when Hale became restive again, dreaming of the spectrographic possibilities of a sixty-inch reflecting telescope. The clear atmosphere of the old Mount Wilson site made it an ideal location for a new observatory. Personal considerations reinforced Hale's scientific ambitions. His wife was ill, unable to face the rigors of another Wisconsin winter at Lake Geneva. "On Margaret's account it will be necessary for us to live in Pasadena for several years," Hale explained to Horace White, a distant relative and one of Carnegie's close friends. "I shall therefore be obliged to give up most, if not all, of my work at the Yerkes Observatory, and therefore compelled to depend upon what I can accomplish here."[49]

Hale, as Secretary of the Advisory Committee on Astronomy in 1902, had recommended a solar observatory to the Carnegie Trustees. The Executive Committee had endorsed his plan, but took no action for want of sufficient funds at that time.[50] Hale had gone ahead, investing his own savings in new instruments, and found a willing patron in John D. Hooker, a Los Angeles iron manufacturer and amateur scientist. In December 1904, however, Hale's repeated applications for aid, and Carnegie's personal expressions of interest in the enterprise, prompted the Carnegie Trustees to underwrite the Solar Observatory.[51]

The heavens had long fascinated Andrew Carnegie, as they had fascinated many wealthy Americans. In one of his earliest public pronouncements on philanthropy, a sequel to his famous essay on the Gospel of Wealth, Carnegie had singled out astronomy as one of "The Best Fields for Philanthropy." Referring to the Lick Observatory, he declared, "If any millionaire be interested in the enobling study of astronomy,—and there should be and would be if they but gave the subject the slightest attention,—here is an example which could well be followed."[52] After 1904 Carnegie studied the revelations of the Mount Wilson reflector with growing enthusiasm. He often mentioned the discovery of "new suns" in letters to his friends, and during the evenings at Skibo, often showed his guests lantern slides made from the latest Mount Wilson photographs.[53]

In 1910 the seventy-five-year-old millionaire visited California to see the great observatory for himself. There he met John D. Hooker, who had recently offered Hale a hundred-inch reflector, the largest in existence, provided others donated the mounting and accessories. Carnegie jumped at the chance to discover even more new suns. Soon after his return to New York he gave the Carnegie Institution another ten million dollars, doubling its endowment.[54] Carnegie's letter showed that enthusiasm for astronomy had motivated this latest gift, and that his sense of gratitude toward his adopted country had not diminished over the years. "I hope the work at Mount Wilson will be vigorously pusht," he wrote, slipping occasionally into his own scheme of simplified spelling, "becaus I am anxious to hear the expected results from it. I should like to be satisfied before I depart, that we are going to repay to the old land some part of the det we owe them by revealing more clearly than ever . . . the new heavens."[55] Andrew Carnegie died in 1919, before the Mount Wilson reflector had begun full operation. Had he lived another decade he would have witnessed revolutionary astrophysical discoveries, and might have contributed to George Ellery Hale's last and greatest project, the Rockefeller-financed two-hundred-inch reflector on Mount Palomar.[56]

In a sense the Carnegie Institution of Washington represented the final step in a search for support that reached back to 1844, when Alexander Dallas Bache had lectured American savants on the needs and prospects of scientific research in America. In its final form, the institution was the closest American equivalent to the nineteenth-century scientist's ideal, the Royal Institution of London. At the same time the Carnegie Institution signaled the beginning of a new era of richly endowed philanthropic foundations. Sustaining the old distinction between the increase and the diffusion of knowledge with modern financing and modern administrative organization, the Carnegie Institution, and others like it, would exert considerable influence on the character of science benefactions in the twentieth century.

10

A Plea for Pure Science

There must be in every community men specially
endowed with scientific tastes and impulses. . . .
Now the social problem here evidently is, so to
order the influences and attune the public sentiment in the community as to allow the ablest minds
to labor in those fields for which they are best
adapted.

Benjamin A. Gould, 1869

CONSIDERING the esoteric nature of original research, American men of science were surprisingly successful in their search for private financial support in the
nineteenth century. Many creative investigators showed corresponding talents as business managers and fund raisers, promoting the claims of research among wealthy patrons whose first-
hand knowledge of science was necessarily limited. Yet as a
group, working scientists usually underrated their accomplish-
ments in this regard. By the end of the nineteenth century they
had standardized their complaints in a familiar rhetoric of
which Henry Rowland's famed "Plea for Pure Science" was a
representative example. "We are tired of mediocrity," he told
the members of the American Association for the Advancement of Science in 1883. "Some men are gifted with more ideas
than they can work out with their hands, and the world is
losing much by not supplying them with extra hands. It is a
fact in nature, which no democracy can change, that men are
not equal—that some have brains, and some hands." Self-sacri-
ficing scientists must wait for recognition, he continued, secure
in the knowledge that it would eventually come, "and know-

ing, also, that we constitute the most important element in human progress."[1]

Rowland's statement was interpreted as a telling indictment of American indifference to basic science. Actually, his uncompromising, frankly elitist pronouncement was an indication that the scientific community was reasonably confident the public would, in fact, sustain them. Rowland's generation could proclaim openly what the Lazzaroni had thought it more prudent to urge in private. They could press for the increase of knowledge without the traditional bow to its diffusion and application. Much of the battle begun in the 1840's had been won. Scientific research had all but achieved the status of a legitimate vocation.[2] What compelled the late nineteenth-century pleas for pure science, and what gave them a special quality of urgency, was a nagging sense of relative deprivation. After three-quarters of a century of striving, the scientific community was too close to affluence not to feel the want of it acutely.

What Rowland's posture of misunderstood genius did betray was a curiously contradictory notion of the effects of the social environment upon the life of the mind. American scientists, like American intellectuals generally, had always advertised their achievements as the product of creative intellect; their lack of success, on the other hand, they habitually attributed to the failure of an unappreciative society to offer its intellectual workers the necessary encouragement and support. It was an attractive thesis, difficult to refute. Either way the intellectual had the best of the argument.[3] But it was also a thesis that conveniently overlooked the controlling effect of personal limitations on the progress of science, and one that misunderstood the characteristically fortuitous nature of the philanthropic support of research.

"It might almost be said to be a law of philanthropy," William Rainey Harper once remarked, "that it is exercised within a territory coextensive with the horizon of the philanthropist. Most men of liberal mind limit their benevolence to those causes with which they themselves may keep in close touch."⁴ Such generally had been the case. Benevolent individuals, counseled by their own experience, most often sought to supply deficiencies of opportunity they felt in their own and perceived in others' lives. The most popular philanthropic objects (schools, libraries, parks, art galleries, and institutions of all kinds for improving physical and spiritual welfare), were well within the social vision of ordinary Americans.

Scientists, preoccupied with their own work, often forgot that the support of research was an example of what Harper termed "benevolent work at a distance." By the middle of the nineteenth century few laymen could any longer keep in close touch with the progress of discovery. New concepts and new information made a high order of native talent and specialized training mandatory for the scientific man. Overwhelmed by the bewildering advancement of knowledge, the gentleman savant of Jefferson's and Adams' day rapidly passed from the scene. Long removed from common understanding, the pursuit of science grew increasingly mysterious even to the liberally educated.

Except for a continuing enthusiasm for astronomy, America's nineteenth-century commercial-industrial elite displayed little spontaneous interest in science, whether pure or applied. Their neglect was seldom the result of conscious anti-intellectualism, as attractive as that thesis might have been to scientists at the time. American indifference to science and scientists was, instead, the perfectly natural consequence of the fact that neither science nor science-oriented technology was a particularly conspicuous feature of nineteenth-century American life. Not until the twentieth century would industrial, agricultural, and military technology force public recognition that research was a national resource. Until then scientists would in general remain, as one of them termed it, "inoffensive but curious and useless members of the social order."⁵ In bustling nineteenth-century America it was remarkable that original research—Veblen called it "idle curiosity"—attracted the patronage it did.

The patronage it did attract contributed significantly to the pace and quality of American scientific enterprise. James Smithson's bounty served as a rallying point for the generation of the 1840's, the first in America to make a profession of scientific investigation. Under Joseph Henry's creative administration the Smithsonian Institution exerted incalculable influence as a source of research and publication funds, as an example to other philanthropists, and as a living symbol of the distinctions between the increase, the diffusion, and the application of knowledge. Similarly the scientific schools, the laboratories, and the numerous astronomical observatories that dotted the country by mid-century formed the foundation of a substantial scientific tradition.

Yet the fortuitous nature of philanthropic giving, while it added richness and variety to the financing of research, also carried its own limitations. The philanthropists who were free to venture capital on the unknown were also free to venture nothing at all; benefactors were always unpredictable, often capricious. At the same time, the increasing complexity and expense of original research in science called for richer and more reliable financing. Men of science themselves were the first to realize the advantages of permanent research funds over piecemeal benefactions. The pooling of capital in research endowments, first by scientists, later by philanthropists like Elizabeth Thompson, and finally in the great tax-exempt foundations of the twentieth century, announced the maturity of private philanthropy as an instrument for the support of scientific research.

Because of the pluralistic nature of American institutions, the theoretically conflicting claims of private giving and public patronage had never been operationally significant. The goal of laissez-faire in the scientific as well as the business world had been a kind of benevolent partnership in which the government helped but did not hinder private enterprise. The final outcome of the heated Congressional investigations of the 1880's made it clear that most Americans who concerned themselves at all viewed scientific research as an endless frontier of opportunities, not as an exclusive and pre-empted domain. The doctrines of self-made manhood applied equally well to Andrew Carnegie, Alexander Agassiz, and John Wesley Powell.

By the middle decades of the twentieth century billion-dollar foundations and massive government R&D contracts had become commonplace. During the decade 1953–63, the complex partnership of public and private agencies increased the national research committment nearly 16 per cent a year, reaching an annual expenditure of $5.9 billion in 1963 alone. Much of the nation's growing scientific effort was born of war and fear of war, and had a correspondingly practical orientation, yet even so nearly one third of the annual research budget was earmarked for basic, "pure" investigation. As they had in the Gilded Age, Americans still chanted the litany of laissez-faire, but in the Age of Big Science nice distinctions between public and private enterprise were lost in daily practice. Federal tax policies virtually underwrote private giving. The principal dispenser of federal research funds was styled the National Science Foundation.[6]

What did concern both scientists and laymen alike was the mounting influence of the scientific establishment, the penetration of science into every aspect of national life. Big Science brought problems and anxieties unimagined a century before. Atomic age investigators confronted head-on the moral and political consequences of their discoveries.[7] University professors mastered the intricate rules of grantsmanship, and learned to walk the narrow path between consultation and conflict of interest. University presidents pondered the alternatives of subsidized research and institutional independence.[8] Dwight Eisenhower, among other concerned laymen, awoke to the politics of pure science, and to the possibility that a "military-industrial complex" might use the tools of science to fashion a brave new world.[9]

Whether for good or evil, the output of discovery increased at an exponential rate. Scientific "breakthroughs" seemed almost routine, predictable, inescapable. Looking back from such a vantage point, scientists (and some historians) often failed to appreciate how far they had come in a century and a half, and how circuitous their route had been. As Samuel P. Langley had warned in the 1880's, historical hindsight could easily give a distorted view of scientific development. "We often hear it," he wrote, "likened to the march of an army toward some definite end; but this, it has seemed to me, is not the way science usually does move, but only the way it seems to move in the retrospective view of the compiler, who probably knows almost nothing of the real confusion, diversity, and retrograde motion of the individuals comprising the body, and [who] only shows us such parts of it as he, looking backward from his present standpoint, now sees to have been in the right direction."[10] The affluence of modern science, seemingly so natural in the mid-twentieth century, was not the product of historical necessity. It was, instead, a product of what the physiologist, Walter B. Cannon, had once termed "scientific serendipity," that happy ability, whether in the laboratory or in the business office, to capitalize upon good fortune.

Notes

The following abbreviations are used for frequently cited manuscript collections:

AHU   Alexander Agassiz Papers, Museum of Comparative Zoology, Harvard University

BLC   Alexander Dallas Bache Papers, Library of Congress

CLC   Andrew Carnegie Papers, Library of Congress

CRHU   Corporation Records, Harvard University Archives

FAPS   John F. Frazer Papers, American Philosophical Society

GFI   Oliver Wolcott Gibbs Papers, Franklin Institute of Philadelphia

GHHU   Historic Letter File, Gray Herbarium, Harvard University

HCLHU Harvard College Letters, Harvard University Archives

HCOHU Harvard College Observatory Records, Harvard University Archives

HCPHU Harvard College Papers, Harvard University Archives

HSI   Joseph Henry Papers, Smithsonian Institution Archives

MPY   Othniel C. Marsh Papers, Peabody Museum of Natural History, Yale University

NLC   Simon Newcomb Papers, Library of Congress

PHU   Benjamin Peirce Papers, Harvard University Archives

PiHU   Edward C. Pickering Papers, Harvard University Archives

RHEH   William H. Rhees Collection, Henry E. Huntington Library and Art Gallery

SI   Smithsonian Institution Archives

UC   University of Chicago Archives

CHAPTER 1

1. *Washington National Intelligencer,* April 2, 3, 1844; Charles F. Adams, ed., *Memoirs of John Quincy Adams* (12 vols.; Philadelphia, 1874–77), XII, 5.

2. *Third Bulletin of the Proceedings of the National Institute for the Promotion of Science, Washington, D.C., February, 1842, to February, 1845* (Washington, 1845), pp. 429–34, 437–39.

3. Alexander Dallas Bache, "On the Condition of Science in Europe and the United States." A holograph copy of the unpublished address, perhaps the copy from which Bache read, is located in HSI.

4. *Ibid.*

5. *Ibid.*

6. Henry Adams, *History of the United States During the Administration of Thomas Jefferson* (9 vols.; New York, 1891), I, 111; Courtney R. Hall, *A Scientist in the Early Republic: Samuel Latham Mitchill, 1764–1831* (New York: Columbia University Press, 1934); Brooke Hindle, *The Pursuit of Science in Revolutionary America, 1735–1789* (Chapel Hill: University of North Carolina Press, 1956); Whitfield J. Bell, Jr., *Early American Science: Needs and Opportunities for Study* (Chapel Hill: University of North Carolina Press, 1955); Samuel Miller, *A Brief Retrospect of the Eighteenth Century* (2 vols.; New York, 1803); John C. Greene, "Science and the Public in the Age of Jefferson," *Isis,* XLIX (1958), 13–25.

7. Noah Webster, *An American Dictionary of the English Language* (2 vols.; New York, 1828), *s.v.* "Science." See also Samuel Johnson, *A Dictionary of the English Language* (2 vols.; London, 1755), *s.v.* "Science." Sidney Ross, "Scientist: The Story of a Word," *Annals of Science,* XVIII (June 1962), 65–85, is disappointing.

8. *North American Review,* XVI (April 1823), 300. On Bacon, see Fulton H. Anderson, *The Philosophy of Francis Bacon* (Chicago, 1948). Thomas Jefferson's classic *Notes on the State of Virginia* (Paris, 1785) is a prime example of American Baconism in practice.

9. *American Journal of Science,* XXXVI (January–April 1839), 202–3; George H. Daniels, Jr., "Baconian Science in America, 1815–1845" (Ph.D. diss., State University of Iowa, 1963), pp. 61–148.

10. American Association for the Advancement of Science, *Proceedings*, 1851 (Washington, D.C., 1852), p. xliii. Hereafter cited as AAAS, *Proc.* The literature repudiating Baconian induction is extensive. See James Spedding *et al.*, eds., *The Works of Francis Bacon* (14 vols.; London, 1857–74), I, 21–67; Alexander Dallas Bache, *Anniversary Address before the American Institute, of the City of New York . . . October 28th, 1856* (New York, 1857), p. 46; *Atlantic Monthly,* III (April 1859), 514–17; Benjamin Peirce, *Ideality in the Physical Sciences* (Boston, 1881), pp. 9–37; *The Nation,* XXXVIII (April 24, 1884), 368–70. See George Daniels, *American Science in the Age of Jackson* (New York: Columbia University Press, 1968), pp. 68–118, for the best account of Baconism.

11. Joseph Henry to ——?, February 27, 1846, HSI.

12. Benjamin Gould to John F. Frazer, November 22, 1856, FAPS.

13. Joseph Henry to J. Varnum, June 22, 1847, HSI. The best secondary accounts of the Lazzaroni are Richard J. Storr, *The Beginnings of Graduate Education in America* (Chicago: University of Chicago Press, 1953), pp. 67–72, 82–92; A. Hunter Dupree, *Asa Gray* (Cambridge, Mass.: Harvard University Press, 1959), 316–30; Edward Lurie, *Louis Agassiz, A Life in Science* (Chicago: University of Chicago Press, 1960), *passim;* Nathan Reingold, ed., *Science in Nineteenth Century America, A Documentary History* (New York: Hill and Wang, 1964), *passim.*

14. Sydney Smith, "Seybert's Statistical Annals of the United States of America," *Edinburgh Review,* XXXIII (January 1820), 69–80.

15. Joseph Henry to Asa Gray, November 1, 1838, GHHU.

16. Joseph Henry to Dallas Bache, August 9, 1838, HSI.

17. Will of James Smithson, October 23, 1826, printed in William J. Rhees, ed., *The Smithsonian Institution, Documents Relative to its Origin and History, 1835–1899* (2 vols.; Washington, D.C., 1901), I, 5–6. Rhees's carefully edited volumes include all significant legislative documents relating to the institution's formative years. For convenience, all citations to legislative documents are to this source.

18. Diary entry for January 10, 1836, C. Adams, ed., *Memoirs of John Quincy Adams,* IX, 27.

19. Matthew F. Maury to William B. Rogers, November 23, 1846, in Emma Rogers, ed., *Life and Letters of William B. Rogers* (2 vols.; Boston, 1896), I, 268–70.

20. Rhees, ed., *Smithsonian Documents*, I, 102, 109–10, 145–46; *New York Herald*, August 28, 1846. The literature on the Smithsonian is vast and uneven. The best general account is Geoffrey Hellman, *The Smithsonian: Octopus on the Mall* (Philadelphia: Lippincott, 1967); the standard scholarly treatment placing the institution in the context of government science is A. Hunter Dupree, *Science in the Federal Government* (Cambridge, Mass.: Harvard University Press, 1957), pp. 66–90; the most informed discussion of Joseph Henry's role is Wilcomb E. Washburn, "Joseph Henry's Conception of the Purpose of the Smithsonian Institution," *A Cabinet of Curiosities: Five Episodes in the Evolution of American Museums* (Charlottesville: University of Virginia Press, 1967), pp. 106–66.

21. Rhees, ed., *Smithsonian Documents*, I, 139.

22. *Ibid.*, pp. 286, 387.

23. *Ibid.*, pp. 195, 197.

24. Diary entry for June 22, 1838, C. Adams, ed., *Memoirs of John Quincy Adams*, X, 23; Rhees, ed., *Smithsonian Documents*, I, 190–92.

25. Richard Rathbun, "The Columbian Institute for the Promomotion of Arts and Sciences," United States National Museum, *Bulletin 101* (Washington, D.C., 1917), pp. 12–19; George Brown Goode, "The Genesis of the United States National Museum," United States National Museum, *Report, 1897*, Pt. 2 (Washington, D.C., 1901), pp. 85–191; Henry King to Garrett R. Barry, January 8, 1842, RHEH.

26. Henry to Bache, August 9, 1838, April 16, 1844, HSI.

27. Rhees, ed., *Smithsonian Documents*, I, 266–68.

28. *Ibid.*, pp. 280–87.

29. Sir Charles Snow's controversial analysis of *The Two Cultures and the Scientific Revolution* (Cambridge: Cambridge University Press, 1961) may be more valid for the nineteenth century than for the twentieth.

30. Rhees, ed., *Smithsonian Documents*, I, 299–301, 375.

31. *Ibid.*, pp. 371–87.

32. *American Review*, IV (August 1846), 213; Benjamin Silli-

man, Jr., to Asa Gray, January 20, 1846, GHHU. Theophilus Parsons took a contrary view of "The Tendencies of Modern Science," *North American Review*, LXXII (January 1851), 94.

33. Rhees, ed., *Smithsonian Documents*, I, 402.

34. *Statutes at Large of the United States*, IX, 102–6.

35. For a useful synopsis of Bache's career, see "Commemoration of the Life and Work of Alexander Dallas Bache and Symposium on Geomagnetism," American Philosophical Society, *Proceedings*, LXXXIV (1941), 123. Dr. Nathan Reingold of the Smithsonian Institution is preparing a full study of Bache and his work.

36. Regent's Meeting of December 3, 1846, in William J. Rhees, ed., *The Smithsonian Institution: Journals of the Board of Regents, Reports of Committees, Statistics, etc.*, Smithsonian Miscellaneous Collections No. 329 (Washington, D.C., 1879), pp. 11–12.

37. Dallas Bache to Benjamin Peirce, October 20, 1846, PHU; Bache to Henry, December 4, 1846, HSI; Asa Gray to James A. Pearce, August 4, 1855, as quoted in Bernard C. Steiner, "James Alfred Pearce," *Maryland Historical Magazine*, XVIII (March 1932), 40–41; Thomas Coulson, *Joseph Henry, His Life and Work* (Princeton, N.J.: Princeton University Press, 1950), pp. 180–84.

38. Bache to Henry, December 4, 1846, HSI.

39. Henry to Bache, September 6, 1846, HSI; Joseph Henry, "Programme of Organization of the Smithsonian Institution," Smithsonian Institution, *Annual Report, 1847* (Washington, D.C., 1848), pp. 3–18.

40. Regent's Meeting of January 26, 1847, in Rhees, ed., *Smithsonian Journals*, pp. 25–26.

41. Joseph Henry to Louis Agassiz, August 13, 1864, as quoted in Reingold, ed., *Science in Nineteenth Century America*, pp. 212–16.

42. Henry to Gray, May 23, December 22, 1848, GHHU; Henry to E. Sabine, November 6, 1849, HSI.

43. Henry to Gray, May 23, 1848, GHHU; Henry to William C. Preston, April 19, 1848, HSI; Peirce to Bache, May 8, 1856, PHU.

44. Smithsonian Institution, *Annual Report, 1850*, pp. 6–9; *Annual Report, 1852*, p. 11; *Annual Report, 1853*, p. 10.

45. Henry to Bache, October 17, 1853. HSI; Dallas Bache, "Eulogy on Hon. James A. Pearce," Smithsonian Institution, *Annual Report, 1862*, pp. 100–3.

46. Regent's Meeting of March 12, 1853, in Rhees, ed., *Smithsonian Journals*, pp. 91–92; Regent's Meeting of May 20, 1854, in *ibid.*, pp. 101–12.

47. Spencer F. Baird to George P. Marsh, November 14, 1853, as quoted in William H. Dall, *Spencer Fullerton Baird* (Philadelphia: Lippincott, 1915), p. 313.

48. Regent's Meeting of January 12, 1855, in Rhees, ed., *Smithsonian Journals*, pp. 114–16.

49. Rhees, ed., *Smithsonian Documents*, I, 511–12.

50. *New York Tribune*, January 19, 1855; Rhees, ed., *Smithsonian Documents*, I, 540–43.

51. Rufus Choate to Charles W. Upham, February 19, 1855, HSI. A somewhat expurgated version of the letter appears in Samuel G. Brown, *The Works of Rufus Choate with a Memoir of His Life* (2 vols.; Boston, 1862), II, 92–108.

52. Rhees, ed., *Smithsonian Documents*, I, 562.

53. *New York Times*, February 12, 1855; Benjamin Peirce to Charles W. Upham, January 29, 1855, HSI.

54. Joseph Henry, "Thoughts on Education," *American Journal of Education*, I (August 1855), 21. For an unusually perceptive, first-hand analysis of the changing state of science in the 1840's, see Benjamin Silliman, Jr., "American Contributions to Chemistry," *American Chemist*, V (August–September 1874), 93–94.

55. Alexander Dallas Bache, "Address on Retiring from the Duties of President," AAAS, *Proc.*, VI (Washington, D.C., 1852), xlviii; Benjamin Peirce, "Opening Address," AAAS, *Proc.*, VII (Washington, D.C., 1856), xviii.

CHAPTER 2

1. *Athenaeum* (London), July 11, 1840, pp. 555–56.

2. Convenient summaries of colonial astronomy include Brooke Hindle, *The Pursuit of Science in Revolutionary America, 1735–1789* (Chapel Hill: University of North Carolina Press, 1956), pp. 146–76; Brooke Hindle, *David Rittenhouse* (Princeton, N.J.: Princeton University Press, 1964), *passim*; Willis I. Milham, *Early American Observatories* (Williamstown, 1938), *passim*; Elias Loomis, *The Recent Progress of Astronomy, Especially in the United States* (New York, 1850), *passim*.

3. Thomas Jefferson, *Notes on the State of Virginia* (Paris, 1782 [1784/5]), p. 120.

4. William Cranch Bond, *History and Description of the Astronomical Observatory of Harvard College* [Annals of the Astronomical Observatory of Harvard College (Cambridge, Mass., 1856)], I, v–vi; Whitfield J. Bell, Jr., "Astronomical Observatories of the American Philosophical Society, 1769–1843," American Philosophical Society, *Proceedings*, CVIII (February 1964), 7–14.

5. Marquis de Laplace, *Mécanique céleste, translated with a Commentary by Nathaniel Bowditch* (4 vols.; Boston, 1829–39), I, v.

6. Benjamin Peirce, "American Astronomical and Magnetic Observers," *The Cambridge Miscellany of Mathematics, Physics and Astronomy*, I (1842), 25.

7. Calvin Durfee, *A History of Williams College* (Boston, 1860), p. 248; Willis I. Milham, *The History of Astronomy in Williams College* (Williamstown, 1937), pp. 8–12.

8. John Bascom, *Things Learned By Living* (New York: G. P. Putnam's Sons, 1913), pp. 47–48; Howard R. Williams, *Edward Williams Morley, His Influence on Science in America* (Easton, Pa.: Chemical Education Publishing Company, 1957), pp. 20–26.

9. Albert Hopkins, "Revivals of Religion in Williams College," *Journal of the American Education Society*, XIII (1841), 341–51; Albert C. Sewall, *Life of Prof. Albert Hopkins* (New York, 1870), pp. 106–61; Frederick Rudolph, *Mark Hopkins and the Log, Williams College, 1836–1872* (New Haven, Conn.: Yale University Press, 1956), pp. 89–100, 135–43.

10. "History of the City Observatory Fund [Philadelphia]" July 22, 1842, American Philosophical Society Archives; Loomis, *The Recent Progress of Astronomy*, p. 291.

11. "National Institute," *American Review*, II (September 1845), 235–55.

12. *The Cambridge Miscellany*, I (1842), 25; Agnes M. Clerke, *A Popular History of Astronomy During the Nineteenth Century* (London: Adam and Charles Black, 1908), pp. 27–51.

13. Matthew F. Maury to William Rogers, November 23, 1846, in Emma Rogers, ed., *Life and Letters of William B. Rogers* (2 vols.; Boston, 1896), I, 269–70; A. Hunter Dupree, *Science in the Federal Government* (Cambridge, Mass.: Harvard University Press, 1957), pp. 62–63, 105–9, 184–85.

14. F. A. Mitchel, *Ormsby MacKnight Mitchel, Astronomer and General* (Boston, 1887), pp. 23–24, 41–48; Edward D. Mansfield, *Personal Memories, Social, Political, and Literary, with Sketches of Many Noted People, 1803–1843* (Cincinnati, 1879), pp. 227, 288, 309–10.

15. Ormsby MacKnight Mitchel, *Siderial Messenger*, I (July 1846), 1–2.

16. F. A. Mitchel, *Mitchel*, pp. 49–51.

17. *Ibid.*, pp. 50–53. Walter B. Hendrickson, "The Western Academy of Natural Sciences of Cincinnati," *Isis*, XXXVII (July 1947), 138–45.

18. F. A. Mitchel, *Mitchel*, pp. 51–53.

19. Increase A. Lapham to Cleveland Abbe, January 12, 1870, Increase I. Lapham Papers, State Historical Society of Wisconsin; Mitchel, *Mitchel*, pp. 53–57.

20. John Quincy Adams to George B. Airy, June 22, 1842, Adams Papers, Letters Received, Reel 522; Mitchel, *Mitchel*, pp. 93–97, 126–32; Wilfred Airy, ed., *Autobiography of Sir George Biddell Airy* (Cambridge, Eng., 1896), p. 151.

21. "The Cincinnati Observatory," *Siderial Messenger*, I (August 1846), 9–11; "Resolutions of the Cincinnati Astronomical Society," July 19, 1843, copy in Adams Papers, Letters Received, Reel 526; John Quincy Adams to O. M. Mitchel, July 25, 1843, Adams Papers, John Quincy Adams Letterbook, Reel 154; Charles F. Adams, ed., *Memoirs of John Quincy Adams* (12 vols.; Philadelphia, 1874–77), XI, 394–95.

22. C. Adams, ed., *Memoirs of John Quincy Adams*, XI, 183, 425–28, 441; Louisa C. Adams to Charles Francis Adams, November 25, 1843, Adams Papers, Letters Received, Reel 527; John Quincy Adams, *An Oration Delivered Before the Cincinnati Astronomical Society, on the Occasion of Laying the Corner Stone of an Astronomical Observatory* (Cincinnati, 1843), *passim*.

23. Mitchel to J. Q. Adams, April 15, 1845, Adams Papers, Letters Received, Reel 531; *Cist's Advertiser* (Cincinnati), January 29, 1845.

24. Mitchel to J. Q. Adams, March 27, 1844, Adams Papers, Letters Received, Reel 528; F. A. Mitchel, *Mitchel*, pp. 153–57.

25. Mitchel published his lectures, together with a long preface recounting his financial plight, as *The Planetary and Stellar Worlds: A Popular Exposition of the Great Discoveries and The-*

ories of Modern Astronomy, in a Series of Ten Lectures (New York, 1858).

26. Mitchel to J. Q. Adams, April 15, 1845, Adams Papers, Letters Received, Reel 531; "Introductory Remarks," *Siderial Messenger,* II (August 1847), 1–3.

27. Mitchel to J. Q. Adams, April 15, 1845, Adams Papers, Letters Received, Reel 531.

28. *Boston Daily Advertiser,* March 2, March 4, March 10, 1843; *Boston Evening Transcript,* March 2, March 9–13, 1843; Benjamin Peirce, "The Great Comet of 1843," *The American Almanac and Repository of Useful Knowledge for the Year 1844* (Boston, 1843), pp. 94–100; Clerke, *Popular History of Astronomy,* pp. 103–5.

29. *Boston Daily Advertiser,* March 14, 1843; *Niles National Register,* March 18, 1843; *Boston Evening Transcript,* March 22, 1843; Ira V. Brown, "The Millerites and the Boston Press," *New England Quarterly,* XVI (December 1943), 592–614.

30. *Boston Semi-Weekly Courier,* March 13, 1843; *Boston Daily Advertiser,* March 16, 1843; *Niles National Register,* April 1, 1843.

31. Peirce, "American Astronomical and Magnetic Observers," p. 25; Bond, *History of the Harvard Observatory,* pp. lxxv–lxxvi.

32. *Boston Daily Advertiser,* March 24, 1843; *Boston Evening Transcript,* March 25, 1843; *Boston Semi-Weekly Courier,* March 27, 1843.

33. *Boston Daily Advertiser,* March 27, 1843, March 29, 1843; *Boston Semi-Weekly Courier,* March 30, 1843; *American Journal of Science,* LXII (September 1851), 296.

34. *Boston Daily Advertiser,* April 1, 1843.

35. *Niles National Register,* April 8, 1843; *Boston Daily Advertiser,* April 6, 1843.

36. First published in the *American Journal of Science,* XLV (April–June 1843), 224–25, the subscription list also appears in Bond, *History of the Harvard Observatory,* pp. lxiii–lxvi.

37. Biographical material on Boston's elite is largely eulogistic, but occasionally informative. Contemporary guides, such as *Our First Men: A Calendar of Wealth, Fashion and Gentility; Containing a List of those Persons Taxed in the City of Boston, Credibly Reported to be Worth One Hundred Thousand Dollars, With Biographical Notices of the Principal Persons* (Boston, 1846), should be used cautiously. Paul Goodman has attempted to sketch the broad outlines of Brahmin culture in "Ethics and Enterprise:

The Values of a Boston Elite, 1800–1860," *The American Quarterly*, XVIII (Fall 1966), 437–51.

38. Bond, *History of the Harvard Observatory*, pp. lxv, 9, prints the 1846 subscription list.

39. A copy of Edward B. Phillips' will, drawn October 9, 1847, and probated August 3, 1848, is filed in the Harvard University Archives. *Boston Evening Transcript*, June 22, June 26, 1843; Albert M. Phillips, *Phillips Genealogies* (Auburn, Mass., 1885), pp. 28–29; Bond, *History of the Harvard Observatory*, pp. cxxxiv, cxlii; Edward S. Holden, *Memorials of William Cranch Bond . . . and George Phillips Bond* (San Francisco, 1897), pp. 29, 64.

40. Bond, *History of the Harvard Observatory*, pp. 8–9; George P. Bond to C. H. F. Peters, January 7, 1863 as quoted in Holden, *Memorials of William Cranch Bond*, p. 196. For the subsequent history of the observatory (largely a compilation of annual reports), see Solon I. Bailey, *The History and Work of the Harvard Observatory, 1839–1927* (New York: McGraw Hill, 1931), *passim*.

41. Benjamin A. Gould, "An American University," *American Journal of Education*, II (September 1856), 292; Louis Agassiz to John F. Frazer, August 17, 1851, FAPS; J. L. Pruyn to Benjamin Peirce, January 15, 1853, PHU; John M. Clarke, *James Hall of Albany* (Albany, 1921), pp. 190–202. The best secondary accounts of the university scheme are Richard J. Storr, *The Beginnings of Graduate Education in the United States* (Chicago: University of Chicago Press, 1953), pp. 67–74, and Samuel Resneck, "The Emergence of a Scientific Community in New York State a Century Ago," *New York History*, XLIII (July 1962), 211–38.

42. *New York Times*, October 14, 1851.

43. *The Dudley Observatory and the Scientific Council. Statement of the Trustees* (Albany, 1858), pp. 3–5.

44. *Ibid.*, pp. 5–6; Clarke, *James Hall*, pp. 198–202.

45. Benjamin Peirce, "Method of Determining Longitudes by Occultations of the Pleiades," AAAS, *Proc.*, IX (Cambridge, Mass., 1856), 97–102; Benjamin Peirce to Dallas Bache, August 25, 1855, BLC. Compare *Dudley Observatory: Statement of the Trustees*, pp. 6–9, 125–30, with Benjamin A. Gould, *Reply to the "Statement of the Trustees" of the Dudley Observatory* (Albany, 1859), pp. 40, 178–79.

46. *Dudley Observatory: Statement of the Trustees*, pp. 8–9; Gould, *Reply*, pp. 181–85.

47. Benjamin A. Gould to Wolcott Gibbs, September 8, 1896, GFI; AAAS, *Proc.*, 1850 (Washington, D.C., 1851), p. 343; *Astronomical Journal*, I (April 1851), 192. The best biographical notice, with a reasonably complete bibliography of Gould's extensive writings, is George B. Comstock, "Biographical Memoir, Benjamin Apthorp Gould, 1824–1896," National Academy of Sciences, *Memoirs*, XVII (Washington, D.C., 1924), pp. 153–80.

48. Gould, *Reply*, p. 44; Benjamin A. Gould to John F. Frazer, November 22, 1856, FAPS. For an informed estimate of Gould's character, see Simon Newcomb, *The Reminiscences of an Astronomer* (Boston: Houghton Mifflin, 1903), pp. 78–82.

49. *The Dudley Observatory: Speeches of John N. Wilder, and Thomas W. Olcott, June, 1858, Before the Trustees, with Resolutions of the Board* (Albany, 1858), p. 15; *Dudley Observatory: Statement of the Trustees*, pp. 81, 134–37; Gould, *Reply*, pp. 29, 54, 104–9.

50. *Dudley Observatory: Speeches of Wilder and Olcott*, p. 18; Joseph Henry to Benjamin Peirce, December 28, 1856, PHU; Clarke, *James Hall*, pp. 200–2; *Dudley Observatory: Statement of the Trustees*, pp. 29, 147; Gould, *Reply*, pp. 216–18.

51. *Dudley Observatory: Statement of the Trustees*, p. 24.

52. Benjamin Peirce, Dallas Bache, and Benjamin A. Gould to Thomas Olcott, August 8, 1856, BLC; Olcott to Bache, August 5, 1856, BLC; Olcott to Henry, November 24, 1856, HSI; Henry to Peirce, November 24, 1856, PHU; Trustees of the Dudley Observatory, *Dudley Observatory* (a promotional tract, circa 1856); *Inauguration of the Dudley Observatory, At Albany, August 28, 1856* (Albany, 1858), *passim*. For the list of contributors to the observatory, see the Appendix to the *Annals of the Dudley Observatory*, Vol. I (Albany, 1866).

53. *Dudley Observatory: Statement of the Trustees*, pp. 73–78, 106, 148–50; Gould, *Reply*, pp. 30–31; Joseph Henry, Diary, January 9, 12, 16, February 6, 8, 1858, HSI; Bache to Olcott, November 18, 1857, BLC; Henry to Gray, January 8, 1858, GHHU.

54. *Dudley Observatory: Speeches of Wilder and Olcott*, p. 9; *Dudley Observatory: Statement of the Trustees*, p. 103.

55. Joseph Henry, Diary, June 29, 1858, HSI; Gibbs to Bache,

June 8, 1858, BLC; *Dudley Observatory: Statement of the Trustees,* pp. 85–103, 106, 123–24; Gould, *Reply,* pp. 293–303.

56. Henry to Bache, October 4, 1858, HSI; Gibbs to Bache, January 20, 1859, BLC; Gould, *Reply,* pp. 356–57. See also the *Defence of Dr. Gould by the Scientific Council of the Dudley Observatory* (2nd ed., Albany, 1858).

57. Gould, *Reply,* pp. iv, 8, 72, 113, and *passim.*

58. Joseph Henry, Diary, June 29, 1858, HSI; James Hall to Dallas Bache, June 18, 1858, BLC. For samples of the pamphlet literature, see *The Dudley Observatory: An Address to the Citizens of Albany . . . from the Committee of Citizens Appointed at a Public Meeting, on the 13th of July, 1858* (Albany, 1858); *A Letter to the Majority of the Trustees of the Dudley Observatory* (Albany, 1858); George H. Thacher, *A Key to the 'Trustees Statement.' Letters to the Majority of the Trustees of the Dudley Observatory, showing the Misrepresentations, Garblings and Perversions of their Misstatement* (Albany, 1858); *Nebular Hypothesis, or General Theory of the Dudley Observatory, in the Abstract* (Albany, 1858).

59. Olcott to Bache, November 23, 1857, BLC.

60. Gould, *Reply,* pp. 39, 55, 86, 94–99.

61. *Boston Daily Advertiser,* September 15, 1858.

62. George W. Blunt to Dallas Bache, January 7, 1859, BLC.

63. Henry to Bache, September 24, September 28, October 18, 1858, HSI; Gibbs to Bache, October 11, December 12, 1858, BLC; Jefferson Davis to Bache, October 22, 1858, BLC; Peirce to Bache, December 23, 1858, RHEH.

64. James Hall to James D. Dana, September 10, 1858, as quoted in Clark, *James Hall,* pp. 350–51.

65. Edward Everett, *The Uses of Astronomy: An Oration Delivered at Albany, on the 28th Day of July, 1856 . . . on the Occasion of the Inauguration of the Dudley Astronomical Observatory* (New York, 1856), p. 20 and *passim;* Ormsby MacKnight Mitchel, *An Address Delivered at the Dedication of the Astronomical Observatory of Hamilton College, July 16, 1856* (Utica, N.Y., 1856), *passim.*

CHAPTER 3

1. *Boston Daily Advertiser,* October 5, 1846; *Boston Evening Transcript,* October 3, 1846. This chapter follows, in part, Edward Lurie, *Louis Agassiz, A Life in Science* (Chicago: University of Chicago Press, 1960), and A. Hunter Dupree, *Asa Gray, 1810–1888* (Cambridge, Mass.: Harvard University Press, 1959). Both are excellent biographies, and together make up the best available history of natural science in nineteenth-century America.

2. Asa Gray to George Englemann, October 8, 1846, in Jane L. Gray, ed., *Letters of Asa Gray* (2 vols.; Boston, 1893), I, 343.

3. Elizabeth C. Agassiz, ed., *Louis Agassiz, His Life and Correspondence* (2 vols.; Boston, 1886), I, 12–13; Lurie, *Louis Agassiz,* pp. 114–18.

4. Charles Lyell to George Ticknor, March 1, 1845, in Katherine M. Lyell, ed., *Life, Letters, and Journals of Sir Charles Lyell, Bart.* (2 vols.; London, 1881), II, 91; *American Journal of Science,* LI (May 1846), 451–52; Lurie, *Louis Agassiz,* pp. 114–18.

5. Louis Agassiz to Benjamin Silliman, February 1, 1846, Louis Agassiz Papers, Houghton Library, Harvard University.

6. Louis Agassiz to Rose Agassiz, December, 1846, in E. Agassiz, ed., *Agassiz, Life and Correspondence,* II, pp. 409–29.

7. Asa Gray to John Torrey, December 9, 1846, January 24, 1847, in J. Gray, ed., *Letters of Asa Gray,* I, 344–45.

8. Louis Agassiz, *An Introduction to the Study of Natural History, in a Series of Lectures Delivered in the Hall of the College of Physicians and Surgeons, New York* (October–November 1847) (New York, 1847), p. 8. The New York lectures were a repetition of the earlier, unreported Lowell Lectures in Boston.

9. Agassiz, *Introduction to Natural History,* p. 58. See also Louis Agassiz, *Twelve Lectures on Comparative Embryology Delivered Before the Lowell Institute, In Boston, December and January, 1848–9* (Boston, 1849), pp. 103–4; Asa Gray to John Torrey, January 24, 1847, in J. Gray, ed., *Letters of Asa Gray,* I, 345–46.

10. Louis Agassiz to Chancellor Favargez, December 31, 1846, in E. Agassiz, ed., *Agassiz, Life and Correspondence,* II, 430–31; Lurie, *Louis Agassiz,* pp. 128–33.

11. Charles Lyell to Charles Bunbury, January 17, 1850, in K. Lyell, ed., *Life and Letters of Charles Lyell,* II, 159–60; Lurie, *Louis Agassiz,* pp. 166–76; Louise H. Tharp, *Adventurous Alliance,*

The Story of the Agassiz Family of Boston (Boston, 1959), pp. 87–159.

12. Edward Everett to Samuel A. Eliot, March 16, March 17, March 19, 1848, HCLHU.

13. Lurie, *Louis Agassiz*, pp. 190–92; Alexander Agassiz, *Annual Report of the Trustees of the Museum of Comparative Zoölogy, at Harvard College, in Cambridge, for 1873* (Boston, 1874), p. 4.

14. Louis Agassiz to Oswald Heer, January 9, 1855, in E. Agassiz, ed., *Agassiz, Life and Correspondence*, II, 514–15.

15. *Ibid.*, p. 515; Lurie, *Louis Agassiz*, pp. 195–96.

16. Louis Agassiz, *Contributions to the Natural History of the United States of America* (4 vols.; Boston, 1857–62), I, x–xi.

17. Charles K. Bolton, "Memoir of Francis Calley Gray," Massachusetts Historical Society, *Proceedings*, XLVII (June 1914), 529–34; *North American Review*, VIII (March 1819), 396–414.

18. Agassiz, *Contributions*, I, vii. A copy of the prospectus, and several letters relating to the publicity campaign, are printed in Elmer Herber, ed., *Correspondence Between Spencer Fullerton Baird and Louis Agassiz* (Washington, D.C.: Smithsonian Institution, 1963), pp. 81–87.

19. Louis Agassiz to Increase A. Lapham, August 24, 1855, Increase A. Lapham Papers, State Historical Society of Wisconsin. The subscription list is printed in Agassiz, *Contributions*, I, xvii–xliv.

20. Edward Lurie has prepared a critical edition of the *Essay* for the John Harvard Library Series (Cambridge, Mass.: Harvard University Press, 1962).

21. Agassiz, *Contributions*, I, 55, 135, 235, 315.

22. Louis Agassiz, "Remarks on the Death of Francis C. Gray," American Academy of Arts and Sciences, *Proceedings*, III (1852–57), 347–49. The text of the Gray donation is printed in the *Report of the Trustees of the Museum of Comparative Zoology, 1861* (Report for the years 1859–1860) (Boston, 1861), pp. 21–23.

23. William H. Prescott to Charles Lyell, January 23, 1859, in George Ticknor, *Life of William Hickling Prescott* (Boston, 1864), p. 440; Lurie, *Louis Agassiz*, pp. 220–27.

24. George Ticknor, Jacob Bigelow, William Gray, "Report of the Committee on the Museum, October 31, 1860," *Boston Evening Transcript*, November 12, 1860.

25. *Private and Special Statutes of the Commonwealth of Massachusetts, 1859*, Chap. 135 (April 2, 1859). For the private subscription list see the Museum *Report, 1861*, pp. 24–29.

26. *Boston Evening Transcript*, November 13, 1860.

27. Louis Agassiz to Rose Agassiz, March 22, 1865, in E. Agassiz, ed., *Agassiz, Life and Correspondence*, II, 624–29. Professor and Mrs. Louis Agassiz, *A Journey in Brazil* (Boston, 1868), went through eight editions in three years.

28. Elizabeth C. Agassiz, "A Cruise Through the Galapagos," *Atlantic Monthly*, XXXI (May 1873), 579–84; Louis Agassiz, "Evolution and Permanence of Type," *Atlantic Monthly*, XXXIII (January 1874), 92–101.

29. *Andover Review*, January 1886, p. 44.

30. Asa Gray to George Englemann, August 28, 1849, GHHU.

31. Dupree, *Asa Gray*, pp. 149–54, 228–32.

32. *Ibid.*, pp. 216–32.

33. American Academy of Arts and Sciences, *Proceedings*, IV (1857–60), 410–16, 424–31; Charles Darwin to Asa Gray, July 22, 1860, in Francis Darwin, ed., *The Life and Letters of Charles Darwin* (2 vols.; New York, 1891), II, 119–20. Later Gray collected his principal Darwin papers in *Darwiniana: Essays and Reviews Pertaining to Darwinism* (New York, 1876), of which A. Hunter Dupree has prepared a critical edition in the John Harvard Library Series (Cambridge, Mass.: Harvard University Press, 1963).

34. Dupree, *Asa Gray*, pp. 155–73; George Englemann to Asa Gray, March 9, 1843, GHHU; Susan D. McKelvey, *Botanical Exploration of the Trans-Mississippi West, 1790–1850* (Jamaica Plain, 1955), pp. xxi–xxii.

35. Asa Gray, "Memorial of George Englemann," *American Journal of Science*, CXXVIII (July 1884), 61–67.

36. George Englemann to Asa Gray, April 9, 1856, GHHU.

37. Thomas Dimmock, "Biographical Sketch of Henry Shaw," Missouri Botanical Garden, *Annual Report, I* (1890), 7–25.

38. George Englemann to Asa Gray, May 13, 1856, GHHU.

39. *Ibid.*, December 29, 1857, May 2 and September 28, 1858, GHHU; Gray to Englemann, October 14, 1858, in J. Gray, ed., *Letters of Asa Gray*, II, 446.

40. Englemann to Gray, December 16, 1858, GHHU.

41. *Ibid.*, April 15, May 13, 1859, GHHU; Asa Gray, "British

National Museums of Natural History," *American Journal of Science*, LXXVII (March 1859), 277.

42. *The Daily Missouri Democrat* (St. Louis), May 27–June 3, 1859.

43. Englemann to Gray, June 15, October 17, 1859, April 10, 1860, GHHU.

44. Gray to Englemann, May 18, 1859, in J. Gray, ed. *Letters of Asa Gray*, II, 452–53.

45. Englemann to Gray, June 2, 1859, GHHU; Gray to Englemann, June 6, 1859, in J. Gray, ed., *Letters of Asa Gray*, II, 453.

46. Gray to Englemann, June 6, 1859, in J. Gray, ed., *Letters of Asa Gray*, II, 453.

47. Englemann to Gray, April 10, June 12, November 1, 1860, GHHU.

48. Henry Shaw to Asa Gray, April 19, 1884, GHHU.

49. Asa Gray to J. D. Hooker, June 9, 1884, in J. Gray, ed., *Letters of Asa Gray*, II, 752–53.

50. Shaw to Gray, August 19, 1884, GHHU; William Trelease and Asa Gray, eds., *The Botanical Works of the Late George Englemann, Collected for Henry Shaw, Esq.* (Cambridge, Mass., 1887).

51. Shaw to Gray, July 29, 1885, GHHU; "A Western School of Botany," *Science*, VI (July 10, 1885), 21.

52. The will and associated documents are printed in the Missouri Botanical Garden, *Annual Report, I* (1890), 29–58.

53. Emma Rogers, ed., *Life and Letters of William Barton Rogers* (2 vols.; Boston, 1896), Vol. II, *passim*; American Academy of Arts and Sciences, *Proceedings*, VI (1862–65), 141–42; Dupree, *Asa Gray*, pp. 314–24; Lurie, *Louis Agassiz*, pp. 312–36.

54. Asa Gray to R. W. Church, December 25, 1863, in J. Gray, ed., *Letters of Asa Gray*, II, 518–19; Asa Gray to Charles Warren, February 16, 1864, in *ibid*, p. 523.

55. Gray to Church, April 4, 1864, in *ibid.*, pp. 523–26.

56. Asa Gray to Alphonse de Candolle, May 30, 1864, in *ibid.*, p. 527.

57. *American Journal of Science*, XC (March 1865), 224–26; American Academy of Arts and Sciences, *Proceedings*, IV (1857–60), 410, 428–31; John A. Lowell, "Darwin's Origin of Species," *Christian Examiner*, LXVIII (May 1860), 449–64; Asa Gray, "Dar-

win and his Reviewers," *Atlantic Monthly*, VI (October 1860), 406–25; Dupree, *Asa Gray*, pp. 327–28.

58. Asa Gray to Charles Wright, June 28, 1865, in J. Gray, ed., *Letters of Asa Gray*, II, 540; Asa Gray to George Bentham, June 12, 1866, in *ibid.*, p. 547.

59. Gray to Wright, June 28, 1871, in *ibid.*, pp. 616–17.

60. Gray to Englemann, November 20, 1886, in *ibid.*, p. 551; Dupree, *Asa Gray*, pp. 334–35.

61. Gray to Church, April 4, 1870, in J. Gray, ed., *Letters of Asa Gray*, II, 604; Dupree, *Asa Gray*, pp. 334–44.

62. Gray to Church, February 27, 1871, in J. Gray, ed., *Letters of Asa Gray*, II, 614–15.

63. Hollis Horatio Hunnewell, ed., *Life, Letters and Diary of Horatio Hollis Hunnewell* (3 vols.; New York: Privately printed [by DeVinne Press], 1906), I, 186–87, 196–200, 212; II, 5, 51–52.

64. Gray to Church, February 27, 1871, in J. Gray, ed., *Letters of Asa Gray*, II, 614.

65. Hunnewell, ed., *Life and Letters of Horatio Hollis Hunnewell*, II, 67–68, 75, 82, 90, 92, 108, 123; William Trelease, "Charles Sprague Sargent," National Academy of Sciences, *Biographical Memoirs*, XII (1928), 247–70; Dupree, *Asa Gray*, pp. 248–49.

CHAPTER 4

1. Jeremiah Day, "Original Papers in Relation to a Course of Liberal Education," *American Journal of Science*, XV (January 1829), 313.

2. Edward C. Kirkland, *Men, Cities and Transportation* (2 vols.; Cambridge, Mass.: Harvard University Press, 1948), is an excellent survey of New England economic growth during the period.

3. *Niles National Register*, September 9, 1843, p. 32; George Tucker, "Progress of Population and Wealth in the United States in Fifty Years," *Hunt's Merchant's Magazine*, IX (December 1843), 515.

4. John G. Palfrey, *Statistics of the Condition and Progress of Certain Branches of Industry in Massachusetts, for the Year ending April 1, 1845* (Boston, 1846), *passim*; Victor Clark, *History of Manufactures in the United States* (3 vols.; New York: McGraw Hill, 1929), I, 580; Harriet Beecher Stowe, *Oldtown Folks* (Boston, 1880), p. 1.

5. Levi Woodbury, *Annual Address delivered before the National Institute, January 15, 1845* (Washington, D.C., 1845), p. 25; Francis Lieber, *The Stranger in America* (London, 1835), pp. 68–72; Frederick Marryat, *A Diary in America* (3 vols.; London, 1839), II, 120–28.

6. Francis Wayland, *Thoughts on the Present Collegiate System in the United States* (Boston, 1842), pp. 40–41.

7. Francis Wayland, *Report to the Corporation of Brown University, on Changes in the System of Collegiate Education, read March 28, 1850* (Providence, 1850), p. 21. In the following discussion I am indebted to Donald Fleming's insightful essay, *Science and Technology in Providence, 1760–1914*, Brown University Papers No. 28 (Providence, R.I.: Brown University Press, 1952). See also George P. Schmidt, "Intellectual Crosscurrents in American Colleges, 1825–1855," *American Historical Review*, XLII (October 1936), 46–47.

8. Wayland, *Thoughts on the Present Collegiate System*, pp. 153–56; Wayland, *Report*, pp. 22, 28–34, 50.

9. Fleming, *Science and Technology in Providence*, pp. 40–41.

10. Emma Rogers, ed., *Life and Letters of William B. Rogers* (2 vols., Boston, 1896), I, 256–57.

11. Treasurer's Report, 1845–46, as quoted in I. Bernard Cohen, "Harvard and the Scientific Spirit," *Harvard Alumni Bulletin*, No. 50 (1948), p. 395.

12. A holograph copy of Peirce's "Plan" is located in HCPHU, Vol. XIII.

13. Peirce, "Plan," HCPHU, Vol. XIII; Edward Everett to Abbott Lawrence, August 19, 1847, HCLHU; Edward Everett, "University Education" (April 30, 1846), *Orations and Speeches on Various Occasions* (7th ed.; 4 vols.; Boston, 1865–68), II, 496–97; Paul Frothingham, *Edward Everett, Orator and Statesman* (Boston: Houghton Mifflin, 1925), pp. 271–73.

14. Minutes of the President and Fellows, November 28, 1846, CRHU, Vol. VIII; James Walker to Edward Everett, January 20, 1847, HCPHU, Vol. XIV; Edward Everett, "Report on the Scientific School," January 30, 1847, HCPHU, Vol. XIV; Jared Sparks to Edward Everett, May 15, 1847, HCPHU, Vol. XIV; Edward Everett to Dr. Holland, July 30, 1847, Edward Everett Papers, Massachusetts Historical Society.

15. Eben Horsford to Edward Everett, February 23, April 23,

1847, HCLHU; Edward Everett, Diary, June 9, 1847, Edward Everett Papers, Massachusetts Historical Society; Charles L. Jackson, "Eben Norton Horsford," American Academy of Arts and Sciences, *Proceedings*, XXVIII (1892–93), 340–46. Horsford's European experiences can be followed in his open letters home as published in *The Cultivator*, n.s. Vol. II (1845), *passim*.

16. Edward Everett, Diary, June 9, 1847, Edward Everett Papers.

17. Nathan Appleton, "Abbott Lawrence," in Freeman Hunt, ed., *Lives of American Merchants* (2 vols.; New York, 1858), II, 331–64.

18. Charles Lyell, *Travels in North America, in the Years 1841–42* (2 vols.; New York, 1845), I, 85–86.

19. *Washington Daily Intelligencer*, April 5, 1844; George P. Fisher, ed., *Life of Benjamin Silliman* (2 vols.; New York, 1866), I, 358, 369; Hunt, ed., *American Merchants*, I, ix.

20. Abbott Lawrence to Samuel Eliot, June 7, 1847, HCPHU. The letter was subsequently published in *American Journal of Science*, LIV (September 1847), 294–97.

21. *Ibid*. Two notable discussions of the professionalization process are Benjamin Silliman, "Address Before the Association of American Geologists and Naturalists, Assembled at Boston, April 24, 1842," *American Journal of Science*, XLIII (July–September 1842), 236, and Daniel Coit Gilman, "Scientific Schools in Europe," *American Journal of Education*, I (March 1856), 314–19, 327.

22. Alexander Dallas Bache, *Anniversary Discourse Before the American Institute, of the City of New York, at the Tabernacle, October 28th, 1856* (New York, 1857), p. 46.

23. Hiram F. Mills, "Charles Storer Storrow," American Academy of Arts and Sciences, *Proceedings*, XL (1904–5), 769–73; Edward Lurie, *Louis Agassiz, A Life in Science* (Chicago: University of Chicago Press, 1960), p. 137.

24. Lawrence to Eliot, June 7, 1847, HCPHU.

25. Samuel Eliot to Edward Everett, July 8, 1847, HCPHU; Minutes of the President and Fellows, August 21, 1847, CRHU, Eliot to Lawrence, October 13, 1848, Houghton Library, Harvard University.

26. Louis Agassiz to Edward Everett, October 3, 1847, HCPHU; Lurie, *Louis Agassiz*, pp. 132–41.

27. Samuel Eliot to Jared Sparks, April 6, 1849, HCPHU.

28. Eben Horsford to Jared Sparks, June 25, 1849, HCPHU;

Edward Everett to Abbott Lawrence, August 19, 1847, HCLHU.

29. Abbott Lawrence to the Harvard Corporation, September 20, 1849, CRHU.

30. Harvard University, *Catalogue of the Officers and Students of Harvard University, 1851–52* (Cambridge, Mass., 1852), p. 72.

31. Cohen, "Harvard and the Scientific Spirit," p. 397.

32. Samuel E. Morison, *Three Centuries of Harvard* (Cambridge, Mass.: Harvard University Press, 1937), pp. 282–86.

33. Charles W. Eliot, "Josiah P. Cooke," American Academy of Arts and Sciences, *Proceedings*, XXX (1894–95), 531.

34. Edward H. Beardsley, *The Rise of the American Chemistry Profession, 1850–1900*, University of Florida Monographs, Social Science, No. 23 (Gainesville, Fla.: University of Florida Press, 1964), pp. 1–13.

35. Josiah P. Cooke to the Harvard Corporation, July 26, 1856, Harvard University Archives.

36. Josiah P. Cooke to John E. Thayer, August 11, 1856, Harvard University Archives.

37. Josiah P. Cooke to James Walker, January 17, 1857, includes the subscription list; Josiah P. Cooke to the President and Fellows, May 30, 1857, Harvard University Archives.

38. William D. Armes, ed., *The Autobiography of Joseph LeConte* (New York: D. Appleton and Company, 1903), pp. 128, 141–42.

39. Daniel P. Tyler, comp., *Statistics of the Condition and Products of Certain Branches of Industry in Connecticut, for the Year Ending October 1, 1845* (Hartford, Conn., 1846), *passim;* Jarvis M. Morse, *A Neglected Period of Connecticut's History, 1818–1850* (New Haven, Conn.: Yale University Press, 1933), pp. 235–40, 283–85.

40. Percy Bidwell, "The Agricultural Revolution in New England," *American Historical Review*, XXVI (July 1921), 683–702.

41. Morse, *Connecticut, 1818–1850*, pp. 223–32.

42. Horace Bushnell, "Agriculture at the East," *Work and Play: or Literary Varieties* (New York, 1864), pp. 227–61. See also Alvan Hyde, "Address Delivered Before the Connecticut State Agricultural Society, October 14, 1859," Connecticut State Agricultural Society, *Transactions, 1859* (Hartford, Conn., 1860), pp. 70–79.

43. Percy Bidwell and John Falconer, *History of Agriculture*

in the Northern United States, 1620–1860 (Washington, D.C., 1925), pp. 315–20; Morse, *Connecticut, 1818–1850*, pp. 220–21.

44. Samuel W. Johnson, "Agricultural Charlatanry," *The Cultivator*, 3rd ser., I (January 1853), 35–36; "Agriculture, Unscientific and Scientific," *The Cultivator*, n.s. IX (November 1852), 365–66.

45. Edward S. Dana, "The American Journal of Science From 1818 to 1918," in Edward S. Dana *et al.*, eds., *A Century of Science in America* (New Haven, Conn.: Yale University Press, 1918), pp. 13–59.

46. The substance of the report was published in *American Journal of Science*, XV (January 1829), 297–351.

47. Advertising sheet, dated January 1, 1844, in *American Journal of Science*, XLVII (October 1844), 4.

48. Benjamin Silliman, Diary, August 8, 28, 1846, Benjamin Silliman Papers, Beinecke Library, Yale University.

49. The most detailed sketch of Norton's career is William Larned, *Memorials of John Pitkin Norton, Late Professor of Analytical and Agricultural Chemistry, in Yale College, New Haven, Conn.* (Albany, 1853). While a student abroad, Norton sent unusually informative letters home. Most are printed in *The Cultivator*, Vols. I–III, *passim*, and in *The American Agriculturist*, Vols. III–VI, *passim*.

50. The memorial is printed in John F. Fulton and Elizabeth H. Thompson, *Benjamin Silliman, 1779–1864: Pathfinder in American Science* (New York: Henry Shuman, 1947), pp. 208–9.

51. William L. Kingsley, ed., *Yale College, a Sketch of its History* (2 vols.; New York, 1879), I, 195.

52. Russell H. Chittenden, *History of the Sheffield Scientific School of Yale University, 1846–1922* (2 vols.; New Haven, Conn.: Yale University Press, 1928), I, 37–39, 41; Kingsley, *Yale College*, I, 150.

53. Kingsley, *Yale College*, I, 150.

54. *Catalogue of the Officers and Students in Yale College, 1847–48* (New Haven, Conn., 1848); John P. Norton and Benjamin Silliman, Jr., to President Woolsey, undated [1847], Memorabilia Collection, Yale Rare Book Room.

55. John P. Norton to Charles Goodyear, April 19, 1849, William J. Craw to Rev. G. Bull, May 8, 1852, both in the Yale

Analytical Laboratory Letterbook, 1848–52, Yale Rare Book Room.

56. John P. Norton to O. Wolcott Gibbs, June 7, 1849, Yale Analytical Laboratory Letterbook.

57. John P. Norton to S. L. Shotwell, December 11, 1851, Yale Analytical Laboratory Letterbook; John P. Norton to William H. Brewer, December 4, 1851, Yale Rare Book Room; John P. Norton (with the endorsement of Edward Salisbury, Denison Olmsted, Benjamin Silliman, and James D. Dana) to the Prudential Committee, December 10, 1850, Yale Rare Book Room; John P. Norton, *Elements of Scientific Agriculture* (Albany, 1850), p. 189; *The Cultivator*, n.s. IX (March 1852), 107–8.

58. John T. Norton to President Woolsey, January 12, 1853, Yale Rare Book Room.

59. Laura H. Moseley, ed., *Diary, 1843–1852, of James Hadley, Tutor and Professor of Greek in Yale College, 1845–1872* (New Haven, Conn.: Yale University Press, 1951), pp. 267, 286, 296, 298–303, chronicles the plight of college finance and fund raising in the period.

60. Chittenden, *Sheffield Scientific School*, I, 55–63.

61. Edward C. Herrick to Joseph Sheffield, August 21, 1854, Beinecke Library, Yale University; Joseph Sheffield to his sons, March 17, 1875, Beinecke Library, Yale University; Henry W. Farnam, "Joseph Earl Sheffield," New Haven Historical Society, *Papers*, VII (1908), 65–119.

62. John A. Porter, "Plan of an Agricultural School," Connecticut State Agricultural Society, *Transactions*, I (1856), 157–65. See also Daniel Coit Gilman and James D. Dana, *Proposed Plan for a Complete Organization of the School of Science Connected with Yale College* (New Haven, Conn., 1856); Daniel Coit Gilman, "Scientific Education, the Want of Connecticut," Connecticut Agricultural Society, *Transactions*, I (1856), 216–24; *New Haven Daily Palladium*, April 18, May 30, June 5, 1856; Fabian Franklin, *The Life of Daniel Coit Gilman* (New York: Dodd, Mead and Company, 1910), pp. 41–43. A fairly complete bibliography of the promotional pamphlets appeared in the *American Journal of Education*, XXVIII (July 1878), 342.

63. Daniel Coit Gilman, "Scientific Schools in Europe," *American Journal of Education*, I (March 1856), 314–19, 327; Henry A.

Dyer and E. H. Hyde, "Report of the Committee on the Agricultural Department of Yale College," Connecticut State Agricultural Society, *Transactions, 1854*, p. 91; *The Country Gentleman*, XII⁷ (March 24, 1859), 192.

64. Joseph Sheffield to James Brewster, April 14, 1856, in Chittenden, *Sheffield Scientific School*, II, 586–87; *New Haven Daily Palladium*, April 16, 1856.

65. Joseph Sheffield to his sons, March 17, 1875, Beinecke Library, Yale University; Joseph Sheffield to John A. Porter, October 19, November 27, 1857, in Farnam, "Joseph Earl Sheffield," pp. 82–84.

66. Sheffield to Porter, November 27, 1857, in Farnam, "Joseph Earl Sheffield," p. 83.

67. John A. Porter, "Agricultural Education," *New Englander*, XVII (November 1859), 1056–65; Samuel W. Johnson to his father, September 22, November 2, 1859, in Elizabeth A. Osborne, ed., *From the Letter Files of S. W. Johnson* (New Haven, Conn.: Yale University Press, 1913), pp. 125–26.

68. Joseph Sheffield to the President and Fellows of Yale College, March 26, 1859, October 2, 1860, as printed in *American Journal of Education*, XXVIII (July 1878), 327–28; Samuel W. Johnson to Joseph Sheffield, October 10, 1860, in Osborne, ed., *S. W. Johnson*, pp. 133–34; Theodore D. Woolsey to Joseph Sheffield, July 28, 1860; Sheffield to Woolsey, July 30, 1860, Woolsey to Sheffield, July 28, 1861; all as printed in *American Journal of Education*, XXVIII (July 1878), 327–29.

69. Joseph Sheffield to his sons, March 17, 1875, Beinecke Library, Yale University; Benjamin Silliman, Jr., to William H. Brewer, January 24, 1863, Memorabilia Collection, Yale Rare Book Room; Chittenden, *Sheffield Scientific School*, I, 166–67.

70. Joseph Sheffield to his sons, March 17, 1875, Beinecke Library, Yale University.

71. Last Will and Codicils of Joseph Sheffield, 1882, New Haven Probate File No. 26,247, Connecticut State Library, Hartford, Conn. Chittenden's two-volume *History* chronicles the subsequent institutional development of the Sheffield Scientific School.

72. Yale University, *Doctors of Philosophy of Yale University with the Titles of their Dissertations, 1861–1927* (New Haven, Conn., 1927), *passim*.

73. Benjamin Silliman, Jr., "American Contributions to Chemis-

try," *American Chemist*, V (August–September 1874), 93–94; "Science in America," *New York Quarterly*, II (October 1853), 447–49.

74. See Daniel Coit Gilman, "Scientific Schools," in Frederick A. P. Barnard *et al.*, eds., *Johnson's (Revised) Universal Cyclopaedia* (8 vols.; New York, 1887), VII, 86–89.

CHAPTER 5

1. Samuel P. Langley, "The New Astronomy," *Century Magazine*, VI (September–October 1884), 712.

2. George Bond to George B. Airy, September 28, 1857, in Edward S. Holden, *Memorials of William Cranch Bond . . . and George Phillips Bond* (San Francisco, 1897), p. 185; Daniel Norman, "The Development of Astronomical Photography," *Osiris*, V (1918), 560–94; Donald Fleming, *John William Draper and the Religion of Science* (Philadelphia: University of Pennsylvania Press, 1950), pp. 26, 35–38; Agnes Clerke, *A Popular History of Astronomy during the Nineteenth Century* (London: Adam and Charles Black, 1908), pp. 125–42.

3. Samuel P. Langley, *The New Astronomy* (Boston, 1896), Preface; *Siderial Messenger*, VII (June 1888), 270; *Science*, XI (January 27, 1888), 39.

4. Oscar Lewis, *George Davidson* (Berkeley: University of California Press, 1954), pp. 58–60, 80.

5. William W. Campbell, *A Brief Account of the Lick Observatory of the University of California* (3rd ed.; Sacramento, 1902), p. 7; Lewis, *George Davidson*, pp. 76–77; Joseph Henry to James Lick, December 13, 1873, SI; Joseph Henry to Thomas Huxley, August 3, 1874, SI.

6. *San Francisco Evening Bulletin*, September 3, 1872; California Academy of Sciences, *Proceedings*, IV (1872), 253–56, V (1873–74), 20–22, 127–30, 190–94.

7. George Davidson to Joseph Henry, February 2, 1873, SI; George Davidson, "Memoranda on his Relations with James Lick," quoted by Milicent W. Shinn, "The University of California: The Lick Astronomical Department," *Overland Monthly*, 2nd ser., XX (November 1892), 482–83.

8. Henry to Lick, March 10, 1873, SI; Davidson to Henry, April 3, 1873, SI; Lick to Henry, October 22, 1873, SI.

9. Ogden Rood to Wolcott Gibbs, November 2, 1873, GFI; George Davidson to Simon Newcomb, November 11, 1873, NLC; Shinn, "The University of California: The Lick Astronomical Department," pp. 481–82; Lewis, *George Davidson*, pp. 77–80.

10. *San Francisco Evening Bulletin*, October 21, 1873.

11. Lick to Henry, October 22, 1873, SI; Davidson, "Memoranda," pp. 482–83; Simon Newcomb, *The Reminiscences of an Astronomer* (New York: Houghton Mifflin, 1903), pp. 182–86.

12. Campbell, *The Lick Observatory*.

13. Davidson, "Memoranda," pp. 482–83; Lewis, *George Davidson*, p. 78.

14. Edward S. Holden, "Schreiben des Directors Prof. E. S. Holden an den Herausgeber," *Astronomische Nachrichten*, No. 2850–51 (July 31, 1888).

15. Lick's will is summarized in the Society of California Pioneers, *Ceremony of the Unveiling of the Lick Bronze Statuary at City Hall Avenue, Thanksgiving Day, Nov. 29, 1894* (San Francisco, 1894), pp. 10–18.

16. James E. Keeler, "The Importance of Astrophysical Research and the Relation of Astrophysics to the Other Physical Sciences," University of Chicago, *University Record*, II (October 22, 1897), 241.

17. *Los Angeles Daily Herald*, June 8, 1887; Harris Newmark, *Sixty Years in Southern California, 1853–1913* (New York: Houghton Mifflin, 1916), pp. 564–87; Carol G. Wilson, *California Yankee: William R. Staats, Business Pioneer* (Claremont, Calif.: Saunders Press, 1946), *passim*.

18. *Los Angeles Daily Herald*, June 7, 1887; Wilson, *California Yankee*, pp. 56–61; Hiram Reid, *History of Pasadena* (Pasadena, 1895), pp. 325–26.

19. Spence v. Widney, 46 Pacific 463 (October 1896); *Los Angeles Daily Herald*, January 19, 23, 26, 30, 1889.

20. Spence v. Widney, 46 Pacific 464–467.

21. George Ellery Hale, "The Beginnings of the Yerkes Observatory," unpublished reminiscences prepared for the American Astronomical Society in 1922. Miss Helen Wright, Hale's official biographer, graciously supplied me with a copy of the reminiscences. See Helen Wright, *Explorer of the Universe, A Biography of George Ellery Hale* (New York: E. P. Dutton, 1966), pp. 93–96.

22. Hale, "The Beginnings of Yerkes Observatory," p. 2.

23. Charles E. Russell, "Where Did You Get it, Gentlemen?" *Everybody's Magazine*, XVII (September 1907), 355. The best summary of Yerkes's Chicago career is Sidney I. Roberts, "Portrait of a Robber Baron: Charles T. Yerkes," *Business History Review*, XXXV (Autumn 1961), 344–71.

24. William Rainey Harper to Charles Hutchinson, January 30, 1892, UC.

25. William Rainey Harper to Frederick T. Gates, February 23, 1892, UC.

26. Thomas Goodspeed to Frederick T. Gates, April 1, 1892, UC; Charles T. Yerkes to Herman Kohlsaat, April 1, 1892, UC; William Rainey Harper to John D. Rockefeller, April 5, 1892, UC; Goodspeed to Gates, June 12, 1892, UC.

27. Yerkes to Harper, April 24, 1897, UC. The story related by Edwin B. Frost, *An Astronomer's Life* (Boston: Houghton Mifflin, 1933), pp. 97–98, and repeated with embellishments by Ray Ginger, *Altgeld's America* (New York: Funk and Wagnals, 1958), pp. 108–9, is in keeping with Yerkes's character but lacks documentary evidence to support it. Frost and Ginger argue that Yerkes, faced with a declining credit rating, *went to Harper* with the offer of an observatory. The university took the bait, so the story goes, Yerkes's public image and credit rating soared, and he multiplied his fortune.

28. G. E. Hale to Harper, September 23, 1892, UC.

29. Hale, "The Beginnings of Yerkes Observatory," p. 2.

30. Harper to Gates, October 10, 1892, UC; Rockefeller to Goodspeed, October 13, 1892, UC; Wright, *Explorer of the Universe*, pp. 97–113.

31. G. E. Hale to Harper, January 15, 1893, UC; Warner and Swasey to Harper, March 21, 1893, UC; Yerkes to Harper, April 6, 1894, UC.

32. Roberts, "Portrait of a Robber Baron," p. 352.

33. *Ibid.*, pp. 354–57.

34. G. E. Hale to Harper, March 14, 1896, UC; Harper to Yerkes, April 19, 1897, UC; Yerkes to Harper, April 24, May 24, 1897, UC; G. E. Hale to Harper, July 26, 1897, UC.

35. *Chicago Times-Herald*, October 22, 1897; *Chicago Tribune*, October 22, 1897.

36. *Chicago Times-Herald,* October 22, 1897; University of Chicago, *University Record,* II (October 22, 1897), 246–49.

37. Roberts, "Portrait of a Robber Baron," pp. 368–71.

38. William E. Hale to Harper, November 24, 1897, UC; G. E. Hale to Harper, May 9, 1899, and March 2, 1900, UC; Yerkes to Harper, November 24, 1900, UC; Harper to Yerkes, October 2, 1901, UC; G. E. Hale to Harper, February 13, 1904, UC.

39. Edward S. Holden to Edward C. Pickering, March 24, 1892, HCOHU; Solon I. Bailey, *History and Work of the Harvard Observatory, 1839–1927* (New York: McGraw Hill, 1931), pp. 56–57; *Los Angeles Daily Herald,* January 19, January 26, 1889.

40. Edward C. Pickering, "A Large Southern Telescope," three-page circular dated Cambridge, September, 1892, PiHU. The circular is printed in *Science,* XX (September 30, 1892), 193–94.

41. Edward S. King, "Edward Charles Pickering," *Dictionary of American Biography,* XIV, 526.

42. Charles K. Wead to Edward C. Pickering, September 15, 1876, PiHU; Edward C. Pickering, "Large Telescopes," *Boston Advertiser,* March 26, 1878; Edward C. Pickering, "The Endowment of Research," AAAS, *Proc.,* 1877 (Salem, Mass., 1878), pp. 63–72; Simon Newcomb, "Aspects of American Astronomy," *Astrophysical Journal,* VI (November 1897), 304–5.

43. *Science,* VIII (September 24, 1886), 267.

44. Edward C. Pickering, "The Endowment of Astronomical Research," *Science,* n.s. XVII (May 8, 1903), 721–22; Edward C. Pickering, "The Endowment of Astronomical Research," *Science,* n.s. XX (September 2, 1904), 292–93; Edward C. Pickering, "The Aims of an Astronomer," *Popular Astronomy,* XIV (December 1906), 586–91.

45. *Science,* VIII (September 24, 1886), 267; *Science,* n.s. XX (September 2, 1904), 297.

46. Edward C. Pickering, "A Large Photographic Telescope," circular dated Cambridge, November 20, 1888, PiHU.

47. Edward C. Pickering, "History of the Bruce Photographic Telescope," MS notebook, HCOHU.

48. *Science,* XVI (July 18, 1890), 34; *American Journal of Science,* CXL (September 1890), 262; Edward C. Pickering, "Aid to Astronomical Research, No. II," circular dated Cambridge, November 11, 1890, PiHU. See also the numerous begging letters in the Bruce Donation File, HCOHU.

49. Edward C. Pickering, "The Endowment of Research," *Science*, n.s. XIII (February 8, 1901), 201–2; "The Endowment of Astronomical Research," *Science*, n.s. XVII (May 8, 1903), 721–29; "The Endowment of Astronomical Research," *Science*, n.s. XX (September 2, 1904), 292–99.

50. Asaph Hall to Wolcott Gibbs, December 3, 1890, GFI; Benjamin A. Gould to Gibbs, July 2, 1894, GFI; Pickering to Gibbs, February 19, 1901, GFI; Seth Chandler to Gibbs, March 7, March 13, 1901, GFI.

51. Edward C. Pickering, "The Aims of an Astronomer," pp. 586–89; *Science*, n.s. XX (September 2, 1904), 299.

52. For an apparently complete tally of her gifts to astronomy, listing date, recipient, and amount, see William W. Payne, "The Late Catherine Wolfe Bruce," *Popular Astronomy*, VIII (May 1900), 237–38.

53. *Astrophysical Journal*, XI (March 1900), 168.

54. *New York Times*, December 30, 1887, January 5, 1888. For fragmentary biographical data on Miss Bruce, see the obituaries in the *New York Tribune*, March 15, March 23, 1900; *Astrophysical Journal*, XI (March 1900), 168–69; and Hyman H. Weeks, *Book of Bruce: Ancestors and Descendents of King Robert of Scotland* (New York, 1907), pp. 326–28.

55. Catherine W. Bruce to Simon Newcomb, November 6, 1890, NLC; Simon Newcomb, "The Place of Astronomy Among the Sciences," *Siderial Messenger*, VII (January 1888), 69–70.

56. Bruce to Newcomb, November 6, 1890, NLC; Edward E. Barnard to William Rainey Harper, July 26, August 11, 1897, UC.

57. *Popular Astronomy*, VIII (May 1900), 237–38; G. E. Hale to Harper, January 4, 1898, UC; Harper to Gates, January 12, 1898, UC; Bruce to G. E. Hale, June 24, 1898, UC.

58. The will, dated May 5, 1892, is recorded in the Surrogate's Court, City of New York, Liber 627, pp. 407–20.

59. Barnard to Harper, July 28, 1897, UC.

60. George Iles, "The Art of Large Giving," *Century Magazine* LIII (March 1897), 769.

61. Charles S. Venable to Benjamin Peirce, September 29, 1870, PHU; Joseph Henry to Leander McCormick, December 29, 1870, HSI; McCormick to Henry, January 2, 1871, HSI; McCormick to Judge Anderson, February 21, 1878, McCormick Collection, State Historical Society of Wisconsin; Samuel A. Mitchell, *Leander*

McCormick Observatory of the University of Virginia (Charlottesville, 1947), pp. 3–4.

62. *Frank Leslie's Illustrated Newspaper,* LI (October 9, 1880), 93; Lewis Swift, *History and Work of the Warner Observatory, Rochester, N.Y., 1883–1886* (Rochester, 1887), *passim;* Ralph Bates and Blake McKelvey, "Lewis Swift, the Rochester Astronomer," *Rochester History,* IX (January 1947), 1–20.

63. Samuel P. Langley, "The Temperature of the Moon," *American Journal of Science,* 3rd ser., XXXVIII (December 1889), 440; W. Lucien Scaife, ed., *John A. Brashear: The Autobiography of a Man Who Loved the Stars* (Boston: Houghton Mifflin, 1925), p. 93; John W. Jordan, ed., *Encyclopedia of Pennsylvania Biography* (21 vols. to date; New York, 1914–), IV, 1344–46. For a partial listing of Thaw's benefactions, see United States Commissioner of Education, *Annual Report, 1903* (2 vols.; Washington, D.C., 1905), II, 1319.

64. Percival Lowell, *Mars* (Boston, 1896), pp. 2–3, 201–12; *Annals of the Lowell Observatory,* Vol. I (1898), Introduction.

65. Smithsonian Institution, *List of Observatories,* Smithsonian *Miscellaneous Collections, No. 1259* (Washington, D.C., 1902).

66. Carnegie Institution of Washington, *Yearbook No. I, 1902* (Washington, D.C., 1903), pp. 88, 112, 128.

CHAPTER 6

1. *New York Times,* October 10, 1872; Joseph Henry to John Tyndall, August 14, 1871, HSI; John Tyndall, *Lectures on Light, Delivered in the United States in 1872–73* (New York, 1873), pp. 10–11; Arthur S. Eve and C. H. Creasey, *Life and Work of John Tyndall* (London: Macmillan and Company, 1945), pp. 166–67.

2. Tyndall, *Lectures on Light,* p. 9.

3. Eve and Creasey, *John Tyndall,* pp. 43–106.

4. Two notable discussions of the dangers of popularization are Frank W. Clarke, "Scientific Dabblers," *Popular Science Monthly,* I (September 1872), 594–600; Thomas C. Mendenhall, "The Relations of Men of Science to the General Public," *Science,* XVI (October 24, 1890), 229–33.

5. Peter Lesley to Benjamin Peirce, August 27, 1871, PHU.

6. Tyndall, *Lectures on Light,* pp. 3–6, 190; John Tyndall to

E. L. Youmans, October 8, 1872, as quoted in John Fiske, *Edward L. Youmans, Interpreter of Science for the People* (New York, 1894), p. 318.

7. Tyndall, *Lectures on Light*, pp. 151–83 and *passim*.

8. *Ibid.*, pp. 179–83; Alexis de Tocqueville, *Democracy in America*, trans. Henry Reeve (2 vols.; New York: Vintage Books, 1945), II, 17–18, 42–49.

9. Tyndall, *Lectures on Light*, pp. 179, 182–83.

10. Eve and Creasey, *John Tyndall*, p. 171.

11. *Proceedings at the Farewell Banquet to Professor Tyndall, Given at Delmonico's, New York, Feb. 4, 1873* (New York, 1873), pp. 6–9, 12.

12. *Ibid.*, pp. 47–48; *New York Times*, February 5, 1873.

13. Tyndall to Henry, April 26, 1872, RHEH.

14. Henry to Tyndall, May 11, 1872, HSI; Joseph Henry, Diary, January 23, 1873, HSI; Tyndall to Henry, February 7, 1873, SI; Tyndall to Henry, January 2, 1873, RHEH; Henry to Tyndall, January 6, 1873, SI; *Proceedings at the Farewell Banquet*, pp. 49–50; *Popular Science Monthly*, III (May 1873), 100–1. See also Michael Pupin, *From Immigrant to Inventor* (New York: Charles Scribners, 1923), 201–6, and *Science*, VI (July 17, 1885), 45.

15. "The Prayer-Gauge Controversy," *The Nation*, XV (October 31, 1872), 281–82; E. L. Godkin, "Tyndall and the Theologians," *The Nation*, XIX (September 17, 1874), 181–82; Eve and Creasey, *John Tyndall*, pp. 168–71.

16. Tyndall, *Lectures on Light*, p. 174.

17. Benjamin A. Gould, "Address on Retiring from the Duties of President," AAAS, *Proc.*, 1869 (Cambridge, Mass., 1870), p. 7. See also "The Future of American Science," *Science*, I (February 9, 1883), 1–3; Frank W. Clarke, "Laboratory Endowment," *Popular Science Monthly*, X (April 1877), 729–36; Thomas C. Mendenhall, "The Relations of Men of Science to the General Public," *Science*, XVI (October 24, 1890), 227–31, 232–33; *New York Times*, September 19, 1873; Henry A. Rowland, "The Highest Aim of the Physicist," *American Journal of Science*, CLVIII (December 1899), 401–11.

18. John W. Draper, "Science in America," *Popular Science Monthly*, X (January 1877), 319.

19. Robert H. Thurston, "The Science of the Advancement of Science," AAAS, *Proc.*, 1878 (Salem, Mass., 1879), p. 56. Thurston

expanded his argument in "The Mission of Science," AAAS, *Proc.*, 1884 (Salem, Mass., 1885), pp. 227–53.

20. Frederick P. Keppel, "The Responsibility of Endowments in the Promotion of Knowledge," American Philosophical Society, *Proceedings*, LXXVII (April 1937), 591–603.

21. Academy of Natural Sciences of Philadelphia, *Proceedings, 1860* (Philadelphia, 1861), pp. 1, 95. In 1888 Jessup's daughter added five thousand dollars for a similar fellowship for women. On the general topic of scientific societies and the promotion of research, see Addison Brown, "Endowment for Scientific Research and Publication," Smithsonian Institution, *Annual Report, 1892* (Washington, D.C., 1893), pp. 624, 635–36. The concrete support of research is conspicuous by its absence in Ralph Bates's discussion of *Scientific Societies in the United States* (2nd ed.; New York: Columbia University Press, 1958).

22. The American Academy v. Harvard College, 12 Gray 582; *The Rumford Fund of the American Academy of Arts and Sciences* (Boston, 1905), pp. 1–7.

23. *The Rumford Fund*, pp. 14–19.

24. Frederick W. True, *A History of the First Half-Century of the National Academy of Sciences, 1863–1913* (Washington, D.C., 1913), pp. 33–34, 361–63.

25. *Statutes at Large of the United States*, Vol. XXIII (1885), Chap. 107; True, *National Academy of Sciences*, p. 58.

26. Joseph B. Patterson to Joseph Henry, December 20, 1877, and Henry to Patterson, January 10, 1878, copies in the Cyrus H. McCormick Papers, State Historical Society of Wisconsin; Joseph B. Patterson to William J. Rhees, April 7, 1880, RHEH. The complete list of contributors appears in the National Academy of Sciences, *Proceedings*, I, Part 2, 135–36.

27. The wills and trust deeds are printed as Appendix VI in True, *National Academy of Sciences*, pp. 361–73.

28. National Academy of Sciences, *Annual Report, 1895* (54 Cong., 1 Sess., Senate Doc. No. 55), p. 15. Wolcott Gibbs was president of the academy from 1895 until his death in 1900. He was influential in establishing many research funds, and in managing the allocation of grants. His correspondence, at the Franklin Institute of Philadelphia, reveals the day-to-day operation of the academy endowment program.

29. AAAS, *Proc.*, 1853 (Cambridge, Mass., 1856), pp. 276–77;

ibid., 1868 (Cambridge, Mass., 1869), p. 358; *ibid.*, 1873 (Salem, Mass., 1874), pp. 439–40.

30. *Ibid.*, 1873 (Salem, Mass., 1874), p. 422.

31. Joseph Henry, letter of introduction for Elizabeth Thompson, December 27, 1877, SI.

32. On Thomas Thompson, see *The American Annual Cyclopaedia, 1869* (New York, 1871), p. 504. On Mrs. Thompson, see Francis E. Willard and Mary Livermore, eds., *A Woman of the Century* (Buffalo, 1893), p. 712; *The American Annual Cyclopaedia, 1899* (New York, 1900), p. 642; *The National Cyclopaedia of American Biography* (55 vols. to date; New York, 1892–), V, 405–6; James E. Willard and Colin Goodykoontz, eds., *Experiments in Colorado Colonization, 1869–1872* (Boulder, 1926), pp. xxvi, 305–11.

33. *New York Times*, October 1, 1878.

34. "A Talk with Elizabeth Thompson," *New York Tribune*, August 25, 1885.

35. See George Jacob Holyoake, *Among the Americans, and A Stranger in America* (Chicago, 1881), pp. 42–43, 232–33.

36. AAAS, *Proc.*, 1884 (Salem, Mass., 1885), p. 707; *Science*, IV (September 19, 1884), 269.

37. "A New Endowment for Research," *Science*, VI (August 21, 1885), 144–45.

38. AAAS, *Proc.*, 1873 (Salem, Mass., 1874), pp. 422–23; *ibid.*, 1891 (Salem, Mass., 1892), p. 451; *ibid.*, 1894 (Salem, Mass., 1895), p. 469.

39. *Science*, VI (August 21, 1885), 145. See also *ibid.*, VIII (July 2, 1886), 1–2; *ibid.*, XIII (June 14, 1889), 461.

40. *New York Tribune*, July 22, July 25, 1899. For the later history of the fund (to 1911), including an outline of granting policies and a list of recipients, see [Charles S. Minot], *The Elizabeth Thompson Science Fund, 1886–1911* (Boston, n.d.).

41. Theodor Heuss, *Anton Dohrn* (Stuttgart und Tübingen: R. Wunderlich, 1948), pp. 114–52; Charles A. Kofoid, *The Biological Stations of Europe*, U.S. Bureau of Education, Bulletin, 1910, No. 4 (Washington, D.C., 1910), pp. 7–10.

42. Emily A. Nunn, "The Naples Zoological Station," *Science*, I (June 1, 1883), 479–81.

43. Anton Dohrn, "The Zoological Station at Naples," *Nature*, XLIII (March 19, 1891), 465–66.

44. Harry L. Russell, "Log of a European Trip Made in 1890 and 1891" (compiled from contemporaneous letters in 1944), Harry L. Russell Papers, University of Wisconsin Archives. Edward H. Beardsley, Russell's biographer, called this and other Russell items to my attention. Mrs. Margaret C. Russell, Madison, Wisconsin, permitted me to quote from the manuscripts.

45. Anton Dohrn published a comprehensive list of American students, their dates of attendance, and the tables they occupied, in *Science*, n.s. IX (April 21, 1899), 596–97.

46. Heuss, *Anton Dohrn*, p. 285; *Science*, XVII (February 27, 1891), 118; *Science*, n.s. I (March 1, 1895), 238–39.

47. Harry Russell, Diary, 1890–91, Russell Papers, University of Wisconsin Archives. On Alexander H. Davis, see Heuss, *Anton Dohrn*, pp. 309–15, and Franklin H. Chase, *From Out of the Past: Catalogue of Historical Objects, Portraits, Relics, etc. . . . in the Onondaga Historical Association Building* (Syracuse, 1930), pp. 101–2.

48. Heuss, *Anton Dohrn*, pp. 309–15; *Science*, n.s. I (March 1, 1895), 238.

49. AAAS, *Proc.*, 1891 (Salem, Mass., 1892), pp. 329, 449–51; *Science*, XIX (March 4, 1892), 130; Charles O. Whitman, "The Question of a Table at the Naples Station," *Science*, XVIII (September 18, 1891), 160.

50. Charles W. Stiles, "Report on the Memorial Presented to the Smithsonian Institution," *Science*, XXI (June 16, 1893), 328–29; *Science*, n.s. I (March 1, 1895), 238; Kofoid, *Biological Stations of Europe*, p. 14.

51. H. Jean Crawford, "The Association to Aid Scientific Research by Women," *Science*, LXXVI (November 25, 1932), 492–93; Kofoid, *Biological Stations of Europe*, pp. 14–15.

52. Kofoid, *Biological Stations of Europe*, p. 14.

53. On organized charities see Daniel Coit Gilman, "Special Training for Special Work in Philanthropy," *The Launching of a University and Other Papers* (New York: Dodd, Mead and Company, 1906), pp. 353–66, and Robert H. Bremner, "Scientific Philanthropy, 1873–1893," *Social Service Review*, XXX (June 1956), 168–73.

54. U.S. Bureau of the Census, *Historical Statistics of the United States, Colonial Times to 1957* (Washington, D.C., 1960), p. 139; *New York Tribune Extra*, June, 1892, edited by Sidney Ratner un-

der the title, *New Light on the History of Great American Fortunes* (New York: A. M. Kelley, 1953), *passim*.

55. U.S. Commissioner of Education, *Annual Report, 1875* (Washington, D.C., 1876), p. lxxxii; U.S. Commissioner of Education, *Annual Report, 1902* (2 vols.; Washington, D.C., 1903), II, 1351–54.

56. The estimated value of scientific research endowments is based on a detailed survey conducted in 1902 by the Carnegie Institution of Washington, and printed in Carnegie Institution of Washington, *Confidential Report of the Executive Committee to the Board of Trustees, November 11, 1902* (Washington, D.C., 1902), Appendix B.

57. George Davidson, *The Endowment of Research*, Presidential Address, California Academy of Sciences, circa 1892 (n.p., n.d.), p. 6.

CHAPTER 7

1. Othniel C. Marsh, "Notice of a New and Diminutive Species of Fossil Horse (Equus parvulus), from the Tertiary of Nebraska," *American Journal of Science*, XLVI (November 1868), 374–75; Charles Schuchert and Clara LeVene, *O. C. Marsh, Pioneer in Paleontology* (New Haven, Conn.: Yale University Press, 1940), pp. 98–99.

2. Royal Society of London, *Transactions*, XXIX (London, 1717), 62–71.

3. Thomas Jefferson, "A Memoir on the Discovery of Certain Bones of a Quadruped of the Clawed Kind in the Western Parts of Virginia," American Philosophical Society, *Transactions*, IV (Philadelphia, 1799), 256; Rembrandt Peale, *Account of the Skeleton of the Mammoth, a non-Descript Carnivorous Animal of Immense Size, Found in America* (London, 1802); Edwin T. Martin, *Thomas Jefferson, Scientist* (New York: Collier Books, 1961), pp. 96–114.

4. Nicholas Collin, "An Essay on Those Inquiries in Natural Philosophy Which at Present are Most Beneficial to the United States of America," American Philosophical Society, *Transactions*, III (Philadelphia, 1793), xxiv.

5. Othniel C. Marsh, "The History and Methods of Paleonto-

logical Discovery," AAAS, *Proc.*, XXVIII (Salem, Mass., 1880), 1–42; Karl A. von Zittel, *History of Geology and Paleontology to the End of the Nineteenth Century* (London, 1901), pp. 363–424.

6. Joseph Leidy, *The Ancient Fauna of Nebraska*, Smithsonian Contributions to Knowledge, VI (Washington, D.C., 1854), 7; Joseph Leidy, "On the Fossil Horse of America," Academy of Natural Sciences of Philadelphia, *Proceedings*, III (Philadelphia, 1847), 262–66; Joseph Leidy, *A Flora and Fauna Within Living Animals*, Smithsonian Contributions to Knowledge, No. 5 (Washington, 1853), pp. 9–10; Henry F. Osborn, "Biographical Memoir of Joseph Leidy," National Academy of Sciences, *Biographical Memoirs*, VII (Washington, D.C., 1913), 366–68.

7. Charles Darwin, *On the Origin of Species by Means of Natural Selection* (London, 1859), pp. 310, 279–311; Loren Eisley, *Darwin's Century* (Garden City, N.Y.: Doubleday, 1961), pp. 91–115; Edward Lurie, *Louis Agassiz, A Life in Science* (Chicago, University of Chicago Press, 1960), *passim*.

8. The best accounts of the western surveys are Richard A. Bartlett, *Great Surveys of the American West* (Norman: University of Oklahoma Press, 1962); William H. Goetzmann, *Exploration and Empire, the Explorer and the Scientist in the Winning of the American West* (New York: Knopf, 1966); and Thomas Manning, *Government in Science, the United States Geological Survey, 1867–1894* (Lexington: University of Kentucky Press, 1967).

9. Osborn, "Biographical Memoir of Joseph Leidy," pp. 339–50.

10. *Ibid.*, p. 365; William B. Scott, *Some Memories of a Paleontologist* (Princeton, N.J.: Princeton University Press, 1939), p. 59. Most of the many discussions of the Cope-Marsh controversy merely reproduce the material in Schuchert and LeVene, *O. C. Marsh*, and Henry F. Osborn, *Cope, Master Naturalist* (Princeton, N.J.: Princeton University Press, 1931). An exception is Nathan Reingold, ed., *Science in Nineteenth Century America, A Documentary History* (New York: Hill and Wang, 1964), pp. 236–50.

11. Phebe A. Hanaford, *The Life of George Peabody* (Augusta, Me., 1875), pp. 80–201; Joseph Henry to Asa Gray, October 31, 1866, March 8, 1867, GHHU; Franklin Parker, "George Peabody, Founder of Modern Philanthrophy" (3 vols.; typescript dissertation, George Peabody College for Teachers, 1956), *passim. Cf.*

Andrew Carnegie, *The Gospel of Wealth and Other Timely Essays* (New York, 1890), and John G. Cawelti, *Apostles of the Self-Made Man* (Chicago: University of Chicago Press, 1965), pp. 167–99.

12. Schuchert and LeVene, *O. C. Marsh,* pp. 21–93.
13. *Ibid.,* p. 76.
14. "Mr. George Peabody's Recent Gifts to Science," *American Journal of Science,* XCIII (January 1867), 131–35; "Additional Gifts to Science from George Peabody," *ibid.* (May 1867), 414–16; Schuchert and LeVene, *O. C. Marsh,* pp. 75–82.
15. On the Yale expeditions, see *Harper's Monthly Magazine,* XLIII (October 1871), 663–71; W. W. Beach, comp., *The Indian Miscellany* (Albany, 1877), pp. 258–69; Schuchert and LeVene, *O. C. Marsh,* pp. 94–138.
16. Osborn, *Cope,* p. 160.
17. *Ibid.,* p. 170.
18. A. Hunter Dupree, *Science in the Federal Government* (Cambridge, Mass.: Harvard University Press, 1957), pp. 204–5.
19. 43 Cong., 1 Sess., *HR Report No. 612* (1874), pp. 16–18; *New York Tribune,* December 4, 1878; Allan Nevins, *Abram S. Hewitt, with Some Account of Peter Cooper* (New York: Harper and Brothers, 1935), pp. 400–9; Thurman Wilkins, *Clarence King* (New York: Macmillan, 1958), pp. 230–38; Manning, *Government in Science,* pp. 38–39.
20. Henry Adams, *The Education of Henry Adams* (Boston: Houghton Mifflin, 1918), pp. 312–13.
21. 45 Cong., 3 Sess., *HR Misc. Doc. No. 5* (Washington, D.C., 1878), pp. 3–5; Wilkins, *Clarence King,* pp. 240–45.
22. *Cong. Rec.,* 45 Cong., 3 Sess. (February 11, 1879), pp. 1203, 1206; Manning, *Government in Science,* pp. 47–58.
23. *New York Herald,* January 12, January 19, 1890. Edward D. Cope, "Editor's Table," *American Naturalist,* XIX (July 1885), 691–93; XX (February 1886), 140–42; XXII (November 1888), 1003–5; XXV (December 1891), 1111–12. Osborn, *Cope,* pp. 360–71. Goetzmann, *Exploration and Empire,* pp. 578–97.
24. John Wesley Powell to O. C. Marsh, November 1, 1878, in 45 Cong., 3 Sess., *HR Misc. Doc. 5* (Washington, D.C., 1878), pp. 24–25.
25. *Cong. Rec.,* 45 Cong., 3 Sess. (February 11, 1879), p. 1209.
26. Grover Cleveland, "Inaugural Address, March 4, 1885," *In-*

augural Addresses of the Presidents of the United States from George Washington 1789 to Harry S. Truman 1949 (Washington, D.C., 1952), p. 141; Horace S. Merrill, *Bourbon Leader: Grover Cleveland and the Democratic Party* (Boston: Little, Brown, 1957), p. 100 and *passim*.

27. Simon Newcomb to O. C. Marsh, June 5, November 16, 1884, MPY; Simon Newcomb to David Gill, December 28, 1885, NLC; "The Government and Its Scientific Bureaus," *Science*, VI (December 18, 1885), 530–31, 536–37.

28. *Joint Commission to Consider the Present Organization of the Signal Service, Geological Survey, Coast and Geodetic Survey, and the Hydrographic Office of the Navy Department, with a View to Secure Greater Efficiency and Economy of Administration of the Public Service in Said Bureaus* . . . , *Testimony*, 49 Cong., 1 Sess., *Sen. Misc. Doc. No. 82* (Washington, D.C., 1886). Hereafter cited as Allison Commission, *Testimony*. See also Newcomb to Marsh, May 10, 1886, MPY.

29. Hilary Herbert to O. C. Marsh, July 13, 1886, MPY; Newcomb to Marsh, May 10, July 19, 1886, MPY.

30. Allison Commission, *Testimony*, pp. 2–3, 177–87.

31. Simon Newcomb, "The Let-Alone Principle," *North American Review*, CX (January 1870), 1–33; Simon Newcomb to Alexander Agassiz, December 8, 1885, AHU; Simon Newcomb to Otto Struve, September 23, 1881, NLC; James A. Garfield to Simon Newcomb, April 3, 1872, NLC.

32. Alexander Agassiz to Sir James Hector, October 19, 1865, AHU; George R. Agassiz, *Letters and Recollections of Alexander Agassiz with a Sketch of His Life and Work* (Boston: Houghton Mifflin, 1913), pp. 19–23, 57–61.

33. Alexander Agassiz to Fritz Müller, November 8, 1868, AHU; G. Agassiz, *Alexander Agassiz*, pp. 85–88.

34. Alexander Agassiz to E. H. Clark, March 1, 1886, AHU; Irvin G. Wyllie, *The Self-Made Man in America* (New Brunswick, N.J.: Rutgers University Press, 1954), analyzes the myth of rags to riches.

35. Alexander Agassiz to Thomas Huxley, April 17, 1886, AHU; Alexander Agassiz, "The Coast Survey and 'Political Scientists,'" *Science*, VI (September 18, 1885), 253–55.

36. Newcomb to A. Agassiz, December 18, 1885, AHU; G. Agassiz, *Alexander Agassiz*, pp. 169, 243–44; Alexander Agas-

siz, *Three Cruises of the United States Coast and Geodetic Survey Steamer "Blake," in the Gulf of Mexico . . . from 1877 to 1880* (2 vols.; Boston, 1888), pp. vii–xxii.

37. Alexander Agassiz to Daniel Manning, September 29, 1885, AHU; Alexander Agassiz to E. L. Godkin, September 30, 1885, AHU; "The President and Professor Agassiz," *Science*, VI (October 9, 1885), 203–4.

38. Alexander Agassiz to Hilary Herbert, November 23, December 2, 1885, AHU; Herbert to A. Agassiz, November 27, December 3, December 11, 1885, AHU; Alexander Agassiz, "Official Science at Washington," *Popular Science Monthly*, XXVII (October 1885), 844–47; Alexander Agassiz, "The National Government and Science," *The Nation*, XLI (December 24, 1885), 525–26.

39. Alexander Agassiz to H. N. Mosely, September 30, 1885, AHU; A. Agassiz to T. Huxley, October 14, 1885, AHU; G. Agassiz, *Alexander Agassiz*, p. 400.

40. "Restricting the Work and Publications of the Geological Survey, and for Other Purposes," 49 Cong., 1 Sess., *HR Report No. 2214* (May 5, 1886), pp. 1–15; Newcomb to Marsh, April 27, 1886, MPY.

41. Allison Commission, *Testimony*, pp. 1074–82.

42. *Ibid.*, pp. 1076–81; Dupree, *Science in the Federal Government*, pp. 215–31, is the best published discussion of the Allison Commission.

43. Newcomb to Marsh, March 18, April 29, 1886, MPY; Allison Commission, *Testimony*, pp. 7–8.

44. Herbert to A. Agassiz, July 5, 1886, AHU; Dupree, *Science in the Federal Government*, pp. 227–31.

45. A. Agassiz to Newcomb, June 24, 1886, NLC; A. Agassiz to John Wesley Powell, June 25, 1886, AHU; A. Agassiz to T. Huxley, June 26, 1886, AHU; A. Agassiz to Marsh, October 24, 1886, MPY; [Alexander Agassiz], "Science and the State," *Popular Science Monthly*, XXIX (July 1886), 412–15.

46. A. Agassiz to George Brown Goode, February 5, 1888, AHU; A. Agassiz to Senator Edward O. Wolcott, July 2, July 20, 1892, AHU.

47. A. Hunter Dupree, "Central Scientific Organization in the United States Government," *Minerva*, I (Summer 1963), 453–69.

48. Royal Commission [Devonshire Commission] on Scientific Instruction and Advancement of Science, *Report* (3 vols.; Lon-

don, 1872–73). Richard A. Proctor, "The Endowment of Scientific Research," *Popular Science Monthly*, VII (July 1875), 354–63; (August 1875), 437–44. C. E. Appleton, "Economic Aspect of the Endowment of Research," *Fortnightly Review*, XXII (October 1874), 519–36.

49. Andrew D. White, "The Relation of National and State Governments to Advanced Education," *Journal of Social Science*, VII (September 1874), 311.

CHAPTER 8

1. Daniel Coit Gilman, *The Launching of a University and Other Papers, a Sheaf of Rembrances* (New York: Dodd, Mead and Company, 1906), pp. 237–51; University of Chicago, *Decennial Publications, 1st Series* (Chicago, 1903), I, xviii.

2. William Rainey Harper to Andrew H. Green, January 19, 1891, UC.

3. John D. Rockefeller, *Random Reminiscences of Men and Events* (New York: Doubleday, 1909), pp. 177–78; Frederick Rudolph, *The American College and University: A History* (New York: Knopf, 1962), pp. 348–54.

4. A tabulation of Rockefeller's university gifts appears in Thomas W. Goodspeed, *A History of the University of Chicago, The First Quarter-Century* (Chicago: University of Chicago Press, 1916), pp. 497–98. For most purposes, Goodspeed's history has been supplanted by Richard J. Storr, *Harper's University* (Chicago: University of Chicago Press, 1966).

5. Gilman, *Launching a University*, p. 9.

6. William Rainey Harper to John D. Rockefeller, September 22, 1890, UC; University of Chicago [William Rainey Harper], *Official Bulletin No. 1* (January, 1891).

7. Allan Nevins, ed., "The Memoirs of Frederick T. Gates," *American Heritage*, VI (April 1955), 74–75; Allan Nevins, *Study in Power: John D. Rockefeller* (2 vols.; New York: Scribner, 1953), II, 181–84.

8. On Leighton Williams, see George H. Hansell, *Reminiscences of Baptist Churches and Baptist Leaders in New York City and Vicinity, from 1835–1898* (Philadelphia, 1899), p. 57; Walter Rauschenbusch, *Christianizing the Social Order* (New York: Macmillan, 1912), p. 94; Dores R. Sharpe, *Walter Rauschenbusch*

(New York: Macmillan, 1942), *passim.* On Mornay Williams, see *New York Times,* June 19, 1926; *National Cyclopaedia of American Biography,* XXII, 334–35; Walter Rauschenbusch, *For God and the People, Prayers of the Social Awakening* (Boston: Pilgrim Press, 1910), pp. 13, 53–54, 71–72.

9. Leighton Williams to William Rainey Harper, January 5, 1891, UC.

10. L. Williams to Harper, January 9, 1891, UC. On Green's public career, see John Foord, *Life and Public Services of Andrew Green* (Garden City, N.Y.: Doubleday, Page and Company, 1913), especially pp. 203–16.

11. *New York Times,* August 4, 1877; December 9, 1890; July 7, 1891. On Ogden's business career, see Thomas Goodspeed, *The University of Chicago Biographical Sketches* (Chicago: University of Chicago Press, 1922), pp. 35–56.

12. *New York Times,* November 25, 1890, December 9, 1890. On American charity law in general and the Tilden bequest in particular, see Howard S. Miller, *The Legal Foundations of American Philanthropy, 1776–1844* (Madison: University of Wisconsin Press, 1961), pp. 40–50, and Carl Zollman, *American Law of Charities* (Milwaukee, Wis.: Bruce Publishing Company, 1924), pp, 28–37.

13. Mornay Williams to William Rainey Harper, June 17, 1891, September 21, 1892, UC.

14. Ogden Rood to Wolcott Gibbs, May 11, 1890, GFI; Brander Matthews *et al.,* eds., *A History of Columbia University, 1754–1904* (New York: Columbia University Press, 1904), pp. 152–71, 282–83; John W. Burgess, *Reminiscences of an American Scholar: Beginnings of Columbia University* (New York: Columbia University Press, 1934), pp. 234–38.

15. Green to Harper, January 12, 1891, UC.

16. Harper to Green, January 19, 1891, UC; Thomas Goodspeed to Harper, January 16, January 19, 1891, UC.

17. M. Williams to Harper, March 16, 1891, UC; L. Williams to Harper, April 4, 1891, UC; M. Williams to Harper, June 9, 1891, UC.

18. M. Williams to Harper, June 17, June 24, 1891, UC; L. Williams to Harper, June 29, 1891, UC.

19. Green to Harper, June 30, 1891, UC; *New York Tribune,* July 7, 1891; *New York Times,* July 7, 1891.

20. Harper to Green, July 1, 1891, UC; "Appointment by the Executors of William B. Ogden," July 11, 1891, UC; Harper and Goodspeed to the Ogden Executors, July 16, 1891, UC.

21. M. Williams to Harper, September 30, 1892, UC; George W. Murray to Harper, November 14, December 6, 1892, UC.

22. *New York Times*, November 26, 1891.

23. *New York Tribune*, December 12, 1892; M. Williams to Harper, February 23, 1893, UC; Harper to Green, March 8, 1893, UC; Murray to Harper, October 5, 1893, UC; L. Williams to Harper, May 25, 1894, UC; Storr, *Harper's University*, pp. 78–79.

24. William Rainey Harper to Frederick T. Gates, December 26, 1891, UC.

25. Henry H. Donaldson, "Memories for My Boys," typescript memoir, December, 1931, Henry Donaldson Papers, American Philosophical Society; G. Stanley Hall, *Life and Confessions of a Psychologist* (New York: D. Appleton and Company, 1923), pp. 258–79.

26. See Louis N. Wilson's perceptive discussion of Clark and Hall in "Some Recollections of Our Founder," *Publications of the Clark University Library*, VIII (February 1927), 1–22.

27. Donaldson, "Memories for My Boys," Donaldson Papers, American Philosophical Society.

28. Hall, *Life and Confessions*, pp. 290–306.

29. Charles L. Hutchinson to William Rainey Harper, January 3, 1892, UC; George Walker to the Trustees, March 17, 1892, UC; Sidney A. Kent to William Rainey Harper, January 1, 1894, UC; Charles O. Whitman to William Rainey Harper, April 9, 1895, UC.

30. John D. Rockefeller to the Trustees, February 23, 1892, UC.

31. Martin Ryerson to William Rainey Harper, June 15, July 18, 1892, UC; Martin Ryerson to the Trustees, November 7, 1892, UC; A. A. Michelson to William Rainey Harper, July 3, 1892, UC; A. A. Michelson to Lord Kelvin, January 30, 1894, UC; Goodspeed, *University of Chicago*, pp. 230–41.

32. Whitman to Harper, August 21, 1894 [?], April 9, 1895, UC; Henry Donaldson, Diary, November 21, 1894, Donaldson Papers, American Philosophical Society.

33. Harper to Hutchinson, January 22, 1894, UC; William Rainey Harper, "The Old and the New in Education," *The Trend in Higher Education* (Chicago: University of Chicago Press, 1905), pp. 127–30.

34. *Chicago Daily Tribune*, August 20, 1925, and *New York Times*, August 20, 1925, for informative obituaries of Helen Culver. See also Albert N. Marquis, ed., *Who's Who in America, 1924–1925* (Chicago: A. N. Marquis and Company, 1924), p. 886.

35. Charles J. Hull, *Reflections from a Busy Life* (Chicago, 1881), as quoted in Goodspeed, *University of Chicago Biographical Sketches*, p. 135.

36. Charles J. Hull to Helen Culver, December 20, 1874, as quoted in Goodspeed, *University of Chicago Biographical Sketches*, p. 138.

37. Jane Addams, *Twenty Years at Hull-House, with Autobiographical Notes* (New York: Macmillan, 1910), pp. 92–94.

38. Harper to Ryerson, December 24, 1895, UC. Ryerson was abroad, and had asked to be informed of university developments, hence the unusually full report. Harper sent a similar though less detailed report to Frederick T. Gates, December 11, 1895, UC.

39. On the identity of the sociologist, see Oberlin College, *Alumni Register . . . 1833–1960* (Oberlin, 1960), p. 52; University of Chicago, *General Register of the Officers and Alumni, 1892–1902* (Chicago, 1903), p. 22. Thomas, whose early scholarly preoccupations centered on the psychology of sex, left Chicago in disgrace in 1918 after being indicted on a violation of the Mann Act. See *New York Times*, April 13–April 20, 1918; Edmund H. Volkart, "Biographical Sketch," *Social Behavior and Personality, Contributions of W. I. Thomas to Theory and Social Research* (New York: Social Science Research Council, 1951), pp. 323–24.

40. Harper to Ryerson, December 24, 1895, UC.

41. *Ibid.;* Helen Culver to William Rainey Harper, December 3, 1895, UC.

42. Harper to Ryerson, December 24, 1895, UC; Harper to Gates, December 11, 1895, UC.

43. Harper to Ryerson, December 24, 1895, UC; Helen Culver to the Trustees, December 14, 1895, UC; Henry Donaldson, Diary, December 10–23, 1895, Donaldson Papers, American Philosophical Society.

44. Culver to Harper, May 18, 1896, May 31, 1897, UC; Helen Culver, "Presentation Address," *University Record*, II (July 16, 1897), 149–50.

45. *The Century Dictionary* (6 vols.; New York, 1889–91), VI, 6642. Peirce related the story to John J. Chapman in 1893. See

Mark DeWolfe Howe, ed., *John J. Chapman and His Letters* (Boston: Houghton Mifflin, 1937), pp. 96–97.

46. Thorstein Veblen, *The Higher Learning in America: A Memorandum on the Conduct of Universities by Business Men* (New York: B. W. Huebsch, 1918), *passim;* Daniel Coit Gilman, "Our National Schools of Science," *North American Review,* CV (October 1867), 514–16; Charles W. Eliot, "The New Education: Its Organization," *Atlantic Monthly,* XXIII (February 1869), 216.

47. Alexander Dallas Bache, "A National University," *American Journal of Education,* I (May 1856), 477–79; Edgar B. Wesley, *Proposed: The University of the United States* (Minneapolis: University of Minnesota Press, 1936), pp. 73–83.

48. Louis Agassiz to S. Weir Mitchell, May 28, 1868, as quoted in Anna R. Burr, *Weir Mitchell, His Life and Letters* (New York: Duffield and Company, 1929), pp. 119–20. See also Truman Abbe, *Professor Abbe and the Isobars: The Story of Cleveland Abbe, America's First Weatherman* (New York, 1955), pp. 64–65.

49. Daniel Coit Gilman, "Education in America, 1776–1876," *North American Review,* CXXII (January 1876), 216, 219.

50. Frank W. Clarke, "American Colleges Versus American Science," *Popular Science Monthly,* IX (August 1876), 467–79.

51. "National Traits in Science," *Science,* II (October 5, 1883), 455–57; William Trelease, "Botanical Opportunity," *Science,* n.s. IV (September 18, 1896), 369; John W. Burgess, *The American University, When Shall it Be? Where Shall it Be? What Shall it Be?* (Boston, 1884), pp. 1, 8, 11, 17–18. See also Laurence Veysey, *The Emergence of the American University* (Chicago: University of Chicago Press, 1965), pp. 121–79.

52. Rockefeller, *Random Reminiscences,* p. 160.

CHAPTER 9

1. Andrew Carnegie, *Autobiography* (Boston: Houghton Mifflin, 1920), p. 255.

2. Andrew Carnegie to Simon Newcomb, January 3, 1902, NLC; Trust Deed by Andrew Carnegie, January 28, 1902, Carnegie Institution of Washington, *Yearbook, No. 1,* 1902 (Washington, D.C., 1903), p. xiv. Edward Kirkland's introduction to the John Harvard Library edition of *The Gospel of Wealth and Other*

Timely Essays (Cambridge, Mass.: Harvard University Press, 1962), pp. vii–xx, is an unusually perceptive treatment of Carnegie's social ideas. On the sale to J. P. Morgan, see Burton J. Hendrick, *The Life of Andrew Carnegie* (2 vols.; New York: Doubleday, Doran, 1932), II, 144–46.

3. A convenient summary of the national university movement, with an extensive bibliography, is Edgar B. Wesley, *Proposed: The University of the United States* (Minneapolis: University of Minnesota Press, 1936).

4. Hoyt's typescript autobiography, 1831–1903 (completed to 1912 by his son, Kepler Hoyt), and titled "The Life of John Wesley Hoyt, A.M., M.D., LL.D.," is preserved in the John W. Hoyt Papers, State Historical Society of Wisconsin. See especially pp. 369–70, 414–17.

5. Lester Frank Ward, "A National University," *Science*, VI (December 11, 1885), 539; Daniel Coit Gilman, "Thoughts on Universities," *Science*, VIII (July 9, 1886), 37–44; Herbert B. Adams, "The Encouragement of Higher Education," *Science*, XIII (March 22, 1889), 219–22; Simon Newcomb, "Why We Need a National University," *North American Review*, CLX (February 1895), 210–16; David Starr Jordan, "The Urgent Need of a National University," *Forum*, XX (January 1897), 600–6; Daniel Coit Gilman, "Another University in Washington and How to Secure It," *Century Magazine*, LV (November 1897), 156–57.

6. Gilman, "Thoughts on Universities," p. 43.

7. "The Washington Academy of Science," *Science*, n.s. VII (February 25, 1898), 253–55; Charles D. Walcott, "Relations of the National Government to Higher Education and Research," *Science*, n.s. XIII (June 28, 1901), 1001–15.

8. Susanna Phelps Gage, "A George Washington Memorial University," *Outlook*, LVIII (February 26, 1898), 521–24.

9. Hoyt, "Life of Hoyt," p. 447.

10. *Ibid.*, pp. 448–50; John W. Hoyt to Andrew Carnegie, March 27, 1900, as quoted in *ibid.*, p. 456.

11. Andrew Carnegie to Andrew D. White, April 26, May 2, 1901, CLC.

12. White to Carnegie, May 13, 1901, CLC; Carnegie to White, May 28, June 18, 1901, CLC; White to Gilman, May 20, 1901, as quoted in Fabian Franklin, *The Life of Daniel Coit Gilman* (New York: Dodd, Mead and Company, 1910), pp. 390–91.

13. Arthur James Balfour to Andrew Carnegie, May 21, 1901, CLC. Hendrick, *Life of Andrew Carnegie*, II, 219, cites this letter as the main influence on Carnegie's decision to found the Carnegie Institution of Washington.

14. Carnegie, *Autobiography*, p. 182.

15. Charles D. Walcott, "Relations of the National Government to Higher Education and Research," *Science*, n.s. XIII (June 28, 1901), 1009–15; Nicholas Murray Butler, "The Washington Memorial Institution," *Review of Reviews*, XXIV (July 1901), 56–59.

16. White to Carnegie, June 21, 1901, CLC.

17. Franklin, *Daniel Coit Gilman*, pp. 393–97.

18. *Ibid.*, p. 394. See also Carnegie's remarks, January 28, 1902, as he presented the trust deed, as quoted in Carnegie Institution of Washington, *Yearbook, No. 1*, pp. xv–xvii.

19. Draft Plan of Organization, "University in Washington," November, 1901, CLC; Andrew Carnegie to Theodore Roosevelt, November 28, 1901, CLC.

20. *Washington Post*, December 10, 1901; *New York Times*, December 10, December 11, 1901; Hoyt, "Life of Hoyt," pp. 466–69.

21. Gilman to White, December 20, December 29, 1901, both as quoted in Franklin, *Daniel Coit Gilman*, pp. 400–1.

22. Articles of Incorporation of the Carnegie Institution of Washington, January 4, 1902, Carnegie Institution of Washington, *Yearbook, No. 1*, pp. vii–viii. The incorporators were John Hay, Edward D. White, John Shaw Billings, Daniel Coit Gilman, Charles D. Walcott, and Carroll D. Wright.

23. Carnegie Institution of Washington, *Yearbook, No. 1*, p. xiii. There is an undated copy of the Draft Plan of November, 1901, revised in Carnegie's hand, in CLC.

24. Carnegie to Newcomb, January 3, 1902, NLC.

25. Carl Snyder, "America's Inferior Position in the Scientific World," *North American Review*, CLXXIV (January 1902), 59–72. On Snyder, see Albert N. Marquis, ed., *Who's Who in America, 1920–1921* (Chicago: A. N. Marquis and Company, 1921), p. 2649.

26. Henry S. Pritchett to Andrew Carnegie, January 14, 1902, CLC.

27. Carnegie to Roosevelt, November 28, 1901, CLC; Carnegie Institution of Washington, *Yearbook, No. 1*, p. xvii.

28. Memorandum, Executive Committee of the Carnegie Institution, April 3, 1902, CLC; Carnegie Institution of Washington, *Confidential Report of the Executive Committee to the Board of Trustees, November 11, 1902* (Washington, D.C., 1902), pp. iv–xi.

29. Carnegie Institution of Washington, *Report of the Executive Committee*, pp. iv–ix; *Science*, n.s. XVI (November 7, 1902), 746–47; Daniel Coit Gilman, "The Carnegie Institution," *The Bookman*, XV (March 1902), 73–74.

30. Joseph Jastrow, "The Carnegie Foundation," *The Dial*, XXXII (February 16, 1902), 109–12.

31. Simon Newcomb, "Conditions Which Discourage Scientific Work in America," *North American Review*, CLXXIV (February 1902), 158.

32. Elihu Root to Andrew Carnegie, December 30, 1901, CLC; Roosevelt to Carnegie, December 31, 1901, CLC.

33. J. McKeen Cattell, "The Carnegie Institution," *Science*, n.s. XVI (September 19, 1902), 469. For specific page citations to the letters to the editor, see the Index to *Science*, n.s. XVI.

34. Hugo Münsterberg, "The Carnegie Institution," *Science*, n.s. XVI (October 3, 1902), 521–24. See also the comments by George Sternberg, Joseph Jastrow, and Morris Loeb, in the same volume, pp. 482, 695, and 485–86, respectively.

35. Henry S. Pritchett, "The Carnegie Institution," *Science*, n.s. XVI (October 10, 1902), 587–88.

36. Edward S. Holden, "The Carnegie Institution," *Science*, n.s. XVI (October 10, 1902), 585–86.

37. J. C. Branner, "The Carnegie Institution," *Science*, n.s. XVI (October 3, 1902), 527.

38. Carnegie Institution of Washington, *Report of the Executive Committee*, pp. xi–xiii.

39. Charles Walcott to Andrew Carnegie, June 19, 1902, January 19, 1903, CLC. See also Charles D. Walcott, "Outlook of the Geologist in America," Geological Society of America, *Bulletin*, XIII (February 2, 1902), 117–18. A brief, though informative sketch of Walcott is Nelson H. Darton, "Memorial of Charles D. Walcott," Geological Society of America, *Bulletin*, XXXIX (1927), 80–116. Pages 103–16 are a bibliography of Walcott's writings.

40. Lewis Boss to Andrew Carnegie, April 7, 1902, CLC.

41. Walcott to Carnegie, January 25, 1903, CLC. See also Henry S. Pritchett to Simon Newcomb, January 16, 1906, NLC, and

Simon Newcomb, "The Organization of Research," *North American Review*, CLXXXII (January 1906), 32–43.

42. Andrew Carnegie, "Popular Illusions About Trusts," *Century Magazine*, LX (May 1900), 144. On Rockefeller, see Allan Nevins, *John D. Rockefeller, The Heroic Age of American Enterprise* (2 vols.; New York: Scribner, 1940), especially I, 622.

43. Carnegie, "Popular Illusions About Trusts," p. 146.

44. Carnegie Institution of Washington, *Yearbook, No. 5* (Washington, D.C., 1906), p. 36.

45. Carnegie Institution of Washington, *Yearbook, No. 4* (Washington, D.C., 1905), pp. 17, 28–30; *Yearbook, No. 5* (Washington, D.C., 1906), pp. 30, 33–35.

46. Carnegie Institution of Washington, *Yearbook, No. 4* (Washington, D.C., 1904), p. 32.

47. Carnegie Institution of Washington, *Yearbook, No. 10* (Washington, D.C., 1911), pp. 8–13. The departments, with their dates of establishment, were: Dept. of Experimental Evolution, Dept. of Marine Biology, and Dept. of Historical Research, December 1903; Dept. of Economics and Sociology, January 1904; Dept. of Terrestrial Magnetism, April 1904; Mount Wilson Observatory, December 1904; Geophysical Laboratory and Dept. of Botanical Research, December 1905; Nutritional Laboratory, December 1906; Dept. of Meridian Astronomy, March, 1907.

48. Mark H. Haller, *Eugenics: Hereditarian Influences in American Thought* (New Brunswick, N.J.: Rutgers University Press, 1963), discusses the work at Cold Spring Harbor.

49. George Ellery Hale to Horace White, March 11, 1904, Horace White Family Papers, in the possession of Amelia E. White, Santa Fe, New Mexico. Professor Joseph Logsdon, White's biographer, called the Hale-White correspondence to my attention. See also Carol G. Wilson, *California Yankee, William R. Staats* (Claremont, Calif.: Saunders Press, 1946), pp. 63–71, 117, 122–25, and Helen Wright, *Explorer of the Universe, A Biography of George Ellery Hale* (New York: E. P. Dutton, 1966), pp. 159–78.

50. Carnegie Institution of Washington, *Report of the Executive Committee*, pp. xxx, 128–44.

51. Hale to White, December 24, 1903, March 11, May 16, 1904, Horace White Family Papers.

52. Originally appearing in the December 1889 issue of the

North American Review, "The Best Fields for Philanthropy" is reprinted in *The Gospel of Wealth.*

53. Hendrick, *Andrew Carnegie,* II, 237–41.

54. *Ibid.;* Wilson, *William R. Staats,* pp. 122–25; Wright, *Explorer of the Universe,* pp. 159–96.

55. Andrew Carnegie to Robert S. Woodward, January 19, 1911, as quoted in Carnegie Institution of Washington, *Yearbook, No. 10* (Washington, D.C., 1911), pp. 7–8.

56. See Helen Wright, *Palomar* (New York: Macmillan, 1952), *passim,* and *Explorer of the Universe,* pp. 387–429.

CHAPTER 10

1. Henry A. Rowland, "A Plea for Pure Science," AAAS, *Proc., 1883* (Salem, Mass., 1884), pp. 104, 108, 110, 120, 122.

2. George H. Daniels, "The Process of Professionalization in American Science: The Emergent Period, 1820–1860," *Isis,* LVIII (Summer 1967), 151–66, places Rowland's remarks in an insightful context.

3. For a recent, extended example of similar reasoning, see Richard Hofstadter, *Anti-Intellectualism in American Life* (New York: Knopf, 1963).

4. William Rainey Harper, *The Trend in Higher Education* (Chicago: University of Chicago Press, 1905), pp. 255–56.

5. John M. Coulter, "Public Interest in Research," *Popular Science Monthly,* LXVII (July 1905), 306.

6. Addison Brown, "The Need of Endowment for Scientific Research and Publication," *The Scientific Alliance of New York, Addresses Delivered at the First Joint Meeting* (New York, 1893), pp. 18–41; Warren Weaver, *U.S. Philanthropic Foundations, Their History, Structure, Management, and Record* (New York: Harper and Row, 1967), is a guide to twentieth-century developments.

7. Alice K. Smith, *A Peril and a Hope: The Scientists' Movement in America, 1945–1947* (Chicago: University of Chicago Press, 1965); Morton Grodzins and Eugene Rabinowitch, eds., *The Atomic Age: Articles from the Bulletin of the Atomic Scientists, 1945–1962* (New York: Simon and Schuster, 1963).

8. Donald Fleming, "The Big Money and High Politics of Science," *The Atlantic,* CCXVI (August 1965), 41–45; Charles V.

236 *Notes*

Kidd, *American Universities and Federal Research* (Cambridge, Mass.: Harvard University Press, Belknap Press, 1959).

9. Dwight D. Eisenhower, "Farewell Address, January 17, 1961," *Public Papers of the Presidents: Dwight D. Eisenhower, 1960–61* (Washington, D.C., 1962), No. 421. See also Don K. Price, *The Scientific Estate* (Cambridge, Mass.: Harvard University Press, 1965), J. Stefan Dupré and Sanford Lakoff, *Science and the Nation, Policy and Politics* (Englewood Cliffs, N.J.: Prentice-Hall, 1962), Donald Cox, *America's New Policy Makers: The Scientists' Rise to Power* (Philadelphia: Chilton, 1964), Ralph Lapp, *The New Priesthood: The Scientific Elite and the Uses of Power* (New York: Harper and Row, 1965).

10. Samuel P. Langley, "The History of a Doctrine," AAAS, *Proc., 1888* (Salem, Mass., 1889), p. 2; Walter B. Cannon, *The Way of an Investigator* (New York: W. W. Norton, 1945), pp. 68–78.

Essay on the Sources

A detailed, formal bibliography would involve a needless repetition of the notes to the text. What follows is, instead, an evaluation of the major categories of source material relating to the support of scientific investigation in nineteenth-century America.

MANUSCRIPTS

To a great extent the social history of science, of which its financial support is a part, remains buried in little-used manuscript collections. Edward Lurie's "Some Manuscript Resources in the History of Nineteenth Century American Natural Science," *Isis*, Vol. XLIV (December 1953), is a useful preliminary guide. Whitfield J. Bell, Jr., and Murphy Smith, *Guide to the Archives and Manuscript Collections of the American Philosophical Society* (Philadelphia: American Philosophical Society, 1966), and Venia Phillips and Maurice Phillips, *Guide to the Manuscript Collections in the Academy of Natural Sciences of Philadelphia* (Philadelphia: Academy of Natural Sciences of Philadelphia, 1963), will, hopefully, serve as models and as inspiration for other depositories. Also useful as a manuscript-finding aid is the periodic *Newsletter* of the Project on the History of Recent Physics in the United States, sponsored by the American Institute of Physics (May 1964–).

The following manuscript collections and institutional archives were of greatest value for this study:

John Quincy Adams Papers, Massachusetts Historical Society, Microfilm Edition. Adams' complete diary, his incoming and outgoing correspondence, and miscellaneous papers are an essential source for the 1830's and 1840's, and contain much material relating to astronomy and to the Smithsonian Institution.

Alexander Agassiz Papers, Museum of Comparative Zoology, Harvard University. An immense collection of incoming and outgoing correspondence and other papers reflecting Agassiz's interests in mining, oceanography, and the Museum of Comparative Zoology.

Alexander Dallas Bache Papers, Library of Congress. Several bound volumes of correspondence relate to the organization of research before the Civil War. Six volumes of a ten-volume "Diary of a Trip to Europe, 1836–37," chronicle a scientific and cultural pilgrimage. Two more volumes are located in the Smithsonian Institution Archives, the remaining two in the Henry E. Huntington Library, San Marino, California.

Alexander Dallas Bache Papers, Smithsonian Institution Archives. An extensive private correspondence with Joseph Henry, 1834–67, plus general private correspondence, trace the activities of the Lazzaroni.

Spencer Fullerton Baird Papers, Smithsonian Institution Archives. Nearly fifty thousand items relate to Baird as naturalist and as Joseph Henry's successor as Secretary of the Smithsonian Institution.

Andrew Carnegie Papers, Library of Congress. Chiefly useful for correspondence and related documents dealing with the Carnegie Institution of Washington.

Henry H. Donaldson Papers, American Philosophical Society. One of America's first neurologists, Donaldson took his doctorate at The Johns Hopkins and taught at Clark and the University of Chicago. Diaries for these years, and a typescript memoir, written in 1931, are unusually frank and factual.

Edward Everett Papers, Massachusetts Historical Society. Correspondence and manuscript diaries for the 1840's are valuable for Everett's presidency at Harvard, and for the establishment of the Lawrence Scientific School.

John Fries Frazer Papers, American Philosophical Society. Frazer, a chemist and the Philadelphia member of the Lazzaroni, corresponded with most American physical scientists in the two decades before the Civil War. He was also active in local scientific organizations in Philadelphia.

Frederick T. Gates Papers, University of Chicago Archives. Gates was John D. Rockefeller's philanthropic adviser. Correspondence with William Rainey Harper, 1891–93, and Gates's incoming letters relating to the university, 1889–1905, chronicle the institution's search for science endowments.

Oliver Wolcott Gibbs Papers, Library of the Franklin Institute, Philadelphia. Scientific correspondence deals with the history of organic chemistry and the organization of research in general. Gibbs took a special interest in the research funds of the National Academy of Sciences, and the papers reveal the everyday workings of the academy in that regard.

Asa Gray Papers, Gray Herbarium, Harvard University. The collection includes his original letters, plus typescript copies of Gray letters in the New York Botanic Garden. The Historic Letter File, consisting of eight file cases of incoming correspondence, 1830's to 1880's, involves nearly every aspect of American science during that half century.

George Ellery Hale Papers, Mount Wilson and Palomar Observatories Library, Pasadena, California, Microfilm Edition. An immense collection, one hundred rolls in the film edition, reflecting Hale's deep involvement in astrophysics and the organization of research. Daniel J. Kevles, ed., *Guide to the Microfilm Edition of the George Ellery Hale Papers, 1882–1937* (Pasadena: California Institute of Technology, 1968), is the indispensable guide.

William Rainey Harper Papers, University of Chicago Archives. Supposedly limited to Harper's non-university correspondence, the collection includes a considerable amount of information on the search for patrons.

Harvard University Archives, Widener Library, Harvard University. The College Papers, College Letters, and Records of the President and Fellows chart the institutional development of science at Harvard. The Records of the Lawrence Scientific School reveal faculty policies during the formative period. The Records of the Harvard Observatory contain much routine material, but also considerable personal correspondence from Edward S. Pickering. The Observatory Records also contain correspondence relating to Catherine Wolfe Bruce, 1890–91, including dozens of begging letters from astronomers throughout the world.

Joseph Henry Papers, Smithsonian Institution Archives. An immense collection of correspondence, diaries, and scientific papers document Henry's position as the elder statesman of the American scientific community. A comprehensive published edition of the Joseph Henry Papers is in preparation under the editorship of Dr. Nathan Reingold.

John Wesley Hoyt Papers, State Historical Society of Wisconsin. Hoyt's massive typescript autobiography, 1831–1903, is a prime source for the national university movement during the second half of the nineteenth century.

Abbott Lawrence Papers, Houghton Library, Harvard University. A few scattered letters relate to the Lawrence Scientific School. Most of Lawrence's personal papers, diligently gathered by the Massachusetts Historical Society for a memorial biography, burned at once during the Great Boston Fire of 1872.

Othniel C. Marsh Papers, Peabody Museum of Natural History, Yale University. A large and valuable collection relating to paleontology, government science, and the affairs of the scientific community at large. Unfortunately there are no copies of Marsh's outgoing correspondence.

Simon Newcomb Papers, Library of Congress. Newcomb's incoming letters alone fill more than 280 file boxes. Extensive correspondence deals with all phases of astronomy and related sciences, and with the Carnegie Institution of Washington.

Benjamin Peirce Papers, Harvard University Archives. Eleven large folders of correspondence, 1825–72, reveal Peirce the man, Peirce the mathematician, and Peirce the strategist of scientific organization.

Edward Charles Pickering Papers, Harvard University Archives. Autobiographical manuscripts and notebooks, and correspondence from the 1850's to the 1870's relate to Pickering's activities as Director of the Harvard Observatory and as a major promoter of organized giving for science.

William H. Rhees Collection, Henry E. Huntington Library, San Marino, California. As Chief Clerk of the Smithsonian Institution, 1852–91, Rhees collected a large number of letters and institutional records relating to the Smithsonian, to Joseph Henry, Dallas Bache, and others. Material in the Rhees Collection fills in many gaps in the present holdings of the Smithsonian Institution Archives.

Joseph Sheffield Papers, Beinecke Library, Yale University. Two volumes of letters deal in part with the foundation of the Sheffield

Scientific School. Of particular interest are Sheffield's *Reminiscences*, written in the 1870's as a series of letters to his sons.

Benjamin Silliman Papers, Rare Book Room, Yale University Library. Silliman's seventeen-volume diary, 1840–64, is a running account of Yale science, and much of American science as well. It is especially useful for the evolution of the Sheffield Scientific School.

Smithsonian Institution Archives, Smithsonian Institution. Under Secretary Joseph Henry the Smithsonian was a very personal institution; there is no clear line between institutional and personal correspondence. Voluminous papers, records of the regents, and miscellaneous letters relate to Smithsonian affairs and to the encouragement and support of research throughout the country. Also hidden away in the archives are eight file cases of the papers of the Columbian Institute for the Promotion of Science, 1816–37, and its successor, the National Institution for the Promotion of Science, 1839–63.

University of Chicago Archives, Harper Memorial Library, University of Chicago. The President's Papers, arranged by subject and correspondent, reflect institutional expansion and the origins of institutional policy.

John Warner Papers, American Philosophical Society. After a priority dispute with Benjamin Peirce, Warner, an amateur naturalist, became the most vocal foe of the Lazzaroni. Two boxes of letters, 1850–64, give important perspectives on the Dudley Observatory controversy and the founding of the National Academy of Sciences.

Yale Memorabilia Collection, Rare Book Room, Yale University Library. Extensive archival material relates to the foundation of the Sheffield Scientific School. The Yale Analytical Laboratory Letterbook, 1848–52, provides an inside view of daily activities in the Norton-Silliman laboratory, seasoned with personal letters from the two chemists.

SERIALS AND NEWSPAPERS

Max Meisel's invaluable *Bibliography of American Natural History: The Pioneer Century, 1769–1865* (8 vols.; Brooklyn: Premier Publishing Company, 1924–29), and the Royal Society of London, *Catalogue of Scientific Papers, 1800–1900* (19 vols.; London, 1867–

1925), are comprehensive guides to technical papers. The three principal American scientific journals, useful for technical papers, general articles, and professional news, are the *American Journal of Science*, often called simply *Silliman's Journal* (1818–), Edward L. Youmans' *Popular Science Monthly* (1872–), and the weekly, *Science* (1883–), the official organ of the American Association for the Advancement of Science. The short-lived *Cambridge Miscellany of Mathematics, Physics and Astronomy* (1842–43) was an important voice for science at Harvard. The *Siderial Messenger* (1846–48) chronicled the rise of the Cincinnati Observatory, while Benjamin A. Gould's *Astronomical Journal* (1849–), *Popular Astronomy* (1893–), and the *Astro-Physical Journal* (1895–) covered American astronomy as a whole. *The American Naturalist* (1867–) contained informative editorials and news items by its controversial editor, Edward D. Cope.

Before the day of numerous specialized journals, general magazines carried considerable scientific information, essays, and book reviews. Chief among them were the *North American Review* (1815–1940), for which there is an index listing the authors of unsigned reviews, the *New Englander* (1843–85), and the *Atlantic Monthly* (1857–). Henry Barnard's *American Journal of Education* was another important outlet, as were such progressive farm journals as *The Cultivator* (1834–65) and *The American Agriculturist* (1842–).

The publications of scientific and learned societies reflected the efforts of their members to secure financial assistance. Ralph Bates catalogues these agencies and their publications in *Scientific Societies in the United States* (2nd ed.; New York: Columbia University Press, 1958). The *Proceedings* of the following organizations were of particular value: The Boston Society of Natural History (1841–), the American Philosophical Society (1838–), the American Academy of Arts and Sciences (1846–), the American Association for the Advancement of Science (1848–). The AAAS *Proceedings* contain the annual addresses of the retiring presidents, an extremely valuable series of nontechnical surveys of the current state of science in America. The *Proceedings* of the National Academy of Sciences (1863–) provide information on the research endowments administered by that agency. The varied publications of the Smithsonian Institution stand in a class by themselves. William J. Rhees, comp., *List of Publications of the Smithsonian*

Institution, 1846–1903, Smithsonian Publication No. 1376 (Washington, D.C., 1903), is a valuable guide to the *Annual Report* of the Secretary, the *Smithsonian Contributions to Knowledge*, the *Miscellaneous Publications*, and much more. The *Yearbook* of the Carnegie Institution of Washington (Washington, D.C., 1902–) reflects major policy trends and lists annual allocations for research.

Newspapers varied in their coverage of day-to-day affairs within the scientific community, but were an indispensable source. *The Boston Daily Advertiser* (1813–1929), the *Boston Evening Transcript* (1830–), the *New York Tribune* (1841–1906), the *New York Times* (1851–), the *Washington National Intelligencer* (1813–69), and *Niles National Register* (1811–49) devoted considerable space to scientific affairs.

BIOGRAPHICAL MATERIAL

Few men of science, and even fewer philanthropists, left autobiographical accounts. John A. Brashear, *The Autobiography of a Man Who Loved the Stars* (Boston: Houghton Mifflin, 1925), is a warm story of a self-made instrument maker. Andrew Carnegie's *Autobiography* (New York: Houghton Mifflin, 1920) is self-conscious but revealing. Edwin B. Frost, *An Astronomer's Life* (Boston: Houghton Mifflin, 1933), chronicles the early years at the Yerkes Observatory. Granville Stanley Hall, *The Life and Confessions of a Psychologist* (New York: D. Appleton, 1923), gives his version of the founding of Clark University. William D. Armes, ed., *The Autobiography of Joseph LeConte* (New York: D. Appleton, 1903), is a useful memoir, particularly for the Agassiz era at Harvard. Simon Newcomb, *The Reminiscences of an Astronomer* (Boston: Houghton Mifflin, 1903), is unusually frank, as are William B. Scott, *Some Memories of a Paleontologist* (Princeton, N.J.: Princeton University Press, 1939), and Harvey W. Wiley, *An Autobiography* (Indianapolis: Bobbs Merrill, 1930). John D. Rockefeller, *Random Reminiscences of Men and Events* (New York: Doubleday, 1909), is a clear statement of his approach to philanthropy, but it should be supplemented by Frederick T. Gates's enlightening "Memoirs," edited by Allan Nevins, *American Heritage*, Vol. VI (April 1955).

Biographies of the "life and letters" variety are primary sources because of the documents they contain. Elizabeth C. Agassiz,

Louis Agassiz, His Life and Correspondence (2 vols.; Boston, 1886), should be read in conjunction with Jane L. Gray, ed., *Letters of Asa Gray* (2 vols.; Boston, 1893). William H. Dall, *Spencer Fullerton Baird* (Philadelphia: J. B. Lippincott, 1915), sheds light on early Smithsonian affairs. Edward S. Holden, ed., *Memorials of William Cranch Bond . . . and of His Son, George Phillips Bond* (San Francisco, 1897), is a capsule history of the Harvard Observatory to 1865. Henry F. Osborn, *Cope: Master Naturalist: The Life and Letters of Edward Drinker Cope, with a Bibliography of His Writings* (Princeton, N.J.: Princeton University Press, 1931), should be compared with the favorable treatment of Cope's bitter rival by Charles Schuchert and Clara Levene, *O. C. Marsh, Pioneer in Paleontology* (New Haven, Conn.: Yale University Press, 1940). Daniel Coit Gilman, *The Life of James Dwight Dana* (New York, 1899), is disappointing. Albert C. Sewall, *The Life of Prof. Albert Hopkins* (New York, 1870), shows the interaction of astronomy and religious zeal. Hollis H. Hunnewell, ed., *Life, Letters and Diary of Horatio Hollis Hunnewell* (3 vols.; New York: privately printed [by DeVinne Press], 1906), unfortunately tells little of Hunnewell's relations with Asa Gray. Elizabeth A. Osborne, ed., *From the Letter Files of S. W. Johnson* (New Haven, Conn.: Yale University Press, 1913), is useful for the early years of the Sheffield Scientific School, and for the history of physiological chemistry generally. F. A. Mitchel, *Ormsby MacKnight Mitchel, Astronomer and General* (Boston, 1887), is a basic source for the founding of the Cincinnati Observatory, but should be supplemented by Russell McCormmach, "Ormsby MacKnight Mitchell's Siderial Messenger, 1846–1848," American Philosophical Society, *Proceedings*, CX (February 1966), 35–47. Emma Rogers, ed., *Life and Letters of William Barton Rogers* (2 vols.; Boston, 1896), is a revealing account. George P. Fisher, *The Life of Benjamin Silliman* (2 vols.; New York, 1866), is frequently more useful than the later study by John F. Fulton and Elizabeth H. Thompson, *Benjamin Silliman, 1779–1864: Pathfinder in American Science* (New York: Henry Schuman, 1947).

Outstanding modern biographies of American men of science include Donald Fleming, *John William Draper and the Religion of Science* (Philadelphia: Lippincott, 1950), A. Hunter Dupree, *Asa Gray* (Cambridge, Mass.: Harvard University Press, 1959), and

Edward Lurie, *Louis Agassiz, A Life in Science* (Chicago: University of Chicago Press, 1960). Merle M. Odgers, *Alexander Dallas Bache, Scientist and Educator* (Philadelphia: University of Pennsylvania Press, 1947), will be supplanted by Nathan Reingold's forthcoming biography. John M. Clarke, *James Hall of Albany* (Albany, 1921), demonstrates the need for a modern study. Thomas Coulson, *Joseph Henry, His Life and Work* (Princeton, N.J.: Princeton University Press, 1950), is best on Henry as a physicist. The best account of Henry as scientific administrator is Wilcomb E. Washburn, "Joseph Henry's Conception of the Purpose of the Smithsonian Institution," in Walter M. Whitehill *et al.*, *A Cabinet of Curiosities: Five Episodes in the Evolution of American Museums* (Charlottesville: University of Virginia Press, 1967), pp. 106–66. Courtney R. Hall, *A Scientist in the Early Republic: Samuel Latham Mitchill, 1764–1831* (New York: Columbia University Press, 1934), paints a sympathetic portrait of the universal savant. Andrew D. Rodgers, *John Torrey: A Story of North American Botany* (Princeton, N.J.: Princeton University Press, 1942), treats the life of Asa Gray's mentor with considerable insight. Helen Wright's official biography, *Explorer of the Universe: A Biography of George Ellery Hale* (New York: E. P. Dutton, 1966), will likely remain the authoritative account. For a great many significant men of science who are virtually unknown outside their fields, one must go to the *Biographical Memoirs* of the National Academy of Sciences (Washington, D.C., 1877–). The *Memoirs* have treated more than five hundred individuals thus far, and often include a complete bibliography of the subject's published works.

Three biographical collections, W. J. Youmans, ed., *Pioneers of Science in America* (New York, 1896), David Starr Jordan, ed., *Leading American Men of Science* (New York: Henry Holt, 1910), and Bernard Jaffe, *Men of Science in America* (New York: Simon and Schuster, 1944), are of uneven quality. On the social origins of the scientific community, J. McKeen Cattell's pioneering surveys are still very useful. See especially "Homo Scientificus Americanus," *Science*, XVII (1903), 561–70; "Families of American Men of Science," *Popular Science Monthly*, LXXXVI (1915), 504–15; "Origin and Distribution of Scientific Men," *Science*, LXVI (1927), 513–16.

Biographers have shown little interest in any but the most

wealthy philanthropists. Burton J. Hendrick, *The Life of Andrew Carnegie* (2 vols.; New York: Doubleday, Doran, 1932), and Allan Nevins, *Study in Power, John D. Rockefeller* (2 vols.; New York: Scribner, 1953), treat the two leading exponents of wholesale giving. Most patrons of science lived quiet lives, and biographical information must be pieced together from scattered eulogies, obituaries, and works such as the *Dictionary of American Biography* (22 vols.; New York: Scribner, 1928–44), *Who's Who in America* (Chicago: A. N. Marquis and Company, 1899–), and the *National Cyclopaedia of American Biography* (55 vols.; New York: J. T. White Company, 1892–). Essential for Boston and vicinity is *Our First Men: A Calendar of Wealth, Fashion and Gentility; Containing a List of Those Persons Taxed in the City of Boston, Credibly Reputed to be Worth One Hundred Thousand Dollars, with Biographical Notices of the Principal Persons* (Boston, 1846, and later editions). In 1892 the *New York Tribune* compiled a generally reliable list of 4,047 American millionaires, with brief biographical notes. It has been reprinted by Sidney Ratner, ed., *New Light on the History of Great American Fortunes: Amedican Millionaires of 1892 and 1902* (New York: A. M. Kelley, 1953).

INSTITUTIONAL HISTORIES

Ralph Bates's survey of American scientific societies, cited above, is the best guide to the many brief, often "official" histories. A few accounts are worthy of special notice. George Brown Goode, ed., *The Smithsonian Institution, 1846–1896. The History of Its First Half Century* (Washington, D.C., 1897), recounts the facts. Geoffrey T. Hellman, *The Smithsonian: Octopus on the Mall* (Philadelphia, 1967), which was originally a series of *New Yorker* "Profiles," captures the spirit. William Cranch Bond, *History and Description of the Astronomical Observatory of Harvard College*, Vol. I of the *Annals of the Harvard College Observatory* (Cambridge, Mass., 1856), is more valuable for the early years than Solon Bailey's *History and Work of the Harvard Observatory, 1839–1927* (New York: McGraw-Hill, 1931). See also Bessie I. Jones, *Lighthouse of the Skies: The Smithsonian Astrophysical Observatory: Background and History, 1846–1955* (Washington, D.C., 1965).

There is no extended discussion of the Lawrence Scientific

School, though I. Bernard Cohen, "Harvard and the Scientific Spirit," *Harvard Alumni Bulletin, No. 50* (1948) is a thoughtful account. Richard J. Storr treats the Lawrence School in his valuable analysis of *The Beginnings of Graduate Education in America* (Chicago: University of Chicago Press, 1953). William L. Kingsley's monumental *Yale College, A Sketch of Its History* (2 vols.; New York, 1879) is often more informative than Russell H. Chittenden's standard *History of the Sheffield Scientific School* (2 vols.; New Haven, Conn.: Yale University Press, 1928). George Brown Goode, "The Origin of the National Scientific and Educational Institutions of the United States," appears with several other important papers on the history of science in America in the United States National Museum, *Annual Report, 1897, Part 2* (Washington, D.C., 1901).

Hugh Hawkins, *Pioneer: A History of the Johns Hopkins University, 1874–1889* (Ithaca, N.Y.: Cornell University Press, 1960), should remain the definitive study. Thomas W. Goodspeed's *History of the University of Chicago, The First Quarter Century* (Chicago: University of Chicago Press, 1916) is an account by an informed "insider." It should be read in conjuction with Richard J. Storr, *Harper's University* (Chicago: University of Chicago Press, 1966). The following set high standards for comprehensiveness and interpretive insight: Walter P. Metzger, *The Age of the University*, Part Two of Richard Hofstadter and Walter Metzger, *The Development of Academic Freedom in the United States* (New York: Columbia University Press, 1955); Laurence R. Veysey, *The Emergence of the American University* (Chicago: University of Chicago Press, 1965); Frederick Rudolph, *The American College and University: A History* (New York: Knopf, 1962), and Rush Welter, *Popular Education and Democratic Thought in America* (New York: Columbia University Press, 1962).

THE HISTORY OF SCIENCE IN AMERICA

There is no synthetic discussion, nor is there anything for the period after 1820 to compare with Whitfield J. Bell's *Early American Science: Needs and Opportunities for Study* (Chapel Hill: University of North Carolina Press, 1955). A. Hunter Dupree's *Science in the Federal Government* (Cambridge, Mass.: Harvard University Press, 1957) is the standard treatment, but based almost entirely on printed sources. For government science in the West, see Thomas G. Manning, *Government in Science: The U.S. Geological Survey, 1867–1894* (Lexington: University of Kentucky Press, 1967), and William H. Goetzmann, *Exploration and Empire: The Explorer and the Scientist in the Winning of the American West* (New York: Knopf, 1966).

Dirk J. Struik, *Yankee Science in the Making* (Boston: Little, Brown, 1948), is a Marxian analysis of science and technology in New England, 1815–40. Donald Fleming, *Science and Technology in Providence, 1760–1840* (Providence, R.I.: Brown University Press, 1952), and Brooke Hindle, *Technology in Early America: Needs and Opportunities for Study* (Chapel Hill: University of North Carolina Press, 1967), deal more satisfactorily with similar themes. Edward S. Dana *et al.*, eds., *A Century of Science in America* (New Haven, Conn.: Yale University Press, 1918), discusses its topic in terms of the *American Journal of Science*. George P. Merrill, *The First One Hundred Years of American Geology* (New Haven, Conn.: Yale University Press, 1924), is unusually comprehensive. Elias Loomis, *The Recent Progress of Astronomy: Especially in the United States* (New York, 1850), and Édouard Mailly, *Précis de l'histoire de l'astronomie aux États-Unis d'amerique* (Brussels, 1860), are essential for the history of the observatory movement. Benjamin Silliman, Jr., "American Contributions to Chemistry," *American Chemist*, Vol. V (August–September 1874), is both a list of papers and a suggestive analysis of science in the 1840's.

Since 1948, when Richard Shryock published his seminal and controversial essay, "American Indifference to Basic Science in the Nineteenth Century," *Archives internationales d'histoire des sciences*, No. 5 (October 1948), a number of significant interpretive essays have appeared. John D. Bernal, *Science and Industry in the Nineteenth Century* (London: Routledge and Paul, 1953), refutes Shryock from a Marxist point of view. For contrasting perspectives see I. Bernard Cohen, "Science in America: The Nineteenth Century," in Arthur Schlesinger, Jr., and Morton White, eds., *Paths of American Thought* (Boston: Houghton Mifflin, 1963), pp. 167–89; A. Hunter Dupree, "The History of American Science: A Field Finds Itself," *American Historical Review*, LXXI (April 1966), 863–74; George H. Daniels, "The Pure-Science Ideal and Democratic Culture," *Science*, CLVI (June 30, 1967),

1699–1705, and the same author's *American Science in the Age of Jackson* (New York: Columbia University Press, 1968); and John C. Greene, "American Science Comes of Age, 1780–1820," *Journal of American History*, LV (June 1968), 22–41. See also the essays in Vol. VIII, No. 4 (1965) of the *Journal of World History*, the entire issue of which is devoted to "Science in the American Context." David D. Van Tassell and Michael Hall, eds., *Science and Society in the United States* (Homewood, Ill.: Dorsey Press, 1966), integrates scientific developments into general American history. A valuable guide to the sociology of science is Bernard Barber, "Sociology of Science: A Trend Report and Bibliography," *Current Sociology*, Vol. V (Paris, 1956).

PHILANTHROPY IN AMERICAN HISTORY

The starting point is the Russell Sage Foundation, *Report of the Princeton Conference on the History of Philanthropy in the United States* (New York, 1956), which contains an extensive bibliography. Merle Curti, "The History of American Philanthropy as a Field of Research," *American Historical Review*, Vol. LXII (January 1957), "Tradition and Innovation in American Philanthropy," American Philosophical Society, *Proceedings*, Vol. CV (April 1961), and Merle Curti and Roderick Nash, *Philanthropy in the Shaping of American Higher Education* (New Brunswick, N.J.: Rutgers University Press, 1965), assess major themes. Robert H. Bremner, *American Philanthropy* (Chicago: University of Chicago Press, 1960), is an encyclopedic survey. The Carnegie Institution of Washington, *Confidential Report of the Executive Committee to the Board of Trustees, November 11, 1902* (Washington, D.C., 1902), Appendix B, contains a unique check-list of nineteenth-century science research endowments.

Considering the influence of the modern private foundation in American life, it is surprising that there are no satisfactory historical analyses of the foundation as a social institution. Frederick P. Keppel's *The Foundation, Its Place in American Life* (New York: Macmillan, 1930) is suggestive but too brief. F. Emerson Andrews' numerous studies, notably *Philanthropic Giving* (New York: Russell Sage Foundation, 1950), and *Philanthropic Foundations* (New York: Russell Sage Foundation, 1956), lack historical insight, as does Warren Weaver's otherwise valuable *Philanthropic Foundations, Their History, Structure, Management, and Record* (New York: Harper and Row, 1967).

Index

AAAS. *See* American Association for the Advancement of Science

Abbe, Cleveland, 86

Academy of Natural Sciences of Philadelphia, 124

Adams, Henry, 6, 141

Adams, John Quincy: supports Smithsonian Institution, 9–13 *passim;* and astronomy, 11–12, 28, 32; mentioned, 167, 184

Addams, Jane, 160

Agassiz, Alexander: biography of, 145–46; opposes government science, 145–50 *passim;* advises Allison Commission, 146–47; criticizes O. C. Marsh, 147; mentioned, 53, 131, 150, 186

Agassiz, Cécile Braun, 51

Agassiz, Elizabeth Cary, 51–52

Agassiz, Jean Louis Rodolph. *See* Agassiz, Louis

Agassiz, Louis: and the Lazzaroni, 8; as promoter of science, 39, 48–58 *passim,* 61, 100; personality of, 49; and popular science, 49–51, 53–55, 59; on the races of man, 59; joins Lawrence Scientific School, 51, 80; and Museum of Comparative Zoology, 52–53, 55–57; opposes Darwinism, 55–58, 136; mentioned, 60, 66, 67, 70, 81, 86, 119, 120, 163. *See also* Gray, Asa; Lawrence, Abbott; Religion: science and

Albany, N.Y.: national university in, 39–40; astronomy in, 39–47 *passim;* mentioned, 8

Alger, Horatio, 146

Allegheney Observatory, 117

Allison, William B.: investigates government science, 144. *See also* Allison Commission; Powell, John Wesley; Herbert, Hilary A.

Allison Commission: investigates government science, 144–49; findings, 148–49; mentioned, 150. *See also* Powell, John Wesley; Agassiz, Alexander

American Academy of Arts and Sciences: debate on Darwinism, 59; research funds, 125; mentioned, 36, 54, 67, 69

American Association for the Advancement of Science: research funds, 127, 129, 132; mentioned, 7, 40, 43, 105, 124, 131, 175, 183

American Journal of Science and Arts, 15, 37, 141

American Philosophical Society: research funds, 124; mentioned, 13, 120, 135

Appleton, Nathaniel, 37

Appleton, Samuel, 37

Appleton, William, 36

Argelander, Friedrich W. A., 41

Armsby, James, 40–47 *passim*

Arnold, James, 68–69

Association of American Naturalists, 131

Association to Aid Scientific Research by Women, 131

Astor, William B., 43